DATE DUE

w/D

NONSENSE LITERATURE FOR CHILDREN

Nonsense Literature for Children

Celia Catlett Anderson and Marilyn Fain Apseloff

Aesop to Seuss

Foreword by William Cole

Afterword by Nancy Willard

LIBRARY PROFESSIONAL PUBLICATIONS
1989

First published in 1989 as a Library Professional Publication,
an imprint of The Shoe String Press, Inc., Hamden, Connecticut 06514

Printed in the United States of America

The paper used in this publication meets the
minimum requirements of American National Standard for
Information Sciences—Permanence of Paper for Printed
Library Materials.
ANSI Z39.48-1984. ∞

Library of Congress Cataloging-in-Publication Data

Anderson, Celia Catlett, 1936–
Nonsense literature for children : Aesop to Seuss / Celia Catlett
Anderson and Marilyn Fain Apseloff : foreword by William Cole :
afterword by Nancy Willard.
p.   cm.
Bibliography: p.
Includes index.
ISBN 0–208–02161–2.
1. Nonsense literature, English—History and criticism.
2. Nonsense literature, American—History and criticism.
3. Children's literature, English—History and criticism.
4. Children's literature, American—History and criticism.
5. Children—Books and reading. I. Apseloff, Marilyn. II. Title.
PR468.N6A53   1989
827'.009—dc19   88-27108   CIP

This book is dedicated to

FRANCELIA BUTLER

A no-nonsense lady who has served
as fairy godmother to many scholars
in the field of children's literature

Contents

Foreword

by William Cole

There's a great deal of common sense about nonsense here. I've never really thought of nonsense as a thing apart, although goodness knows I'm full of it. It's even featured in one of my titles. In compiling my eight anthologies of silliness for children, I looked for whatever made me laugh or smile; I looked for poems that my instinct told me I would have laughed at when I was a boy. Funny stuff, ridiculous, loony, impossible, upside-down. Come to think of it, nonsensical may be the word. Or the title of one of Spike Milligan's books would cover it—*Silly Verse for Kids*.

And speaking of Spike, the English comedian and poet, one of the many things I like about this book on nonsense is that he's given the recognition he deserves; indeed, I think of him as the "King of Nonsense." Spike Milligan has never been published in the United States, except in anthologies. I've just flipped through my own, and found that I've used his silly verses twenty-one times. One poem, in fact, is in three different books, something I always try to avoid. Here's the poem, the first line of which is the title: "A thousand hairy savages / Sitting down to lunch / Gobble gobble glup glup / Munch munch munch." I wish I'd said that.

Although Milligan's given recognition, I wish that there was more on Tomi Ungerer, another nonsense master. I've done seven books in collaboration with Tomi, the kinds of collaboration where I'd give him something and he'd improve it. An example: in 1967 we did *A Case of the Giggles*. This was four little books in a box: *Limerick Giggles*, *Nonsense Giggles*, *Joke Giggles*, and *Rhyme Giggles*. I was in his studio one morning when he was hand-lettering all four covers, back and front. He finished lettering the front of *Nonsense Giggles*. "Ze front," he said. "Now ze beck." (He's from Alsace). He applied himself to the task, swiftly and carefully, and finished—"Here, Beel—ze beck." The title had been magically transposed to *Gonsense Niggles*. That, I submit, was the very spirit of nonsense. Or gonsense.

Oh, yes, and let's not forget the two wonderful books written and illustrated by Mark Alan Stamaty, *Who Needs Donuts?* and *Small in the Saddle*. When I first encountered *Small* in 1975, I was so excited that I looked Mark up in the phone book and gave him a fan call. Here's an outlaw in a cowboy town who doesn't shoot people—he tickles 'em. In rides a small stranger, and by golly he gets rid of the outlaws—because he's *not ticklish!* Inspired lunacy, with all manner of lagniappe on each page: birds with horse heads and vice versa, a frog on horseback, a poster showing two leaves—"Wanted—for rustling." *Donuts* is just as funny (even though I deplore that spelling of doughnuts). Great nonsense, but out of print, as it seems most good books go.

How do people write nonsense? Well, for myself, I think up opposites or "upside-downnesses." My long poem, "A Boy Named Mary Jane," is a string of those, starting with the title. Then I placed a town called Washington in Spain, then a father who teaches crocheting and a mother who's a plumber. Then a cat named Rover and a dog named Scat and on and on. But nonsense must have one foot on the ground. Or at least a toe. Me, I don't enjoy Gertrude Stein. I find her silliness not attached to anything. The authors say she's "relished by young and old." Well, I've been both, and remain unrelished.

To go back to out-of-print for a moment. There are two fine bibliographies of nonsense at the back of this book; a treasure trove of nonsense. Looking them over, I would guess that a large percentage of the books listed are out of print, though still available in many libraries. The attitude of most publishers is, if it doesn't sell so many copies a year, off with its head!

But enough lamenting about what isn't available; this book is a celebration. Nonsense is one of the great things a parent can share with kids. When I used to read to mine—there are four—I'd search out nonsense books that would give us all pleasure. (Funny, as I wrote that, Walt Kelly's *Pogo* swam into mind.) Laughing together with little ones is one of the greatest joys in the world. The authors show us here that nonsense is not to be taken lightly. Quality in anything is always a serious matter.

And with that I will close for the nonce, and simply say, as I used to say nonsensically to the other kids, "Goombye!"

Preface

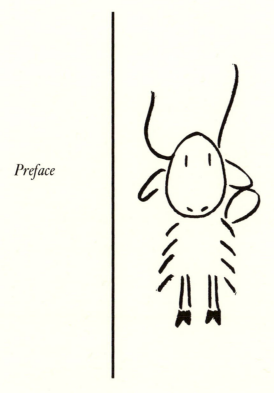

This book is intended as a resource work for anyone interested in nonsense literature for children. We hope that it will be especially useful for those who work with young people, whether as teachers or librarians, counselors or therapists. In addition, parents, grandparents, and any adult fond of reading to children and providing them with enjoyable books will find something of value among the many poetry, fiction, and picture books we discuss. Academics in literature, art, library science, education, and psychology will find the bibliographies of both primary and secondary sources an aid for further research.

The material included is appropriate for a wide age range. We comment on and give examples of nursery rhymes for preschoolers, nonsense creatures for these and slightly older children, longer works of nonsense fiction and examples of wordplay and riddles for those in the middle and upper grades. On the theoretical side, the contributing authors have analyzed a number of critical perspectives on the oral, literary, graphic, and psychological nature of nonsense.

As coauthors and coeditors we are responsible for most of the material, but, to give added perspectives, we called on psychologist Leo Schneiderman, drama expert Blair Whitney, and children's author Nancy Willard (whose seminal essay on nonsense is reprinted in part as the afterword) to help us. Because we have covered many facets of the nonsense tradition, considering its form in text and illustration, its value as an educational or psychological tool, we think that this volume can serve as either textbook or supplemental reading for college level courses on children's literature and courses for early childhood and elementary grade teacher programs, or as supplemental reading in courses on child psychology. It can serve both as a bibliographic aid and a stimulus for instructors teaching at the primary and secondary levels.

The format of the book provides easy access to specific topics. Part 1 establishes our definition of nonsense, gives a history of the development of nonsense into a genre intended mainly for children, and covers a number of authors, from ancient to modern times, who have included nonsense elements in their writing. Part 2 covers the linguistic, intellectual, and psychological benefits that can accrue from an exposure to this type of humor, while Part 3 categorizes nonsense in various ways: by format, as it appears in drama, verse, and prose; by subject matter, as it deals with creating impossible worlds and creatures or with mocking other literary traditions. In Part 4 we consider the visual forms of nonsense, and for an afterword we are fortunate enough to have an abridged version of Nancy Willard's "The Game and the Garden: The Lively Art of Nonsense." Separate bibliographies of primary and secondary sources expand on the reference lists given for each chapter, and an index is provided for quick reference on an individual author or work.

As is true of many scholarly works, we have, of course, been selective rather than all-inclusive in our choice of material. We have, for instance, concentrated on nonsense written in English. Although some of what we cover is in translation, we have not analyzed the stylistic elements of any examples first written in a foreign language. Naturally, we have chosen primarily from works intended for children, mentioning adult nonsense literature and art mainly for purposes of comparison. We have restricted ourselves to those tales and verses from folklore and childlore that have found their way into print, although we are well aware that the rich oral tradition currently enjoying a revival in many storytelling festivals and sessions around the country can supply lively examples of nonsense. We do not investigate nonsense in films for children or in Saturday-morning cartoons. Blair Whitney's essay, however, does analyze the connection between "Sesame Street" and the theater of the absurd. Finally, while we do give examples of riddles and jokes, puns and other forms of wordplay, these are subsumed under various appropriate categories rather than discussed in sections devoted specifically to them. In sum, we have tried to discover what nonsense is in art and literature and to give a sufficient number of examples and sources to set our readers on a path to many hours of amusement and intellectual challenge.

We wish to thank the many people who helped make this book possible. First of all we thank William Cole for agreeing to write the foreword, Nancy Willard for permitting us to use her essay as an afterword, the two contributors for their excellent essays, and Stanford Apseloff for his help with the material on the theater of the absurd that appears in chapter 3. Carl Meigs, a colleague at Eastern Connecticut State University with an expertise in linguistics superior to that of either of the authors, read chapter 4 and made some helpful suggestions. Kenneth Moorhead, Jody Newmyer, and Nicholas Welchman, librarians, gave invaluable help in finding and checking sources. We are grateful to those publishers and authors who granted us permission to reproduce a number of the illustrations that appear in the text. We have been fortunate enough to work with Virginia Mathews as our editor and William Rutter as designer, and have appreciated their sound professionalism and their patience. Finally, we wish to thank Francelia Butler, who instigated and inspired this book and to whom it is dedicated.

CELIA CATLETT ANDERSON

MARILYN FAIN APSELOFF

Contributors

LEO SCHNEIDERMAN, author of chapter 7, "Psychological Aspects of Nonsense Literature for Children," teaches psychology at Eastern Connecticut State University at Willimantic, Connecticut. He has published frequently on the interconnection of literature and psychology, and is the author of *The Psychology of Myth, Folklore and Religion*, among other works. He is currently the editor of the *Connecticut Review*.

BLAIR WHITNEY, author of chapter 8, " *'Sesame Street'* as Theater of the Absurd," is assistant director for Academic Affairs, Illinois Board of Higher Education. He has taught at various universities in the midwest and has written extensively on the literature and history of that area. His book, *John G. Neihardt*, is a critical study of that Nebraska author, and in the field of drama his play, *Vachel*, about Vachel Lindsay, was a prize winner.

List of
Illustrations

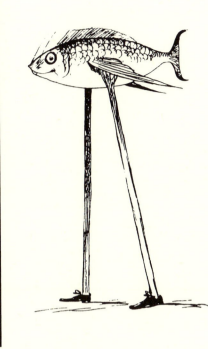

Part I

THE WHAT, WHEN, AND WHO OF NONSENSE

1

If the butterfly courted the bee,
  And the owl the porcupine;
If churches were built in the sea,
  And three times one was nine;
If the pony rode his master,
  If buttercups ate the cows,
If the cat had the dire disaster
  To be worried, sir, by the mouse;
If mamma, sir, sold the baby
  To the gipsy for half a crown;
If a gentleman, sir, was a lady—
  The world would be Upside-Down!
If any or all these wonders
  Should ever come about,
I should not consider them blunders,
  For I should be Inside-Out!

William Brighty Rands,
"*Topsy-Turvy World*" *in* Lilliput Levee

Some Definitions of Nonsense

Nonsense literature is as old as written records, but commentators have yet to agree upon a single, clear definition. Roger Lancelyn Green writes in his introduction to *The Book of Nonsense*: "Many learned and sensible people have tried to decide what Nonsense is—or at least they have tried to discover the difference between Nonsense and Tommy Rot. . . . But no one has really discovered the secret" (xv).

SOME DEFINITIONS

The first definition of nonsense that the *Oxford English Dictionary* gives is "That which is not sense; spoken or written words which make no sense or convey absurd ideas; also absurd or senseless action." Similar definitions are given in *Webster's Ninth New Collegiate Dictionary*: "words or language having no meaning or conveying no intelligible ideas" or "language, conduct, or an idea that is absurd or contrary to sense." *Webster's* editors define the adjective "nonsense" as "consisting of an arbitrary grouping of speech sounds or symbols." Their separate definition for nonsense verse reads: "humorous or whimsical verse that features unique characters and actions and often contains evocative but meaningless nonce words." The last entry cited is the most relevant to literary nonsense; we wish, however, to expand it to include forms of writing other than verse: nonsense stories, wordplay (such as riddles, puns, and palindromes) and to include the visual nonsense of illustrations. We are not concerned with random senselessness, accidently produced and never incorporated into an intentional construct. We consistently argue that literary and graphic nonsense always implies a contrast to some linguistic, spatial, emotional, or ethical form that is accepted as sense. As Susan Stewart puts it in her book *Nonsense: Aspects of Intertextuality in Folklore and Literature*, "Our ways of making nonsense will depend upon our ways of making common sense" (viii).

Some writers restrict nonsense to its extreme form, "pure nonsense," variously defined. Myra Cohn Livingston, in "Nonsense Verse: The Complete Escape," holds that it does effect a "complete escape" to "an *impossible* world" which, she concedes, "must use the touchstones of reality" (124). The *Princeton Encyclopedia of Poetry and Poetics* has a similar description, calling it "the rejection of what most people consider logical or even normal and an acceptance of the conventions of a completely different universe" (572) and "essentially a poetry of escape" (574) that creates "an autonomous world, a world which operates according to its own laws and into which sane people can never really penetrate" (572–73). All art creates autonomous worlds, what J. R. R. Tolkien dubbed "subcreations." Stewart discusses this facet of artistic endeavor and notes that the idea also occurs in philosophy with "William James's idea of 'sub-universes of meaning' " (15).

The editors of *Poetry and Poetics* also add that nonsense entails "a conscious refusal to communicate anything which could be considered positive" (574). This attitude is an example of what Susan Stewart means when she points out that nonsense has been relegated to second-class citizens: the child, the servant, the mad, "the chronically foolish and playful" and that "Nonsense becomes a negative language" because it "does not count in the eyes of common sense discourse" (5).

Although we certainly agree with Stewart that nonsense is intentionally in the "domain of the 'never happened' . . . 'could not happen' " (16), we do not believe that nonsense literature should be confined to "pure nonsense." As Joyce Thomas writes, "the term is pretty much a misnomer, since, given the necessary adherence to language and its inherent sense, probably only a madman's babbled jibberish properly qualifies as pure nonsense" ("'There Was an Old Man . . .' : The Sense of Nonsense Verse," 120). Nonsense escapes into its own universe, but so does all art. Farther removed from everyday reality than the categories of realism, myth, and irony that Stewart uses to subdivide verbal art, nonsense is never totally detached. We argue that it is always the mirror image of sense, a carnival or fun-house mirror perhaps, but dependent on what stands before the mirror for the effects it can produce. To those who protest our inclusion of "impure" nonsense, borrowing a retort from William Cole, we say, *"Fiddle-faddle! Twiddle-twaddle! Bushwa! And Balderdash!"* (*Oh, What Nonsense!*, 10).

Nonsense is not the absence of sense but a clever subversion of it that heightens rather than destroys meaning. The very notion of topsy-turvy implies that there is a right side up. Essentially dyadic, nonsense consists of humorous absurdities with double or split meanings, of contrasts, reversals, and mirror images. We will consider all of these ploys: nonsense as the world turned upside down, inside out (or slightly tilted); nonsense as absurd connections, the juxtaposition of perfectly ordinary but incongruous ideas or objects to create the ridiculous. Other forms of nonsense, such as over-exaggeration (tall tales), figurative language taken literally (for example, the Amelia Bedelia books), taking ideas or situations to absurd lengths (as in *The Phantom Toll Booth*), and using logic as a base for illogical events (the mad tea party), all pair the everyday with the bizarre. A similar duality applies to wordplay with its subtle misconnections. Children (and anyone, for that matter) must understand legitimate words before they can appreciate nonce words. They must know multiple meanings of words before the humor of puns becomes accessible to them. In like fashion, they must recognize visual reality before they can laugh at the pictorial distortions of it. Nonsense is a type of escape, but it is a circular flight that returns us to the ground.

NONSENSE TECHNIQUES

Those who create nonsense use a number of techniques to achieve this double effect of grounding in and flight from reality. Sentences are carefully phrased to bring out the double or the inappropriate meaning of a word. Juxtaposition is a frequent device for calling attention to incongruous relationships. The inclusion of a matter-of-fact narrator can anchor the nonsense in reality. The use of parody can highlight both the sensible and potentially silly elements in the original. Conventions of verse forms, such as the strict adherence to regular rhyme and meter or heavy use of alliteration and assonance, keep the nonsense from spinning off into a nightmare world of chaos. As Nancy Willard so aptly phrases it in a passage not included in our excerpted reprint of her essay on nonsense, "well-regulated babble is as essential . . . as abracadabra to the magician. Like the wizard's charmed circle, it draws a boundary between the game and the real world and lets us make light of the most dreadful events" (*Angel in the Parlor*, 262). These poetic conventions impose order on disorder and create a nonsense universe which, simply by its separateness, makes us more aware of the everyday world.

Illustrators have their own methods for highlighting contrasts between the sensible and the silly. For example, in some instances the language is ordinary and the narrative realistic, while the illustrations provide the nonsense. Also, some writers and illustrators combine sense and nonsense in a way that speaks to a dual audience, the adult and the child, entertaining both. Visual as well as linguistic puns abound for a mixed audience, some for children but others obviously intended for adults. Children may see only the silliness, whereas adults may recognize social satire masking as nonsense. We are, in other words, dealing with a highly complex form of art. It is to children's great credit that they instinctively take to this type of intellectual play, gathering insights and gaining an oblique angle of vision and the ability to view the world actively rather than passively.

THE NEED FOR NONSENSE

Children live and move in an adult world that they did not make and whose terms they do not readily understand. Besides the "blooming, buzzing" physical universe, as William James described the child's world, there are all the customs and contradictions of human relationships and all the rules and nuances of language. Looking back on childhood, we may forget how much hard work growing up involves, and how much stress. It is small wonder that children turn so often to both laughter and tears. Humor is a major ingredient in a healthy childhood, and the extreme type of humor that is called nonsense is especially useful. Nonsense exchanges can give children their first lessons in distinguishing between logic and illogic, between what is to be taken seriously and what is comic. It has always had a special appeal for the young, partly because such blatant humor allows children to get the joke more readily than they do with other more subtle forms. In his book *The Language of Humour*, Walter Nash comments, "I have been struck by the complexity of the subject—by the realization of what we are required to know, what social competence we must possess, what intellectual operations we may have to perform before we can grasp even a simple joke" (xi). And Nash goes on to note that humor tends to be referential, highly topical, and therefore accessible only to those who share an understanding of the specific people and events that are the butt of the humor. There are nonsensical satires and parodies that require special knowledge, but nonsense humor usually homes in on very basic human traits and conditions, one more reason why children appreciate nonsense.

Another benefit is that it can help children gain linguistic control by allowing them to play with sound and meaning. Nonsense jokes, rhymes, and riddles provide a release from the stress of trying to make sense of complex, often puzzling, language and surroundings, and also provide practice in the oral acquisition of language. Rhymes and phonetically simple nonsense words serve the child over many years. Rhyme, long acknowledged as an aid to children in learning language, is not an essential ingredient of the nonsense tradition, but much nonsense is written in verse. What is central to the connection between nonsense and learning is that children are amused by patterned but meaningless strings of sound, by misconceptions engendered by a too literal interpretation of words, by puns, and by adult logic that is ultimately absurd, all fertile grounds for nonsense constructions and all excellent means by which children gain control of their world.

Whether found in a casual exchange among a group of children or as part of the play between child and parent, or formalized in literature, nonsense affirms that not everything we encounter does or has to make sense. Children, like Edward Lear's Jumblies, who quite successfully "went to sea in a Sieve" (*Complete Nonsense*, 71), can rejoice in the risks of life and sing with the Jumblies, "Timballo! How happy we are, / When we live in a sieve and a crockery-jar!" (73).

Carroll, Lewis. *The Annotated Alice: Alice's Adventures in Wonderland & Through the Looking Glass*. Annotator, Martin Gardner. New York: World, 1972.

Cole, William, ed. *Oh, What Nonsense!* New York: Viking, 1966.

Green, Roger Lancelyn, ed. *The Book of Nonsense by Many Authors*. New York: Dutton, 1956.

Juster, Norton. *The Phantom Tollbooth*. New York: Random, 1964.

Lear, Edward. *The Complete Nonsense of Edward Lear*. Ed. Holbrook Jackson. New York: Dover, 1951.

Livingston, Myra Cohn. "Nonsense Verse: The Complete Escape." In *Celebrating Children's Books*. Eds. Betsy Hearne and Marilyn Kaye. New York: Lothrop, 1981. 129–39.

Nash, Walter. *The Language of Humour: Style and Technique in Comic Discourse*. White Plains, NY: Longman, 1985.

Oxford English Dictionary (Compact Edition). New York: Oxford University Press, 1971.

Preminger, Alex, ed. *Princeton Encyclopedia of Poetry and Poetics*. Princeton: Princeton University Press, 1974.

Rands, William Brighty. "Topsy-Turvy World" in *Lilliput Levee*, London, 1864. Qtd. in Green.

Stewart, Susan. *Nonsense: Aspects of Intertextuality in Folklore and Literature*. Baltimore: Johns Hopkins University Press, 1979.

Thomas, Joyce. " 'There was an Old Man . . .': The Sense of Nonsense Verse." *ChLAQ* 10.3 (Fall 1985): 119–22.

Webster's Ninth New Collegiate Dictionary. Eds. Frederick C. Mish et al. Springfield, MA: Merriam-Webster, 1983.

Willard, Nancy. "The Game and the Garden: The Lively Art of Nonsense." *Angel in the Parlor: Five Stories and Eight Essays* San Diego: Harcourt, 1983. 258–82.

2

Fraga quot in pelagi fluctibus orta putes?
Salsa quot alecum millia sylva ferat.

Wallace Tripp's Latin for:
The man in the wilderness asked of me,
How many strawberries grew in the sea?
I answered him, as I thought good,
As many as red herring grew in the wood.

In Granfa' Grif Had a Pig, *46*

A Capsule History of Nonsense Literature from Ancient Greece to Victorian England

When we view nonsense as a subversion or undercutting of sense, we find its threads woven into many oral and literary traditions. We cannot trace those strands to their first spinning in the case of folklore, but we know that tall tales, and riddles, and nonce phrases in refrains have existed from the earliest recorded days of most cultures.

NONSENSE AS OLD AS THE HILLS

Fortunately, we do have some ancient examples of nonsense in literature. One that dates back almost twenty-five hundred years is perhaps the most famous: the refrain from the frog chorus in Aristophanes' play *The*

Frogs. These vain and noisy creatures, the "Frogswans" chant the nonsense refrain:

> Brekeke-kex, Ko-ax, ko-ax,
> Ko-ax, ko-ax, ko-ax!

(1.1.164)

In act 2, the character Aeschylus "demolishes" the solemn prologues that the character Euripides recites by interposing the phrase "lost his bottle of oil" (200–1) every few lines. Finally convinced that he should desist, Aeschylus then interrupts a lyric with cymbal crashes and another nonsense sequence: "Flat-a-thrat-a-flat-a-thrat" (202–3). That these are nonce words in Greek is made clear when the character Dionysus asks, "What is all this flat-a-thrat? A bit of Persian you picked up at Marathon, Aeschylus?" (203). The use of cymbals is merely a slapstick technique, but the other three instances are good examples of, first, an onomatopoetic nonsense refrain ("Brekeke-kex, Koax") similar to some found in Mother Goose rhymes, second, an absurdity created by placing a simple object or act ("lost his bottle of oil") in an inappropriate context, and, third, a string of nonce words ("Flat-a-thrat").

A more intellectual form of nonsense existed in Greek philosophy; many of their paradoxes create a sealed world of logic, perfect in its inner workings, but absurd in terms of common sense. It is, practically speaking, nonsense to say that the swift-footed Achilles can never overtake the slow turtle, but once we grant the premise that in the abstract world of mathematics anything (including time and space) is infinitely divisible, we have made that last, infinitesimally small, overtaking step impossible. Susan Stewart discusses the paradoxical nature of nonsense, and we cover this in detail in chapter 6, "Nonsense and Philosophy."

In his anthology *The Book of Nonsense by Many Authors*, Roger Lancelyn Green includes a selection of five nonsense verses by later Greek writers, among them one by Nicarchus who lived about A.D. 200.

> I boiled hot water in an urn
> Till it was cold as ice;
> I blew the fire to make it burn,
> Which froze it in a trice.

(qtd. in Green, 246)

In this quatrain we have an example of the reverse reality, the upside-down world that is so common in nonsense constructions. We may also have a riddle. But as to its answer, we must repeat the Mad Hatter's reply to his own query, " 'Why is a raven like a writing-desk?' " and say " 'I haven't the slightest idea' " (Carroll, *Wonderland*, chap. 7).

NONSENSE RIDDLES

Riddles are one of the oldest known forms of word play. "At the heart of all this wordplay," Walter Nash says, "seems to be a concern with two ancient and related processes: naming and riddling" (*Language of Humour*, 146). Riddles are seeming paradoxes that are resolved when shared characteristics of different objects or actions are discovered or when a missing element, such as time, is applied to the puzzle. Riddles fall under the category of nonsense because on the surface they suggest impossible or highly incongruous combinations that cross everyday boundaries of meaning, and because they are involved in phonetic, semantic, or logical reversals. As Walter Nash puts it, answers to riddles usually fall "into one of two categories; i.e. the play on sound and meaning or the breach of logical/discursive expectations" (50). In other words, riddles share characteristics with puns or misleading questions or misread answers, as the examples below illustrate.

One Old English riddle that demonstrates a typical punning/metaphoric use of words reads in part:

> It walked swiftly
> On its only foot, this odd-shaped monster,
> Travelled in an open country without
> Seeing, without arms, or hands,
> With many ribs, and its mouth in its middle.
> (*Exeter Book* "Riddle 32: Ship," Rafael, 56)

In *The Annotated Mother Goose*, the Baring-Goulds recount the apocryphal story that Homer is supposed to have died of shame when he could not guess the answer to "All that we caught, we left behind, and carried away all that we did not catch" (271)—which answer is "fleas." In a modern children's book written by that Anglo-Saxon scholar J. R. R. Tolkien, the riddles that Gollum sets for Bilbo Baggins are characterized by such internal contradictions. "Dark" is described as something that cannot be seen or felt but can fill holes, and Bilbo has trouble answering

> Alive without breath
> As cold as death;
> Never thirsty, always drinking,
> All in mail, never clinking.
> (*The Hobbit*, 82)

The answer is a "fish." The "riddle" that finally frees Bilbo, breaks the rules by leaving the domain of wordplay and asking a straightforward question whose answer depends on fact, not on understanding the snarled categories of a riddle: Bilbo simply asks what is in his pocket.

Games with time are the central feature of many riddles. One poses the problem, how can something be at once

> As white as milk,
> And not milk;
> As green as grass,
> And not grass;
> As red as blood
> And not blood;
> As black as soot,
> And not soot.
>
> (qtd. in *Annotated Mother Goose*, 278)

The answer, as the Baring-Goulds inform us, is "a blackberry" and the color contradiction disappears when we consider the time sequence from blossom to ripe berry. This is similar to that very old riddle "How could there be a cherry without a stone?," the central query that runs through many English and American versions of a ballad that "was probably old when it was first written down in the middle of the fifteenth century" (Baring-Goulds, 162). The answer is, of course, "When the cherry is in blossom, there is no stone" (163). Centuries later Beatrix Potter had the owl pose to Squirrel Nutkin a companion riddle: "A little wee man in a red red coat; / A staff in his hand, and a stone in his throat," as a description of a red cherry.

Susan Stewart holds that what is considered nonsense varies from culture to culture. Some riddles can travel across borders and still be turned back into prosaic sense; others are language-specific and depend on a play on words not easily translated. For example, another of the rhymes that Tolkien employs in that central scene in *The Hobbit* in which Bilbo Baggins holds a riddling contest with Gollum calls for an answer readily available only in English. Bilbo almost stumps Gollum with

> An eye in a blue face
> Saw an eye in a green face.
> "That eye is like to this eye"
> Said the first eye,
> "But in low place,
> Not in high place."

(82)

Gollum has been away from the reality of sunlight for so long that the riddle seems without meaning until he finally recalls that both the sun and a common meadow flower can be thought of as the "day's eye" and answers, "Sun on the daisies" (82). The solution of this riddle depends in part on the recognition of a metaphor that entered our language as a word in Anglo-Saxon times. It is time-bound as well as culture-bound, not immediately heard or seen in contemporary English pronunciation and spelling, but quite accessible in times when "day's eye" and "daisy" shared the same phonetic values. The riddle itself dates back to the era of Old English, an era when both humorous and high poetry often took this form.

NONSENSE IN FABLES

Another type of literature related to nonsense that has roots in the distant past is the fable. Fables do indeed aim to teach wisdom, but they do this most frequently by including a nonsensical character, a fool who is duped by a second character, the trickster. Stewart notes that the trickster, a "nonsense-making character who has received particular attention from symbolic anthropology" is "the personificiation of ambivalance" (61–62).

In fables and folktales with a trickster hero, the nonsense element is found in the premise on which the plot or trick hinges. Many fables center on a fool who cannot distinguish between common sense and nonsense or between real and false causes. Typically, the trickster figure lures the character who serves as gull to accept a false premise, to slide over some false reasoning, or to forget the consequences of some simple, everyday action and thereby lose life or goods. In "The Fox and the Cock," versions of which are found in Aesop, the Reynard cycle, and Chaucer's *Canterbury Tales*, the trick of flattery is used twice, once by the fox and then by the initially gullible rooster in order to persuade the other to close eyes or open the mouth. Consequently, the vanity-blinded rooster cannot see the fox's predatory leap, and the fox forgets that if he opens his mouth to brag, he will release his prey. In the story "The Elephants and the Moon" (Aesop), a small rabbit plays on the inability of the King of the Elephants to distinguish one level of reality from another and leads him to believe that the reflection of the moon in a rippling pond is actually the moon trembling with rage.

In other cases, the character is a fool all on his own. The dog who loses his piece of meat by opening his mouth to bark at his own reflection in the water is responsible for his own nonsensical behavior. Yet other fables show how a missing premise can make nonsense of the best laid plans. The mice's brave project to bell the cat (and thereby have warning of her presence) is turned to absurdity by the fact that no mouse could carry out such an action.

A further trait that fables share with later nonsense literature is the pairing of incongruous animals. Long before Edward Lear put his owl and pussy cat in one boat, an owl in one of Aesop's stories aspired to marry the eagle's daughter. In another, a raven dies in attempting to be a swan. More happily, a bee and a dove sustain a friendship. One final example from Aesop ("The Jay and the Nightingale") demonstrates the nonsense that can be engendered by an empty use of language. When Master Jay angrily demands of the Lord Eagle that the jay and not the nightingale be called "The King of Song of the Woods," the eagle replies "I have no objection. . . . You may go back to your family and say I have named you the 'King of Song of the Woods' if you like" (143). When the jay goes screeching his new title through the woods, the other animals laugh at him until, offended, he returns to the Lord Eagle to ask why and learns: "My young friend, I certainly gave you the name of 'King of Song of the Woods,' in answer to your request. But to *call* you so is one thing—to *make* you so is another!" (144). Throughout the fables, it is the subversion of sense by the trickster and the dupe's misunderstanding of reality that engender the foolish, nonsensical behavior used to teach a lesson about good sense.

Illustration by Edward Lear from "The Owl and the Pussy-Cat."

CHAUCERIAN NONSENSE

Chaucer expanded the beast fable about the mating aspirations of birds when he wrote his *Parliament of Fowls*, a delightful contribution to nonsense literature; we claim it on the grounds that the elements of satire and fantasy are often subsumed by the sheer absurdity of his birds' behavior and speech. He gives us, for instance, the ridiculous picture of the female eagle blushing (lines 442–47) and a mixture of speech and bird cries:

> The goos, the cokkow, and the doke also
> So cryede, "Kek, kek! kokkow! quek quek!" hye,
> That thourgh myne eres the noyse wente tho.
> The goos seyde, "Al this nys not worth a flye!"
>
> (lines 498–501)

When the duck argues against the idea that a rejected lover should continue faithful, saying "That men shulde loven alwey causeles, / Who can a resoun fynde or wit in that?" (lines 590–91), the "gentil tercelet" rejoins "Out of the donghil cam that word ful right!" (line 597). Chaucer is obviously having great fun in juxtaposing the adjective "gentil" which could mean "refined" and the vulgar reference to a dunghill in the tercelet's speech. The scatalogical undertone in *Parliament of Fowls* is one more element found in some nonsense. The oral tradition of nonsense taunts and chants that children have handed down from generation to generation is frequently scatological as the Opies have shown and as Linda Geller mentions in her book *Wordplay and Language Learning for Children*. The oral tradition of song and poetry gives us many more examples of nonsense that seem to date back nearly to Chaucer's time, although, as is always true of story and song passed from mouth to mouth long before it was recorded in writing, we can never be sure of exact dates. But it seems unlikely that the numerous nonce refrains of the early Renaissance period or that upside-down nonsense, like that in the very popular poem "The Land of Cockayne," appeared suddenly with no antecedents. By the time Shakespeare is writing in the sixteenth century, the convoluted humor of nonsense is very much a part of the English literary scene.

SHAKESPEARIAN NONSENSE

As Eric Partridge maintains in an essay on nonsense literature included in his book of essays *Here, There and Everywhere*, William Shakespeare, Edward Lear, Lewis Carroll, and James Joyce are the masters of nonsense in the Western world. Partridge catalogs a number of nonce words they coined (the list is incomplete, especially in Joyce's case). But in Shakespeare's writing the nonsense exchanges between his characters may be even better examples of his talent for absurd humor. They occur in the comedies and the tragedies alike. The wonderfully nonsensical dialogues between Hamlet and Polonius are examples from a tragedy. In the first, Hamlet keeps turning Polonius's set phrases into literal statements:

> *Polonius.* Will you walk out of the air, my lord?
>
> *Hamlet.* Into my grave.
>
> *Polonius.* Indeed, that's out of the air. [*Aside*] How pregnant some-
> times his replies are! a happiness that often madness hits
> on, which reason and sanity could not prosperously be
> delivered of.
>
> (2.2.208–15)

Polonius, the consummate pompous fool of literature, has a moment of wisdom here; the case for nonsense could not be better stated. And as he has said a line earlier, "If this be madness, yet there is method in't" (2.2.207). The spectator knows that Hamlet is playing with Polonius and that there is indeed a humorous method in disjoining the answer from the intended meaning of the question. In a later exchange, Hamlet uses nonsense banter to hide the emotion he feels at confirming his uncle's murder of the king. Polonius informs Hamlet that his mother the queen wishes to see him and receives for a reply:

> *Hamlet.* Do you see yonder cloud that's almost in shape of a
> camel?
>
> *Polonius.* By the mass, and 'tis like a camel, indeed.
>
> *Hamlet.* Methinks it is like a weasel.
>
> *Polonius.* It is backed like a weasel.
>
> *Hamlet.* Or like a whale?
>
> *Polonius.* Very like a whale.
>
> (3.3.393–99)

Ogden Nash, one of our century's nonsense versifiers, knew what he was about when he entitled a poem on trite metaphors "Very Like a Whale."

In the comedies we can find examples of nonsense in exchanges like those between Elbow (that literary ancestor of Mrs. Malaprop) and the magistrate in *Measure for Measure*. Of course, Shakespeare's masterpiece of nonsense occurs in the unintended parody of "Pyramus and Thisbe" that is staged by the uneducated artisans in *Midsummer Night's Dream*. Roger

Lancelyn Green includes Quince's prologue in his nonsense anthology. With its constant reversals ("If we offend it is with our good will" (5.1.108) and "To show our simple skill, / That is the true beginning of our end" (5.1.110–11), the prologue is certainly a good example of this kind of nonsense. But it is the other absurd elements that for centuries have elicited the most laughter from audiences. Casting a character to play the wall through which the lovers communicate sets the tone, and thereafter we are not surprised to see a man with a lantern play the moon. The functions of the senses are casually confused in such lines as, "I see a voice: now will I to the chink, / To spy an I can hear my Thisby's face" (5.1.193–96), or "Sweet Moon, I thank thee for thy sunny beams" (5.1.276), a conceit that is a staple of nonsense whether it occurs in the schoolyard verse that begins "One bright day in the middle of the night" or in Carroll's "The Walrus and the Carpenter."

NONSENSE IN PROTO-CHILDREN'S LITERATURE

The categories we have dealt with so far predate literature written consciously and deliberately for children. We have, in the past, had literary masterpieces so universally accepted that even though they were written for a mature audience, they have been taken over by children and are most popularly known (and marketed) as juvenile literature. *Aesop's Fables* is the most ancient example. Defoe's *Robinson Crusoe* and Swift's *Gulliver's Travels*, which are later works, are also major examples. And the young continued to co-opt these adult masterpieces even after a special body of writing aimed specifically at a child audience began to emerge in the seventeenth century. These early works for juveniles were at first mainly religious and somber rather than humorous. Although, as Warren Wooden among others has noted, "The various permutations and progeny of the beast fable in Renaissance England down through the talking animals of nursery rhymes and ballads have never been adequately mapped" (*Children's Literature of the English Renaissance*, xiii). Wooden holds that English nonsense verse for children has its origins in John Taylor (1580–1653), a popular writer who published and sold his own chapbooks. Chapbooks, it should be noted, were cheap paper texts that children of the past ages bought and read in much the same way twentieth-century children buy and read comic books.

Wooden says that an early work by Taylor "stands near the beginning of a type of children's literature perfected only in the nineteenth century: nonsense verse" (129). Taylor's long poem was published in 1622, but "as part of the fooling, the title page sports the futuristic date of 1700"

(Wooden, 129). The title page of the work sets the tone: *Sir Gregory Nonsence His Newes from no place. Written on purpose, with much study to no end, plentifully stored with want of wit, learning, Iudgement, Rime and Reason, and may seeme very fitly for the understanding of Nobody.* The prose proem contains such nonsense as placing Christmas Eve near Easter, just after Whitsuntide (Pentecost, the seventh Sunday after Easter), and speaking of "walking in a coach from London to Lambeth by water" (129–30). A fellow traveler narrates the poem in "Vtopian speech what I haue heare with most diligent negligence translated into the English Language, in which if the Printer hath placed any line, letter or sillable, whereby this large volume may bee made guilty to bee vnderstood by any man, I would haue the Reader not to impute the fault to the Author" (130). However, the author then flies in the face of this disavowal by printing an errata list for words and pages not to be found in the work.

The poem itself, as Wooden notes, relies mainly on "two tropes, oxymoron [the yoking together of opposites] and chiasmus [an inversion of syntactical relationships]" (131). We get such strange or impossible combinations as "discourteous friendly," "tempestuous calmes," "Father *Madge* and Mother *Iohn*," and when we read that the seafarers split their "maine top-mast, close below the keele" (131), it is tempting to think that Lewis Carroll found his inspiration here for that wonderfully nonsensical line in *The Hunting of the Snark*, "Then the bowsprit got mixed with the rudder sometimes" ("Fit the Second," line 25). In the course of the poem the narrator meets a variety of impossible creatures and descends with Aesop into the underworld. The work does seem to contain prototypes for almost every imaginable sort of nonsense humor. Near the end of the poem, the author sums up, saying,

> Thus do I make a hotch potch messe of *Nonsence*,
> In darke Eniguaes, and strange sence vpon sence:
> It is not foolish all, nor is it wise all,
> Nor is it true in all, nor is it lies all.
>
> (qtd. in Wooden, 132–33)

NONSENSE WRITTEN FOR A CHILD AUDIENCE

By the eighteenth century, literature for children had become accepted and popular enough to bring profit to such publishers as John Newbery, whose landmark book *A Little Pretty Pocket-Book: Intended for the Instruction and Amusement of Little Master Tommy and Pretty Miss Polly* (1744) was among the first to capitalize on the growing popularity of humorous verse for children. Although essentially a reading tool and an alphabet book, *A Little Pretty Pocket-Book* contains enough spritely nonsense in its verses to set it apart from strictly didactic books. In the same year M. Cooper had printed *Tommy Thumb's Pretty Song Book*, and imitations and pirated editions of Cooper's and Newbery's books were commonplace thereafter.

Many of the verses in such books appear to have come from an oral tradition, but we have no earlier written versions of them. For instance, that contagious ABC rhyme used to "explain" the "Great R Game" of reading:

> Great A, little a,
> Bounceing B;
> The Cats in ye Cupboard,
> And She can't See.
>
> (qtd. in Baring-Goulds, 240)

may, according to James O. Halliwell, date back to the fifteenth century. The proliferation in print of such lighthearted, game-like approaches to instruction for juveniles, along with whimsical poems like *The Butterfly's Ball, and the Grasshopper's Feast*, which "Saw the Children of Earth, and the Tenants of Air,/For an Evening's Amusement together repair" (in *Flowers of Delight*, de Vries, ed., 212), created the cultural environment that could appreciate Edward Lear and Lewis Carroll when their works entered the nurseries of Victorian households.

Victorian Nonsense

As we have shown, the atmosphere for producing such works had been slowly formed during the preceding few centuries. Childhood and a childlike wonder at the often ludicrous workings of human society were growing concerns of the human consciousness. As Stephen Prickett says of Lear and Carroll in his book *Victorian Fantasy*,

> In childhood, dreams, and the frontiers of consciousness, in the marvelous, the grotesque, and the monstrous they [the Victorians] discovered the possibility of quite different rules from those of the prevailing consensus: the rules of "Nonsense." (114)

Edward Lear and Lewis Carroll are so prominent as the masters of nonsense that we scarcely need to discuss their work at length here. We make sufficient reference to them throughout the book. However, some points about Lear and Carroll need to be established at the onset. What these two did with language and logic underlies much of what we mean when we use the term "nonsense" in the twentieth century. What Lear did, for example, was to make the culture at large more aware of "upside down" and of null categories in human language and experience: he sets language on its head with his many nonce words; he mixes categories until we question what belongs where. Carroll, in his capacity as mathematician-artist, revived for general readers what does and does not make sense in the game of logic. For Carroll, logic is never a dry-as-dust exercise but a means of penetrating the fibre of the world around us. He shows us that logic is a tool sharpened, not dulled with use (and that it sharpens the mind that uses it).

The secret of their success is that both Lear and Carroll could step outside the categories of their century. To quote Prickett again, they found nonsense "in the received conventions of society which had become frozen and reified, acquiring the status of objective 'laws' of nature. To discover nonsense, all one had to do was to step through the framework of unquestioned assumptions that form the boundaries of our normal world" (132). This is why their appeal remains so great in our age, which is constantly rebuilding itself on the sands of relativity. Lear and Carroll show us that we, like Alice, must stretch our arms wide enough around the mushroom/world to pull off some nourishment from opposites, because it is through a balance of contraries that we remain a sane size, and that, like the Jumblies, we can and must set to sea in a sieve and must recognize and nurture the worth of each new generation of what the 1877 "Nonsense Botany" dubbed "Queeriflora Babyoides."

Aesop. *Aesop's Fables*. Retold by Blanche Winter. New York: Airmont, 1965.

Aristophanes. *The Wasps, The Poet and the Women, The Frogs*. Trans. David Barrett. Baltimore: Penguin, 1970.

Baring-Gould, William S. and Ceil Baring-Gould. *The Annotated Mother Goose*. New York: World, 1972.

The Butterfly's Ball and the Grasshopper's Feast. London: J. Harris, 1807; rpt. in *Flowers of Delight: An Agreeable Garland of Prose and Poetry, 1765–1830*. Ed. Leonard de Vries. New York: Random/Pantheon, 1965.

Carroll, Lewis. *The Annotated Alice: Alice's Adventures in Wonderland & Through the Looking Glass*. Annotator, Martin Gardner. New York: World, 1972.

Chaucer, Geoffrey. *The Parliament of Fowls*. In *The Poetical Works of Chaucer*. Ed. F. N. Robinson. Boston: Houghton, 1933.

Cooper, Helen, ed. *Great Grandmother Goose*. New York: Greenwillow, 1978.

Cooper, M. *Tommy Thumb's Pretty Song Book*. London, 1744.

DeVries, Leonard, ed. *Flowers of Delight: An Agreeable Garland of Prose and Poetry for the Instruction and Amusement of Little Masters and Misses and their Distinguished Parents*, New York: Pantheon, 1965.

Geller, Linda Gibson. *Wordplay and Language Learning for Children*. Urbana, IL: NCTE, 1985.

Green, Roger Lancelyn, ed. *The Book of Nonsense by Many Authors*. New York: Dutton, 1956.

Lear, Edward. *The Complete Nonsense of Edward Lear*. Ed. Holbrook Jackson. New York: Dover, 1951.

Nash, Walter. *The Language of Humour: Style and Technique in Comic Discourse*. White Plains, NY: Longman, 1985.

Newbery, John. *A Little Pretty Pocket-Book: Intended for the Instruction and Amusement of Little Master Tommy and Pretty Miss Polly*. London, 1744.

Partridge, Eric. "The Nonsense Words of Edward Lear and Lewis Carroll." In *Here, There, and Everywhere: Essays Upon Language*. London: Hamish Hamilton, 1950.

Potter, Beatrix. *The Tale of Squirrel Nutkin*. London: Warne, 1903; rpt. 1931.

Prickett, Stephen. "Consensus and Nonsense: Lear and Carroll." In *Victorian Fantasy*. Bloomington: Indiana UP, 1979.

Raffel, Burton, trans. *Poems from the Old English*, 2d ed. Lincoln: U of Nebraska P, 1964.

Shakespeare, William. Hamlet, Measure for Measure, and *Midsummer Night's Dream*. *Twenty-Three Plays and the Sonnets*. Ed. Thomas Marc Parrott. New York: Scribner's, 1966.

Stewart, Susan. *Nonsense: Aspects of Intertextuality in Folklore and Literature*. Baltimore: Johns Hopkins UP, 1979.

Swift, Jonathan. *Gulliver's Travels*. New York: Oxford UP, 1977.

Tolkien, J. R. R. *The Hobbit*. 1937. New York: Ballantine, rev. ed. 1982; rpt. 1984.

Wooden, Warren W. *Children's LIterature of the English Renaissance*. Lexington: UP of Kentucky, 1985.

"But, Miss Golly, you can't *leave*. What would we do without you?" . . . .

Ole Golly looked up, and Harriet saw a flush of pride on her face. "I thank you for that, Mrs. Welsch. . . . I think, however, that in many ways the time has come. Not only for me, but for Harriet as well."

On the stairs, Harriet felt profound shock. . . . Ole Golly *must* mean that she, Harriet, was able to take care of herself. Is that true? she asked herself. And she had no answer.

Ole Golly held the stage. The other three looked at her in wonder. She seized her moment and spoke: """The time has come," the Walrus said—'"

""""To talk of many things—"""" Harriet knew the words so well that without a second's thought she found herself. . .saying them. . . .

Ole Golly continued: """"Of shoes—and ships— and sealing wax—""""

""""Of cabbages—and kings—"""" Harriet found herself laughing down at Ole Golly's smiling face as they went on, alternating the lines.

""""And why the sea is boiling hot—"""" Ole Golly had the funniest look, halfway between laughter and tears.

Harriet shouted the last with glee: """"And whether pigs have wings."""" She had always loved that line. It was her favorite.

Louise Fitzhugh, Harriet the Spy, *105–06*

Nonsense Literature in the Twentieth Century

A Potpourri of Modern Masters

The creation of nonsense has not declined in the twentieth century but has, if anything, been strengthened by writers of both adult and children's literature. The many traditions that have nurtured nonsense over the ages may be found both in their original forms and in evolved forms. Aesop continues popular; riddle books are published yearly; many versifiers for the young follow traditional nursery rhyme patterns when they write nonsense jingles. L. Frank Baum and his successor Ruth Thompson peopled the American wonderland of Oz with a variety of impossible creatures and characters, and in the kingdom found beyond the Phantom Tollbooth, Norton Juster carries on a Swiftian tradition of intellectual nonsense. On the editorial pages of newspapers, political cartoonists allude to nonsense characters (scenes from the Alice books are frequent) and also create fresh nonsense by picturing the foibles of the modern world in extreme and absurd forms. Children often first meet historical figures through cartoon caricatures, which appear not only in adult publications but in the illustrations for nursery rhymes as well. For example, Wallace Tripp uses Hitler, Napoleon, and Churchill in his drawings for Mother Goose rhymes. Other creators of nonsense have given us variations on the old formulas. That twentieth-century phenomenon of adult literature, the theater of the absurd, has pushed beyond Aristophanes and Shakespeare in its experiments with nonsense elements in drama. And in some of his writings James Joyce seems to have reached the outer limit of wordplay and outrageous jesting.

Adult Nonsense: Joyce, Beckett, Ionesco, Albee

Nonsense is often an organized and coherent statement that appears incoherent on the surface and is therefore declared senseless by readers unaware of the design and intent of the author. Such literature can be the best of all nonsense. In the twentieth century, for example, Joyce and Samuel Beckett, two writers of immense influence, use just such a technique. Others, including Eugene Ionesco and Edward Albee, contributed to what we can best designate as the legitimizing of nonsense in both fiction and drama. These authors explored a distortion of language that parallelled the similar distortions found in impressionism, expressionism, and surrealism.

James Joyce used a wide range of styles, his most extreme prose style occurring in *Finnegans Wake*. Its greatly distorted language is sometimes taken as complete nonsense because it ignores conventions of syntax, creates new words, and blends English and a variety of other languages. *Finnegans Wake* begins

> riverrun, past Eve and Adam's, from swerve of shore to bend of bay, brings us by a commodius vicus of recirculation back to Howth Castle and Environs.
>
> Sir Tristram, violer d'amores, fr'over the short sea, had passencore rearrived from North Armorica on this side of the scraggy isthmus of Europe Minor to wielderfight his penisolate war. (3)

The passage is thick with multilingual puns. Passing politely over "commodius vicus of recirculation" and translating that merely as "a convenient place for recycling," let us consider "violer d'amores," which could be translated "violator of loves" and is an outrageous pun on "viola d'amore," a seventeenth-century stringed musical instrument. "North Armorica," appropriately given the American rather than the British spelling for "armor," strikes closer to home with its implications of American militarism. Joyce's opening of *Finnegans Wake* illustrates the way writers can use language "nonsensically" to create meaning that can escape the imperceptive or unilingual reader.

Samuel Beckett is another very influential writer of sensible nonsense. Beckett defends the compatibility of sense and nonsense in the couplet at the end of his short poem "Echo's Bones":

> the gantelope of sense and nonsense run
> taken by the maggots for what they are
>
> (*Poems in English*, 46)

Beckett and Eugene Ionesco helped create what is now called the theater of the absurd, a type of play where strange characters and sometimes stranger action exhibit the absurdity of the world and of life. Such plays, comic and serious at the same time, are good examples of sensible nonsense. As Blair Whitney demonstrates in part 3, their techniques have been adapted for a child audience in such television shows as "Sesame Street."

Sometimes, as in Ionesco's *The Lesson*, the scene and the initial action are quietly realistic, that realism unraveling as the dialogue slips from sense to insanity. *The Lesson* opens with a perfectly normal professor-pupil exchange and ends in a surreal climax during which the now tyrannically angry professor drives home the final lesson—"the knife kills"—by stabbing the pupil. It is a madder school session than any the Gryphon attended, proceeding to its final violence by way of wonderland arithmetic and such silly linguistic theories as: "The word 'front' is the root of 'frontispiece.' It is also to be found in 'affronted.' 'Ispiece is the suffix, and 'af' the prefix'" (*The Lesson*).

Among American (not "Armorican," please) playwrights, Edward Albee is perhaps the best known dramatist of the absurd. Although not as absurd in its action as *The American Dream* or *The Sand Box*, one play of his that is very apropos the nonsense tradition is *Tiny Alice*. The name may be an allusion to Carroll's Alice, but, however that may be, the essential feature of the stage set, a huge doll's house, is a metaphor for the possibility of infinite regression that nonsense gives us. The doll's house is an exact replica of the grand mansion in which it stands, and there is yet another smaller replica in the first. "You don't suppose," the butler says, "that within that tiny model in the model there, there is——— another room like this, with yet a tinier model within it, and within——— ———" (*Tiny Alice* 2.2). Julian, another character, continues the thought: "———and within and within and within and———" (2.2).

These examples of literature for adults exhibit a high level of nonsense, perhaps the highest level of the modern scene, and yet they are regarded as major literature that conveys a meaningful message. As Martin Esslin argues in his book *The Theatre of the Absurd*, "in expressing the tragic sense of loss at the disappearance of ultimate certainties the Theatre of the Absurd . . . is also a symptom of . . . a genuine religious quest in our age . . . an effort to make man aware of the ultimate realities of his condition" (351).

Nonsense Shared by Children and Adults

Other authors who write primarily for adults have produced some works of nonsense that are more lighthearted and are relished by both young and old. Gertrude Stein, T. S. Eliot, Carl Sandburg, E. E. Cummings, James Thurber, and Ogden Nash and cartoonists like Charles Addams and Walt Kelly are good examples in this category. Others, like Edward Gorey and Nancy Willard, write so effectively for both audiences that they are difficult to categorize. And as for those who have written or drawn nonsense mainly for children, their names are legion. Prominent among them are A. A. Milne, Carolyn Wells, Theodor Seuss Geisel (Dr. Seuss), David McCord, William Cole, Shel Silverstein, Peggy Parish, Dennis Lee, James Marshall, Arnold Lobel, and Muppet-master Jim Henson. Among these rich choices, the works in prose are frequently the most distinctively twentieth century in flavor and make a fitting conclusion to our history of nonsense. We will consider the modern artists and author-illustrators who draw as well as write nonsense and the modern nonsense poets in the sections on illustration and verse.

Nonsense Prose for Children

In the stories he wrote for *Winnie-the-Pooh* (1926) and *The House at Pooh Corner* (1928), A. A. Milne made an interesting contribution to the nonsense tradition by splitting the role of the child into two perspectives: that of the sensible Christopher Robin and that of the dreamy and

childlike but very inventive Pooh. In other words, both sense and nonsense are projected through characters that represent the child. Alice is
indeed the usually sensible observer of the antics of various crazy characters in Wonderland and Looking-Glass Land, but these characters represent the nonsense of the adult world rather than the whimsical misinterpretations of the child mind. In her book *Wordplay and Language Learning*,
Linda Geller sums up the worlds of Christopher Robin and Pooh very
well and shows why the book appeals to a wide range of ages:

> A. A. Milne's *Winnie the Pooh* series tends to explore strategies
> of play—those derived from linguistic ambiguities—that are en-
> joyed by the older elementary ages. The central character, how-
> ever, the bear named Winnie-the-Pooh, is, in thought and feeling,
> more like children in the early elementary years. (49–50)

But, one should add, like very clever children. Pooh, whose intellectual
modesty resembles that of the Scarecrow in *The Wizard of Oz*, thinks that
he is "a Bear of Very Little Brain," but actually the abnormal slant of his
vision enables him to find solutions—most of the time. In the very first
story, Pooh's aberrant and childlike reasoning leads him to believe that he
can fool the bees and steal their honey by hanging from a balloon and
posing as a small black cloud. But in a later adventure, when the world is
quite literally topsy-turvy because he and Owl and Piglet are trapped in
Owl's storm-toppled tree house, Pooh thinks of a way out for them:

> Pooh sat on the floor which had once been a wall, and gazed up
> at the ceiling which had once been another wall, with a front door
> in it which had once been a front door, and tried to give his mind
> to it. (Milne, *The World of Pooh*, 279)

His brain comes up with a plan to hoist Piglet up to the mailbox to escape
and go for help. "'Astute and Helpful Bear,' said Owl," and, proving
Geller's point that the series also contains wordplay, "Pooh looked proud
at being called a stout and helpful bear" (280).

Carl Sandburg is another well-known author who used the short story
form for writing nonsense. His books *Rootabaga Stories* (1922) and *Rootabaga
Pigeons* (1923) have delighted children for decades with their creative
characters, places, situations, and wordplay. The fun begins immediately
when Gimme the Ax "decided to let his children name themselves. 'The
first words they speak as soon as they learn to make words shall be their
names,' he said" (3–4). The results are the names "Please Gimme" for the
son and "Ax Me No Questions" for the daughter. When the threesome

decide to sell everything they own and leave, Gimme the Ax tells the railroad ticket agent that he wants a ticket to "far as the railroad rails go and then forty ways farther yet" (9). They are obviously seeking a destination beyond everyday reality and common sense. Later when they meet another train coming towards them on the same track, it is no problem because "this is the Over and Under country. Nobody gets out of the way of anybody else. They either go over or under" (11), a solution that would work only in a nonsense land.

As the stories continue, so do the improbable names: Wing Tip the Spick (a little girl), Potato Face Blind Man, Any Ice Today, the Village of Liver and Onions, Henry Hagglyhoagly, Blixie Bimber. These and others rival the inventiveness and the level of alliteration typical of nonsense from Mother Goose to Seuss. Joanne Lynn, in her essay "Hyacinths and Biscuits in the Village of Liver and Onions: Sandburg's *Rootabaga Stories*," observed that "naming things, being fascinated with one's own name, with the names of objects, with others' names are qualities shared by children and poets" (122), and we can add that bestowing outlandish names is the special province of nonsense authors. There are further absurdities in each story although some of them have a poignancy intermingled with nonsense, as in "Two Skyscrapers Who Decided to Have a Child" in *Rootabaga Pigeons*. Their child must be free, not rooted to one place, and so they have the Golden Spike Limited, a train that goes to the mountains, the sea, everywhere, until one day there is a terrible train wreck.

At times there is moralizing beneath the nonsense, as when Googler and Gaggler come home from school and describe the war between the pen wipers and the pencil sharpeners, where each side intends to fight until the last one is killed: "no matter how many million we kill, we are going to kill and kill" (*Pigeons*, 79). The same theme, the senselessness of war, is further demonstrated in the boys' second war tale about the people in Thimble country where the left-handed people were against the right-handed. "And the smoke-stacks did all the fighting. They all had monkey wrenches and they tried to wrench each other to pieces. And they had monkey faces on the monkey wrenches—to scare each other" (83–84). Authors before and after Sandburg have used nonsense for similar purposes. Swift has Gulliver recount the absurd Lilliputian disputes, whether between factions in the king's court as in the case of the "two struggling Parties . . . under the Names of *Tramecksan* and *Slamecksan* from the high or low Heels on their Shoes" ("A Voyage to Lilliput," chap. 4.35) or between the monarch and the rebellious "Big-Endians," who continue to break their eggs at the large end, even though Lilliputian law commands that eggs be broken at the small end (36). A generation after the *Rootabaga*

Stories Dr. Seuss wrote in a similar vein of the nonsensical quarrel between the Sneetches with and the Sneetches without stars on their bellies (*Sneetches and Other Stories*), and recently Seuss continued the tradition in his book about the ultimate absurdity of total war, *The Butter Battle Book*.

Joanne Lynn has written about the quality of Sandburg's tales as they "celebrate the wonder and absurdity of the American experience in a form that has enduring literary appeal for both children and adults. In spite of apparent irrationality and sheer nonsense, these tales are deeply rooted in the physical realities of the American Midwest, its geography, its economy, its folkways, its language" (118). Sandburg's stories give a classic proof of our contention that nonsense is inevitably tied to sense. Lynn also supports another of our theses, that there is a connection between poetry and nonsense, when she points out the relationship of the stories to poetry: "Sound and image, the tools of poetry, are far more important in Rootabaga country than plot and character, the tools of prose fiction" (121). She continues:

> Cast an eye quickly over the table of contents for samples: "The Story of Blixie Bimber and the Power of the Gold Buckskin Whincher," "How the Five Rusty Rats Helped Find a New Village," "How Dippy the Wisp and Slip Me Liz Came in the Moonlight where the Potato Face Blind Man Sat with His Accordian." Sheer length and incongruous specificity added to alliteration and internal rhyme promise a high vein of nonsense. The titles prefigure the elements of his nonsense poetry. (121–22)

Furthermore, "the 'craziness' of the Rootabaga Stories comes from incongruity, a device common to poetry and high nonsense" (124). The element of incongruity has an appeal for a dual audience but especially for children, who take particular delight in it. The *Rootabaga Stories* demonstrate quite clearly that the nonsense tradition was alive and strong on the North American continent in the first quarter of this century.

It was also thriving in England and Europe. For example, in *Mary Poppins* and the other books in that series, P. L. Travers skillfully combines reality with the nonsensical. The reader is introduced to the Banks family in a straightforward, realistic fashion, and the advent of a new governess, presumably as straight-laced as governesses are supposed to be does not seem to herald much possibility for nonsense. But with the appearance of Mary Poppins the governess (who seems to be blown into the gate and then against the front door) reality turns upside down. The first obvious break is when the two oldest Banks children, Jane and Michael, see her slide up rather than down the bannister. When she unpacks from what they saw was an empty carpetbag, out come "seven flannel nightgowns, four cotton ones, a pair of boots, a set of dominoes, two bathing-caps and a postcard album. Last of all came a folding camp-bedstead with blankets and eiderdown complete" (13). Her powers of transcending ordinary reality are displayed throughout the book, and the scene in which the children and their governess take their tea floating near the ceiling is the epitome of nonsense.

A children's favorite from the continent is the *Pippi Longstocking* series, which has continued to delight children since its first volume appeared in 1945. Author Astrid Lindgren constrasts realistic characters, Thomas and Annika, with Pippi and her extraordinary capabilities and lifestyle. As Bettina Hurlimann noted in *Three Centuries of Children's Books in Europe*, "it has now been generally accepted that the three books published in England as *Pippi Longstocking* [1950], *Pippi Goes Aboard* [1956], and *Pippi in the South Seas* [1957] are full of the most splendid and comical nonsense" (82). Take, for instance, that delightful chapter "Pippi Goes to School." From the time that Pippi (full name: Pippilotta Delicatessa Windowshade MacKrelmint Efraim's Daughter Longstocking) gallops into the school-yard in time for what she calls "pluttifikation" until she rattles the schoolhouse windows as she rides away, she subverts the assumptions on which the school day is built. Arithmetic goes by the way after Pippi first thinks the teacher really does not know the answer to simple questions about addition, and then, given the same answer for eight and four as for seven and five, Pippi exclaims, "that is carrying things too far. You just said that seven and five are twelve. There should be some rhyme and reason to things even in school" (*Pippi Longstocking*, 55). Reading lessons are also set aside because Pippi, informed the first letter of "ibex" is called "i," declares, "That I'll never believe . . . . I think it looks exactly like a straight line with a little fly speck over it" (55). Neither can she understand the symbolic value of the letter "s" which sets her off on a long tale about her fight with a snake in India. Pippi charms the reader with her independence, but school-age readers, while they applaud Pippi's triumph over the teacher, are well aware that her perspective is cock-eyed. She has superior experience in the oddities of the world, but is their inferior in orderly intellectual skills. This dichotomy gives the books much of their sharp humor.

Hurlimann discusses other writers in her chapter, "Fantasy and Reality: Nonsense from Peter Pan to Pippi Longstocking." She mentions the skill of the German writer, James Kruss: "he asks questions, he plays with words, and he lets children play with words until they understand what the craft of words actually is" (85). Hurlimann also classifies Maurice Druon's *Tistou of the Green Thumbs* as "a nonsense story containing strong surrealistic elements, which an adult reader will interpret differently from an eight-year-old child" (90). In general she demonstrates how strong an element nonsense has been in children's literature over the last century.

Gertrude Stein, who is noted for her attempt to push back the boundaries of language usage, contributed a rather original type of nonsense with her long story *The World Is Round* (1939). In this tale of Rose and Willie, Stein casually blends prose and verse and mixes light humor with fever-dream intensity as the story spirals to its conclusion. For example, in a prose passage (or at least it is a passage whose typographical arrangement signals it as prose) we learn

> An then there was Rose.
> Rose was her name and would she have been Rose if her name had not been Rose. She used to think and then she used to think again.
> Would she have been Rose if her name had not been Rose and would she have been Rose if she had been a twin.
> (qtd. in Butler, *Sharing Literature with Children*, 411)

The same questions and other equally unanswerable ones are posed in verse form in Rose's song:

> I am a little girl and my name is Rose
> Rose is my name.
> Why am I a little girl
> And why is my name Rose
> And when am I a little girl
> And when is my name Rose
> And where am I a little girl
> And where is my name Rose
> And which little girl am I
> Am I the little girl named Rose
> Which little girl named Rose.
>
> (412)

Willie, more confident if less metaphysically speculative, proclaims in his song that "I would be Willie if Henry was my name" (413). Both the prose and the poetry do indeed go round and round in the round world whose roundness makes Rose cry. Stein included some suggestions for reading her circular prose on the jacket flap of the first edition:

> This book was written to be enjoyed. . . . Don't bother about the commas which aren't there, read the words. Don't worry about

the sense that is there, read the words faster. If you have any trouble read faster and faster until you don't. (qtd. in Butler, 411)

Following these instructions creates a dizzying blend of sense and nonsense. Try reading the following passage very fast:

> And then as she looked she saw that one mountain had a top and the top was a meadow and the meadow came up to a point and on the point oh dear yes on the point yes Rose would put a chair and she would sit there and yes she did care yes there she would put a chair there there and everywhere she would see everywhere and she would sit on that chair, yes there. (421)

Besides pulling us along with the whirling rush of her prose, Stein plays games with the concept of roundness. For example, Rose "had to think about number 142. Why. Numbers are round" (421). One of Willie's songs is a delightful jingle on the subject:

> Round is around.
> Lions and tigers
> Kangaroos and canaries abound
> They are bound to be around.
> Why
> Because the world is round
> And they are always there.
>
> (417)

The more timid Rose speculates:

> If the world is round
> would a lion
> fall
> o
> f
> f.
>
> (419)

Throughout the story Stein refuses to let her reader rest; even when Rose reaches the mountaintop with her chair in tow, sits down and "is so pleased with sitting she just sat" (428), her mind keeps churning out songs: "When I see I saw I can / I can see what I saw" (428). One of Rose's rhymes reads like a page from Dr. Seuss:

Am I asleep or am I awake
Have I butter or have I cake,
Am I here or am I there,
Is the chair a bed or is it a chair.
Who is where.

(428)

Stein's story is a masterful combination of linguistic nonsense and psychological sense. As J. D. O'Hara puts it in his essay on Stein's story, "pretending to be a mere tots' tale about childish dream adventures, told in a cheerful kind of baby talk, it is actually the Halloween skeleton of a series of often grim psychological experiences" (in Butler, 446). "Grim" may be too strong a word, but Stein has used nonsense to explore some deep questions about identity, the search for self, and the individual's relationship with the round world all around.

Another writer thought of more in connection with his literature for adults is E. E. Cummings who, in addition to a number of lyrical nonsense poems that we will cover in the section on verse, wrote four tales for his daughter. Beautifully illustrated by John Eaton, they were published posthumously as *Fairy Tales* (1965). The first story, "The Old Man Who Said 'Why?,'" was obviously Cummings's reaction to his daughter's repeated questioning. It is a witty, inventive tale that focuses on an old man who sits on top of a church steeple on the moon and drives everyone crazy with his one-word reply to everything: "Why?" The faerie asked to remedy the situation soon becomes frustrated and angry and finally sends the man to earth. As he travels from the moon, the man grows younger and younger "until, just as he gently touched the earth, he was about to be born" (14).

The next two tales are about incongruous twosomes. In "The Elephant and the Butterfly" we have an example of the mismatched animal mates found so often in nonsense literature. But in spite of their extreme differences, these two characters meet and fall in love, "and they loved each other always" (22). The second couple is even more unusual, crossing the clearly disparate categories of inanimate and animate: "Once there was a house who fell in love with a bird" (24). The bird also loves the house. When three people discover and plan to take over the house, a sudden cacophony of clocks fortunately drives them away, leaving bird and house alone once more, and "so they were as happy together as happy could be" (31). The story's title (wonderful nonsense in itself), "The House That Ate Mosquito Pie," refers to the delicacy that the two make in celebration of finding each other.

Cummings's last tale, "The Little Girl Named I," in its wordplay more closely resembles his adult writings than do the previous three. The story is a conversation between a man and a child, the man asking the little girl questions as he tells her a story. A repeated exchange that continues through various encounters (horse, pig, elephant) runs:

> "And who do you suppose she meets?"
> "A cow, I suppose."
> "Yes, that's right . . . . and what does this cow say?"
>
> (32)

When "this little girl named I sees another little girl just like her" (39), the wordplay begins in earnest. The new little girl says, "You is my name because I'm You" (39). The last exchange, which in both style and topic resembles passages from Stein's *The World Is Round*, is delightful:

> Then I said to You "Would you like to have some tea?" I said. And You said "Yes. I would" You said. So then You and I, we went to my house together to have some tea and then we had some fine hot tea I suppose and some delicious bread and butter too, with lots and lots and lots of jam. (39)

Cummings has created his nonsense in the guise of fairy tales but with a highly original cast of characters and situations. He has shown how to stretch the boundaries of sense until they burst into nonsense in a variety of fresh, inventive ways.

Other authors have turned the never-never land of fantasy and fairy tale into nonsense land. James Thurber, perhaps best known in children's literature for his 1943 Caldecott Medal Book *Many Moons*, has contributed other fantasies as well that contain even more nonsensical elements. In *The White Deer*, for example, Thurber has a fine time with wordplay as King Clode gets his tongue tangled: "Try twice that trick on Tlode . . . and we will wid these wids of woozards" (16). The chapter, "The Perilous Labor of Prince Thag," is also rife with tongue tanglers like "Hag's thad enought" (50). There are also wingless birds and musical mud, a barking tree, snowflakes that become butterflies, and lengthy sentences rife with alliteration. One reads in part: "along the pearly path, across the valley of violets, over the ruby ridge and the misty moor [echoes of *Beowulf*], through the fiery fen and the golden glade and the bronze bog and the silver swamp" (21). His characters are equally ridiculous, especially the Royal Physician who is ill and who explains to the King, "As a physician, I must take my temperature every three hours . . . but as a patient, I must not be told what it is" (33). Therefore, "he shook the mercury down without looking at it" (33). Thurber has crammed this spoof of a fairytale with absurdities and parodies of literary conventions.

Thurber's story *The Great Quillow* contains wild exaggeration in describing the giant Hunder and his demands on the villagers, and thereby qualifies as nonsense under the tall-tale tradition. Thurber again has fun with words. He plays with possible pronounceable orderings of "Lobo" and names the blacksmith's horses "Lobo, Bolo, Olob, and Obol" (22). (One wonders why there are not four more horses named Bloo, Bool, Loob, and Oobl.) However, his wordplay in *The Great Quillow* is not to the extent evident in *The White Deer*. And Thurber does not have as much fun with wordplay in either of these as he does in *The Wonderful O*.

In *The Wonderful O*, he humorously investigates the nature of analogy and especially the traps of false or overstretched analogies. His villain Black has hopelessly confused the levels of reality represented by actual objects on one level, the mere names of these objects on the next, and, on an even more abstract level, the arbitrary letter symbols that spell these names. Black has had a hatred of the letter "O" "ever since the night my mother became wedged in a porthole. We couldn't pull her in and so we had to push her out" (4). A quest for treasure leads Black and his cohorts to the island of Ooroo where they find no jewels but loads of things whose names contain the letter "O": "owls in oaks, moss and moles, toads and toadstools, roots and rocks" (7). Black becomes obsessed with a plan to banish "O" from the universe, first forbidding his subjects to use anything that has an "O" in its name and eventually banning the "O" words themselves.

Nonsense sentences creep in well before the edicts abolishing words with "O" when Black enunciates sentences like "I'll squck his thrug till all he can whupple is geep" (8). But the language becomes more ridiculous as the edicts against the letter "O" increase. When even words with "O" can no longer be used, both words (Ooroo becomes "R") and vocabulary shrink. Such important abstractions as "love" and "freedom" are lost. Although Thurber's extended use of this one verbal joke begins to wear a bit thin, his manipulation of language remains enjoyable. The book abounds in alliteration and random sprinklings of rhyme; "corduroy and bombazine, organdy and tricotine, calico and crinoline" (22), even rhyming sequences of names: "Lancelot and Ivanhoe, Athos, Porthos, Cyrano, Roland, Rob Roy, Romeo. . . . Ichabod and Captain Hook—names enough to fill a book" (60–61). In the end, sense triumphs over the nonsense of an O-less world, and Black's misguided machinations are defeated.

As these humorous tales demonstrate, Thurber liked to knock the verbal world askew. He also brought his nonsense vision to the many cartoons he drew for the *New Yorker*. A famous and frequently reproduced one shows a couple in a bed that has a seal peeping over the headboard while one of the characters complains of hearing a seal bark. The Thurber dog, which appeared in so many of his drawings, conveys in its minimal lines an air of patience, long-suffering, and boredom that is simplistic humor at its best. Edward Lear might well have envied Thurber that dog. Cartoonists have contributed a fair share of this century's nonsense, but some of the best examples have been aimed at an adult audience and, therefore, outside the scope of this study. A few have bridged the generation gap and had wide appeal for both adults and children. Thurber is a member of this select group, as is Charles Addams.

Addams, the famed *New Yorker* cartoonist whose memorable characters became part of the televison series "The Addams Family", added his inimitable brand of visual nonsense to many of the familiar nursery rhymes in *The Charles Addams Mother Goose*. In the somewhat sinister nonsense of his nursery rhyme illustrations, Jack Sprat and his wife eat a man (only his spectacles, watch and collar are left); Tom, the piper's son, is running away with a pig's skeleton; the broken Humpty Dumpty has a small dragon inside; and a monstrous spider with a leering expression creeps up behind Little Miss Muffet. These are just a few samples of his macabre sense of humor.

His single-panel cartoons, though often quite sophisticated, have also engaged a young audience over a number of years. Such captionless drawings as the one in which an adult commuter looks out his train window and sees an enormous young boy manipulating a Lionel model train switch (*Homebodies*, 66) or the one in which an astronaut is tied down a la Gulliver by a swarm of tiny Martians (*Black Maria*, frontispiece) are in the mainstream of the nonsense tradition. In a number of his cartoons the fairytale world and the real world mix: a policeman on his rounds is astounded to see elves working in a shoe-repair shop, or a miner is amazed to see the White Rabbit in the beam of the lantern on his miner's cap (*Homebodies* 6, 12). Similarly, in a collection entitled *Addams and Evil*, a brother and sister read the label on the Gingerbread House: "CONTAINS GLUCOSE, DRY SKIMMED MILK, OIL OF PEPPERMINT, DEXTROSE . . ." (n.p.). Addams's captioned cartoons turn fairy tale conventions upside-down: The grandmother of the Addams family finishes her bedtime story with "Then the dragon gobbled up the handsome young prince and his lovely bride and lived happily ever after" (*Homebodies*, 66). Until his death in 1988, Addams contributed an occasional cartoon to the *New Yorker*, but currently, Edward Gorey seems to have inherited the role of chief propagator of eerie nonsense.

Children in the second half of the twentieth century have been, of course, more frequently influenced by nonsense routines that appear on the television screen rather than on the printed page. Much of what they see is repetitious slapstick, although the Saturday morning animated cartoons do contain some legitimate nonsense conventions such as reversibility, most popularly depicted by the flattened character who reinflates. And fortunately a few series show intelligence and imagination. Jim Henson, whose Muppets have appeared on "Sesame Street" and the "Muppet Show," has managed to combine material drawn from children's literature, vaudeville, and the theater of the absurd to produce some very successful nonsense sequences, which Blair Whitney analyzes in his essay on the subject in part 3 of this book.

An undercurrent of seriousness runs beneath a froth of nonsense in a number of works written for the juvenile book market. A work like Maurice Sendak's *Outside Over There* moves more in the world of the surreal than in the world of light humor. And yet through its illustrations, it deals with burgeoning sunflowers, storms, and flights through space that would not be out of place in Oz. In Sendak's *Higglety Pigglety Pop, or, There Must Be More To Life*, the dog–heroine's acting out of the nursery rhyme is high nonsense at several removes from reality. It is a spoof on a spoof. The nursery rhyme on which it is based reads

> Higglety, pigglety, pop!
> The dog has eaten the mop;
> The pig's in a hurry,
> The cat's in a flurry,
> Higglety, pigglety, pop!

This was American moralist Samuel Griswold Goodrich's scornful challenge to what he considered the mindlessness of nonsense verse. The nonsense tradition, without blinking an eye, incorporated the jingle, swallowed, and digested it as unconcernedly as the dog ate the mop. On the surface *Higglety Pigglety Pop* may seem the most lighthearted of Sendak's nonsense, and yet it is an elegy of sorts; he wrote and illustrated the book as a way to cope with the loss of the pet who is the heroine. Nonsense, it seems, may serve many purposes.

Nancy Willard's story "Gospel Train" in *Sailing to Cythera* also deals with the idea of death by using the conventions of nonsense. Funeral Latin and a cat with the cozy name of Plumpet are comfortably juxtaposed. A "Gospel Train" takes the young protagonist Anatole along imaginary tracks to the christening party for Plumpet's Aunt Pitterpat who has just "gone to get a new skin" (5), her ninth skin. It is a lovely but improbable journey that Anatole takes on the train filled with animals,

"He scrambled to his feet and there, waiting to be noticed, crouched the Blimlim."

From *Sailing to Cythera* by Nancy Willard, illustrated by David McPhail.

some clothed, some not. The story seems to be, at heart, something of a celebration of the whole nonsense tradition, although with somber under-tones.

At twilight the train is ferried across to the underworld, here named Morgentown. They find Aunt Pitterpat riding a merry-go-round in her ninth and eternal skin. Glad to see them, she nevertheless warns that if they do not leave by that night's train, they must stay forever. When the fox conductor overimbibes on blackberry wine and fails to return to drive the train, Anatole, experienced as he is on Lionel trains, drives. Recross-ing the River Styx proves a problem. They rouse the ferryman, who from Plumpet's description ("He looks like a thistle . . . . White hair, white beard, white coat, white boots'" (14), seems more like God the Father than Charon. The bargaining over the fare is an example of that strange mixture of lyricism and nonsense that is Willard's hallmark:

> "This is my river, and my lions are the boat," said the old man.
> "What will you pay me for taking you across?"
> "What do you want?" asked Anatole.
> "The fox always gives me a piece of the sky."
>
> (15)

Unable to supply this, Anatole gives the old man his heirloom pocket watch and his raggedy sneakers.

> Then the old man glanced up at Anatole's shirt and sighed.
> "What a wonderful shirt! What is that inscription on it?"
> "My T-shirt? It says *Oxford, Michigan, Gravel Capital of the World.*
> I got it when I went to visit my grandma."
> "Your grandma lives in a gravel pit?" inquired the old man. (17)

Willard pulls off this and other outrageous combinations. That is just what the best nonsense does.

There are also some subgenres of humorous prose that should be mentioned. Nonsense parodies of fairy tales are popular. Thurber's *The White Deer* represents one type of these. Besides playing with language so cleverly, it also brings together diverse fairy tale conventions and stands them on their heads. For example, all three brothers succeed in the task set, an eventuality ruled out in a serious fairy tale. Countless authors and illustrators have given a humorous twist to a particular fairy tale. In the fifties, Jules Feiffer wrote and drew a satiric version of Cinderella in which a chimney sweep becomes a bosomy, famous movie star thanks to her "friendly neighborhood Godmother" who speaks to her via a blank television screen (*Passionella*, n.p.). Recently (1987), James Marshall has added his zany illustrated version of "Little Red Riding Hood" to the many humorous retellings of that tale (Thurber's among them). These are only two examples from among thousands that have appeared in cartoons and stories in this century.

Nonsense biographies, though less prevalent, also have their niche in children's literature. Two of Robert Lawson's books are a case in point. He has created absurd biographies of Benjamin Franklin (*Ben and Me*) and Paul Revere (*Mr. Revere and I*), told, respectively, by a mouse and a horse. For what the title page describes as "A new Astonishing Life of Benjamin Franklin as written by his Good Mouse Amos" the small rodent author takes "pen to paw" to set the record straight about his part in perfecting the Franklin stove, experimenting with electricity in a hair-raising fashion, and contributing to the Declaration of Independence, which is allegedly derived from a mouse manifesto. The horse's version of Revere's exploits is similarly irreverent.

Nonsense can be found in other subgenres. There are nonsense detective stories, Dean Hughes' Nutty series for one example, and many humorous science fiction stories for children, Jane Yolen's, for example. But the majority of such works of parody fall into the category of social satire in which the trenchant sense outweighs the nonsense and, therefore, we shall not deal with these subgenres at greater length.

This survey of some twentieth-century nonsense practitioners began with a quotation from *Harriet the Spy*, a book that although humorous is not, strictly speaking, nonsense literature. What Harriet's exchange with Ole Golly reveals, however, is the important place that a nonsense poem can have in the life of a child. More profoundly, it reveals the way in which nonsense humor can serve as a buffer against pain that might otherwise overwhelm. Hamida Bosmajian writes, in her essay "Louise Fitzhugh's *Harriet the Spy*: Nonsense and Sense": "*Harriet the Spy* meshes two modes of fiction—satire and psychological realism—through which the sense and nonsense of the story are revealed. Both modes are ironic, but satire often employs irony through nonsensical and comic aggression, whereas psychological realism seriously examines the nonsense of human life" (in *Touchstones*, 1: 73). This deeper level on which nonsense affects us is not its only lasting benefit. Nonsense does much more than simply move us to immediate laughter. It wears the motley coat of a court jester and it serves us as the jester served the king: mocks pompousness, reveals false sentiments and false logic, and, most importantly, keeps us from taking ourselves too seriously. For the young it serves as a release from the demands of the sometimes threatening world of grown-ups and allows children to negotiate in that world in a playful way.

Addams, Charles. *Addams and Evil* New York: Simon, 1947.
———. *The Charles Addams Mother Goose.* New York: Windmill Books, 1967.
———. *Black Maria.* New York: Simon, 1960.
———. *Homebodies.* New York: Simon, 1954.
Albee, Edward. *Tiny Alice: A Play.* New York: Atheneum, 1965.
Becket, Samuel. *Poems in English.* New York: Grove, 1961.
Bosmajian, Hamida. "Louise Fitzhugh's *Harriet the Spy*: Nonsense and Sense." In *Touchstones: Reflections on the Best in Children's Literature* 1: 71–85. Ed. Perry Nodelman. West Lafayette, IN: ChLA, 1985.
Cummings, E.E. *Fairy Tales.* New York: Harcourt, 1965.
Dr. Seuss. *The Butter Battle Book.* New York: Random, 1984.
———. *Sneetches and Other Stories.* New York: Random, 1961.
Esslin, Martin. *The Theatre of the Absurd.* Garden City, NY: Doubleday, 1969.
Fitzhugh, Louise. *Harriet the Spy.* New York: Dell, 1983; rpt. from Harper, 1964.
Geller, Linda Gibson. *Wordplay and Language Learning for Children.* Urbana, IL: NCTE, 1985.
Hurlimann, Bettina. "Fantasy and Reality: Nonsense from *Peter Pan* to *Pippi Longstocking.*" In *Three Centuries of Children's Books in Europe.* London: Oxford UP, 1967.
Ionesco, Eugene. *The Lesson. Four Plays by Eugene Ionesco.* Trans. Donald M. Allen. New York: Grove, 1958.
Joyce, James. *Finnegans Wake.* New York: Viking, 1959.
Lawson, Robert. *Ben and Me.* Boston: Little, 1951.
———. *Mr. Revere and I.* Boston: Little, 1953.
Lindgren, Astrid. *Pippi Longstocking.* 1945. Illus. Louis S. Glanzman. New York: Viking, 1950, 1963.
Lynn, Joanne. "Hyacinths and Biscuits in the Village of Liver and Onions: Sandburg's *Rootabaga Stories.*" *Children's Literature* 8 (1980): 118–32.
Milne, A. A. *The World of Pooh.* New York: Dutton, 1957.
O'Hara, J. D. "Gertrude Stein's *The World Is Round.*" In *Sharing Literature with Children: A Thematic Anthology.* Ed. Francelia Butler. New York: Longman, 1977. 446–49.
Sandburg, Carl. *Rootabaga Stories.* New York: Harcourt, 1967.
———. *The Wedding Procession of the Rag Doll and the Broom Handle and Who Was in It.* Illus. Harriet Pincus. New York: Harcourt, 1967.
Sendak, Maurice. *Higglety Pigglety Pop, or, There Must Be More To Life.* New York: Harper, 1967.
———. *Outside Over There.* New York: Harper, 1981.
Stein, Gertrude. *The World is Round.* William R. Scott, 1939 & 1967. Rpt. in *Sharing Literature with Children: A Thematic Anthology.* Ed. Francelia Butler. New York: Longman, 1977. 411–30.
Thurber, James. *The Great Quillow.* Illus. Doris Lee. New York: Harcourt, 1944.
———. *The White Deer.* Illus. author and Don Freeman. New York: Harcourt, 1949, 1968.
———. *The Wonderful O.* Illus. Marc Simont. New York: Simon, 1957.
Travers, P. L. *Mary Poppins.* 1934. New York: Harcourt, 1962.
Willard, Nancy. *Sailing to Cythera and Other Anatole Stories.* New York: Harcourt, 1974.

Part II

THE BENEFITS OF
NONSENSE

4

Its name is quite a hard one, but you'll learn
it soon, I hope.
   So try:
      Tri-
         Tri-anti-wonti-
            Triantiwontigongolope.
. . . .

And unless you call it softly it will stay away
and mope.
   So try:
      Tri-
         Tri-anti-wonti-
            Triantiwontigongolope.

C. J. Dennis, "The Triantiwontigongolope,"
qtd. in Fisher and Allen, Amazing Monsters, 16

Nonsense

Sound and Sense

"Take care of the sense and the sounds will take care of themselves," the
Duchess admonishes Alice during the croquet game. Lewis Carroll's
phrasing is good advice for expository writing, but, as Bruce Ross
suggested in a paper delivered to the 1986 Modern Language Association
session on nonsense, a reversal of the axiom—"Take care of the sounds
and the sense will take care of itself"—may be a better dictum for
nonsense writing. Certainly, playing with possible mixtures of sound and
meaning (or non-meaning) is a major element in the nonsense tradition.
This importance of sound over sense is undoubtedly one reason why
children take so readily to nonsense literature and games. As Linda Geller
says, "Sound is the sensory aspect of speech that young children can
manipulate to better acquaint themselves with that system's structures"
(Wordplay and Language Learning, 18).

There are a number of important points to consider when analyzing the types of sounds and the sound patterns that frequently occur in nonsense language:

1. Nonsense literature (even in prose form) shares many strategies with poetry.
2. Nonsense employs many devices that derive from oral tradition.
3. Nonsense may emphasize sound at the expense of sense, but, with rare exceptions, nonce words (sound units empty of assigned meaning) are within the phonemic system of their language.
4. Nonce words are usually straightforwardly phonetic in their spelling.
5. Nonsense language gives children a nonthreatening medium for practicing the subtle variations in the sound patterns of their language and allows for what could be called a second, more sophisticated babbling stage.
6. Nonsense, although it may emphasize sound, can, paradoxically, enhance an understanding of meaning and of the nature of language.

Let us consider these points in turn.

Nonsense Shares Many Strategies with Poetry

"Verbal play, like poetry," says Geller, "is characterized by economy of written expression and density of meaning" (60). And Walter Nash notes in his book *The Language of Humour* that "Jesting language is frequently 'layered,' working its effects combinatively through sounds, through vocabulary, and through grammar and syntax. In this convergence of linguistic elements, it resembles—obviously—the language of poetry" (124). He also says, "humorous language shares a characteristic of poetic language in the frequent convergence of stylistic traits; rhyme or alliteration, for example, may sharply contour a striking grammatical structure that houses some form of lexical play" (12). Nonsense uses many such sound patterns that are conventions of traditional poetry. In fact, it overuses them to the point where pattern and emphasis no longer enhance meaning, as they do in serious poetry, but distort or reverse meaning or push it over the limit into absurdity.

Rhyme and nonsense verse are virtually synonymous as the term *nursery rhymes* suggests, but rhyme is not an essential ingredient of all nonsense. Alliteration and assonance, however, are stylistic devices that inform nonsense constructions in both prose and poetry and in both written and oral traditions. Look, for example, at Edward Lear's work, where a random sampling of his verse in Holbrook Jackson's edition of *The Complete Nonsense* harvests "mumbian melody" ("Daddy Long-legs and the Fly," 68), "willeby-wat" and "flippity flup" ("Calico Pie," 79), and "Fimble Fowl" and "Bisky Bat" ("The Quangle Wangle's Hat," 253–54). In his prose story *The Story of Four Little Children Who Went Round the World*, there are alliterative phrases like "Tropical Turnspits" (94), and "Diaphanous Doorscraper" (*Complete Nonsense*, 106). Lear also has some subtle permutations of sound in *The Scroobious Pip* where the refrain by the mysterious, mixed-creature Pip is initially:

> Chippetty flip! Flippetty chip!
> My only name is the scroobious Pip!
>
> (Sec. 1)

After this answer to the fox, the later refrains in sections 2 to 5 reverse and vary the first line: "Flippetty Chip! Chippety flip!" (to the birds), "Pliffity flip! Pleffity flip!" (to the fish), "Wizzeby wip! Wizzeby wip!" (to the insects), and finally "Chippetty tip! Chippety tip!" (to all creation). Lear has given us a fine example of how a nonsense writer uses literary tropes, here alliteration and assonance combined with onomatopoeia, to create a nonsensical surface and an underlying meaning.

If we turn to some modern nonsense writers, we find similar patterns. For instance, Spike Milligan, who is as popular with British young people as Shel Silverstein is with their American counterparts, has a nonsense verse ("On the Ning Nang Nong") which uses alliterative sequences, like that of the title, to play through a series of vowel changes. Another example of this is his teapots that "Jibber Jabber Joo" (Cole, *Oh What Nonsense*, 56). Not as consistently nonsensical as Milligan's, Shel Silverstein's language walks a linguistic tightrope above the abyss of nonsense and occasionally executes a laugh-provoking fall. Silverstein's humor depends more on impossible happenings than on nonsense words, but "Ickle Me, Pickle Me, Tickle Me too" (*Where the Sidewalk Ends*, 16–17) and "Ski-hi-dee, fly-hi-dee, why-hi-dee-go / . . . Where-hi-dee, there-hi-dee, scare-hi-dee-boo" (*A Light in the Attic*, "Hippo's Hope," 88), which use assonance in the form of internal rhyme, are as zany as any sequence in Milligan or Mother Goose. Silverstein certainly shares the love of outrageous sounds that characterizes nonsense writers. His language is often reminiscent of children's own outpourings. He uses words that mimic noises: "CRASH! . . . BASH! . . . BANG! . . . WHOOSH!" (*Sidewalk*, "The Fourth," 15) and "sloosh-woosh" and "glug-glug" (*Sidewalk*, "Skinny," 142).

Nursery rhymes are rich in alliteration and assonance. Read the list in

TABLE 1. REFRAINS IN MOTHER GOOSE RHYMES

Hickere, Dickere Dock (31.8)
Nauty Pauty (32.12)
High diddle, diddle (56.45)
Sing jig my jole (89.95)
Diddle Diddle Dumpling (106.129)
rub a dub dub (106.139)
Dingty, diddledy (116.152)
Diddlety, diddlety, dumpty (118.159)
Bumpety, bumpety, bump!
• • •
Lumpety, lumpety lump! (123.162)
Trisky, whisky, wheedle!
Fiddle. faddle. feedle! (124-25.165)
Tweedledum and Tweedledee (125.167)
Fiddle cum fee (128.179)
With a ring a ting tang (146.216)
Petrum, Partrum, Paradise, temporie
Perrie, Merrie, Dixie, Dominie (162.270)
Higglety-pigglety pop (164 note 74)
Hyer iddle diddle dell (164.274)
Hey diddle dinkety, poppety pet (164.275)
Hickety, pickety (171.299)
Chickle, chackle, chee (173.308)
Hi cockalorum, jig, jig, jig (228.559)
Dingle, dingle, doosey (231.573)
Incey, wincey spider (234.579)
Ziccary zan
• • •
Spittery spot
• • •
Twiddleum twaddleum
• • •
Hink Spink (249.628)
Looby, looby, looby (252.637)
A dis, a dis, a green grass
A dis, a dis, a dis (256.645)
Hittity Hot! (258.647)
Slitherum, slatherum (260.658)
Highty, tighty, paradighty (277.714)
Hoddley, poddley (319.846)
Oh, Pillykin, Willykin, Winky Wee! (326.875)

Source: William S. and Ceil Baring-Gould, *The Annotated Mother Goose*
(New York: World Publishing, 1972). The numbers in parentheses
represent the page and the number assigned to the verse.

Table 1 and listen to the refrains that bounce throughout the various Mother Goose collections that the Baring-Goulds brought together in *The Annotated Mother Goose*.

Of these examples drawn from thirty-one verses, fifteen employ assonance, in most cases creating internal rhymes, and (not counting simple repetition) twenty use alliteration. These devices both highlight nonsense phrases and provide a lively lesson in pronunciation.

Note that some of the sequences ring changes on a word to create nonce words ("Fiddle, faddle, feedle" and "Chickle, chackle, chee") or otherwise play with similar sound combinations ("spittery spot" and "Slitherum, slatherum"). This type of playing with sound dances around meaning and sense, delights in testing the limits of a given language, and creates phonemic units that could be words but are not (at least for the moment). A similar playfulness has given us "hippies" and "yippies" and "yuppies" in our century. Children spontaneously work through such sequences. Geller recorded frequent instances among the three-year-olds she observed, one of the most interesting by a child named Kimberly who, asked to tell a story, produced:

> Shama sheema
> Mash day 'n' pash day
> 'N' mash day 'n' cash day
> 'N' mash day 'n' much day
> 'N' much day 'n' push day
> 'N' lush day 'n' push day.
>
> (21)

The girl was, as Geller astutely notes, unconsciously "experimenting with substituting initial phonemes" (21), ringing the changes on both consonants and vowels. It is a technique that Theodor Seuss Geisel employs consciously in the language play in his books.

Walter Nash includes rhyme and rhythm among the "coupling mechanisms" (*The Language of Humour*, 22) that can signal humorous intent and comments that "Comic rhymes are effective either because they are banal and easily predictable, or because they are so remote as to defy expectation" (155), and that comic rhythm is also of two types: banal, "one that marches exactly, in relentless synchronization, with its governing metre"; and lawless, "one that accepts or discards metrical rule, as the rhymester's convenience dictates" (161). Similarly, nonsense constructions not only exaggerate and overuse such poetic devices as rhythm, rhyme, alliteration, and assonance, but they also distort them to mirror a world that is slightly askew. Ogden Nash provides good examples of warped rhyme:

Higgleby, piggleby, my black hen,
She lays eggs for gentlemen;
Sometimes nine, and sometimes ten,
Higgleby, piggleby, my black hen!

From *Granfa' Grig Had a Pig*, compiled and illustrated by Wallace Tripp.

> The ostrich roams the great Sahara.
> Its mouth is wide, its neck is narra.
>
> > (*Verses from 1929 On*, qtd. in
> > Cole and Calmenson, 257)

He also wrenches the meter whenever it suits him. Walter Nash quotes Ogden Nash's lines:

> Let us pause to consider the English,
> Who when they pause to consider themselves they
> > get all reticently thrilled and tinglish.
> > ("England Expects," qtd. in *The Language of Humour*, 162)

He comments that although "rhyme and meter generally go together, . . . in Ogden Nash's verse the expectation of metrical law is frustrated. . . . But each gobbet of gabble ends with a rhyme, pulling the reader back to the notion of regularly-timed verse" (162). Such abuse of meter, as well as overly strict adherence to metrical rules, signals humor and highlights nonsense.

Naturally, nonsense prose does not make such heavy use of poetic devices, but some devices , such as subtle alliteration, help to emphasize nonsense phrases. In Lear's *The Story of the Four Little Children Who Went Round the World* one passage reads:

Illustration by Edward Lear from "The Story of the Four Little Children Who Went around the World."

> After sailing on calmly for several more days, they came to another country, where they were much pleased and suprised to see a countless multitude of white Mice with red eyes, all sitting in a great circle, slowly eating Custard Pudding with the most satisfactory and polite demeanour. (97)

Notice the preponderance of "s" and "z" sounds. The passage is scarcely a tongue-twister, but its humor is heightened by the light mimicry of this form. Later in the story when the children encounter the Blue-Bottle Flies "who discoursed . . . with a slightly buzzing accent" (99), the same sounds are used in manner that makes whole phrases into onomatopoeia: "occasioned a fizzy extraneous utterance" (99) and "buzz at once in a sumptuous and sonorous manner" (100).

Lewis Carroll slyly pokes fun at the very nature of alliteration by crossing the boundary between the literary and the graphic arts. At the mad tea party the Dormouse describes the three sisters who lived in a treacle well as "learning to draw . . . and they drew all manner of things—everything that begins with an M————. . . such as mouse-traps, and the moon, and memory, and muchness" (*Wonderland*, chap. 7). Clearly, both Lear and Carroll have a similar incisive vision and similar methods.

Nonsense Employs Devices from Oral Tradition

The nonsense refrains in nursery rhymes have become formalized in English as agreed upon nonce sequences that have carried over from generation to generation. They are enduring—and memorable—in part because their characteristic repetition, rhyme, and alliteration are aids to the memory, what Walter J. Ong describes as "the heavy mnemonic patterning found in the original oral cultures of all mankind" (*Interfaces of the Word*, 205). Ong further notes that "a child in technological society today passes through a stage something like that of the old oral culture" (299). This is one reason why children who are not yet literate and who still live in a world where language comes to them primarily through the ear, not the eye, enjoy nursery nonsense so greatly. Even after learning to read and becoming at least partially literate, children retain their love for, and use of, sound games. Still in what psycholinguists call the age of resonance, children continue through grade school to learn by ear and to relish sequences where a phonetic rather than an intellectual logic rules.

This phenomenon is perhaps the answer to the Opies' query on how "children who cannot remember their eight-times table for half an-hour, can nevertheless carry in their heads assemblages of rhythmical sounds, and do so with such constancy that gibberish remains recognizable although repeated in different centuries, in different countries and by children speaking different languages" (*Children's Games*, 44). It is not altogether mysterious. Oral cultures transmitted legends through centuries, almost intact, and, as we said, children, before they become fully literate, retain an ability for aural/oral retention that literate peoples have let atrophy. On a very deep linguistic level a set of phonetically related sounds has a more "sensible" order than a times table, or the majority of sentences for that matter. In times tables or sentences, the sound sequence is, as sound, random, nonsensical, one might say. To the ear of a person who does not

From *Four-and-Twenty Watchbirds*, written and illustrated by Munro Leaf.

understand the language code or the mathematical logic that informs a sequence, there is no discernible pattern.

That children relish phonetically linked sequences is evident from the frequent use of alliteration in the game chants they share with each other in a continuing oral subculture that transmits skip rope, hide and seek, chasing, and counting-out rhymes from one school-age group to the next. The tradition has been noted in scattered references as far back as Plato, whom the Opies quote as mentioning games that "children find out for themselves when they meet" (*Children's Games*, 6). Many of the Mother Goose rhymes seem to have originated with street games or other activities of children. The Baring-Goulds inform us that the nonsense phrase "slitherum slatherum" occurs in a rock-skipping rhyme and that "Hittity Hot!" is part of a jingle repeated in a glove-dropping game, and of course everyone knows that the song "London Bridge is falling down" is associated with a children's game.

These child-invented (or at least child-perpetuated) chants were not systematically documented until the nineteenth century when collectors like James O. Halliwell began, in *Popular Rhymes and Nursery Tales* (1842) to note their possible origins. By the end of the nineteenth century the interest was growing and such books as *Games and Songs of American Children* (1884) by William Wells Newell and the two-volume *Traditional Singing Games of England, Scotland, and Ireland* (1894–98) by Alice Bertha Gomme appeared. Throughout this century there have been similar collections: Henry Bett's *The Games of Children: Their Origin and History* (1929), Carl Withers *A Rocket in My Pocket: The Rhymes and Chants of Young America* (1946), the many books by Iona and Peter Opie such as *I Saw Esau: Traditional Rhymes of Youth*, *The Lore and Language of School Children*, and *Children's Games in Street and Playground*, and recently, Francelia Butler's international collection called *Skipping around the World: The Ritual Nature of Folk Rhymes*.

The Opies collected such game chants directly from children throughout England. Alliteration and rhyme and rhythm, those memory aids so strong in all oral traditions, are present in most of these. One famous example is "Eeny, meeny, miney, mo," a counting-out rhyme for which the Opies give more than twenty variations, some in foreign languages, like "Ene, mene, ming, mang" in Danish (*Children's Games*, 45). There is a more varied use of alliteration and assonance in a Chinese Counting rhyme:

> Addi, addi, chickare, chickare,
> Oonie, poonie, om pom alarie,
> Ala wala whiskey,Chinese Chunk.
>
> (*Children's Games*, 39)

And there is a very heavy use of alliteration in one Manchester counting-out chant (or "dip" as English children say):

> Zig Zag Zooligan
> Zim zam bum
>
> (*Children's Games*, 17)

The Opies give thirty-five zestful variations of one "dip" of which the four examples given below give the phonetic flavor.

Iggy oggy,	Iddle oddle,
Black froggy,	Black poddle,
Iggy oggy out.	Iddle oddle out.
(Girl, 13, Dulwich: 32)	(Somerset, 1922: 32)
Ickle ockle	Eettle ottle,
Black Bottle	Black bottle
Ickle ockle out.	Eettle ottle out.
(Girls, Swansea: 32)	(Aberdeen, several: 33)

Although versions of this dip have been traced to the beginning of this century (and of course may be even older), it is difficult to know which version is closest to whatever words were originally chanted. As the Opies point out, the variations can be " 'correct' for particular areas" (*Children's Games*, 32). Perhaps the slacker pronunciation found south of the Scottish border accounts for the "Iddle oddle," and the glottal stop found in parts of southern England (and in Boston) for the "Ickle ockle."

However that may be, that children do change and sometimes conflate the sounds of game chants is supported by the authors' childhood memories. In Brookline, Massachusetts, players were called in from hide and seek with

Allie allie in free!

While in the east end of Louisville, Kentucky, the call was
Ollie ollie oxen tree!

and in the west end of town,
Holler over the ocean. Holler over the sea.
All who're out may come in free.

(The Opies cite a chasing chant from Arncliffe in West Riding that is similar: "Charlie over the water, Charlie over the sea,/ Charlie caught a blackbird, and can't catch me," 80). The variations raise interesting questions. Is one version the source? If so, which version? Is "Ollie" a corruption of "Holler" or a variation on "Allie" (meaning "all")? At any rate, the variations on these and other chants result from the same process at work in the game called "Gossip" or "Secret" or "Whisper" or "Telephone" where a message is transmitted sotto voce from person to person around a group and emerges radically changed. It is, in fact, the process by which all language evolves—a slight mishearing, a slight change in reproducing the sounds of a word or phrase. It is a common route to nonsense words and phrases in oral tradition. There are also literary examples, like the carol that Walt Kelly has Pogo sing, "Deck us all with Boston Charlie" (*Songs of Pogo*, 147) and Ramona's title for our national anthem, the "dawnzer" song in Beverly Cleary's *Ramona the Pest* (14). And every family with a child learning to talk can give examples such as

Fee, fi, fo, fum, I smell the blood of an English muffin.
(Lynn Susan Apseloff, age 3 or 4)

We laugh at such aural/oral confusions whether they are spontaneous and confined to an immediate group or crafted into enduring nonsense words in a work of literature—or handed down through centuries from mouth to mouth in the rich oral tradition of song and rhyme.

There has been much commentary on Lewis Carroll's creation of portmanteau words, which result from a semiconscious intellectual conflation of two words, but Carroll was equally aware of the role that mishearing plays in the creation of nonsense. While a tutor at Oxford, Carroll wrote a letter to his sister and brother, Henrietta and Edwin Dodgson, that reads in part:

> My one pupil has begun his work with me, and I will give you a description how the lecture is conducted. . . . I sit at the further end of the room; outside the door (*which is shut*) sits the scout [a tutor's go-for]; outside the outer door (*also shut*) sits the sub-scout; halfway down stairs sits the sub-sub scout; and down in the yard sits the *pupil*.
>
> The questions are shouted from one to the other, and the answers come back the same way. . . . The lecture goes something like this.

> *Tutor*. "What is twice three?"
> *Scout*. "What's a rice tree?"
> *Sub-Scout*. "When is ice free?"
> *Sub-sub-Scout*. "What's a nice fee?"
> *Pupil* (timidly). "Half a guinea!"
> *Sub-sub-Scout*. "Can't forge any!"
> *Sub-Scout*. "Ho for Jinny!"
> *Scout*. "Don't be a ninny!"
> *Tutor* (looks offended, but tries another question).
> (*Selected Letters*, Jan. 31 [?1855], 15–16)

Quite obviously, many of the humor-breeding confusions and misconstructions of nonsense literature have their origin in the spoken language, and some were formalized in an oral tradition before being recorded in writing.

Nonce Words and Phonemic Systems

Nonsense must be grounded in accepted conventions. If it becomes complete gibberish, it is simply mad ravings rather than humor. A very unambiguous example of this dependence on convention is that virtually all the nonce words invented by writers of nonsense stay within the phonemic system of the language (that set of sounds used to form meaningful words). For example, the French have many fine vocalic distinctions that do not exist in English while, on the other hand, English speakers distinguish between the sounds of "th" and "t" but French speakers do not. Any speech sound that falls outside a language's phonemic system is difficult for a native speaker to hear or pronounce clearly. For this reason, nonsense words that survive and enter the tradition of folklore and literature are likely to be those constructed from the basic, recognizable sound elements and accepted sound sequences of the language that contains them. The simple spelling of nonce words may spring from this same cause.

In *The Phantom Tollbooth*, Norton Juster acknowledges the language specific nature of the sounds that make up both nonce and real words. Several officials of King Azaz, ruler of Dictionopolis, explain the Word Market to Milo:

> "Once a week by Royal Proclamation the word market is held here in the great square and people come from everywhere to buy words they need or trade in the words they haven't used."
>
> "Our job," said the count, "is to see that all the words sold are proper ones. . . . For instance, if you bought a word like *ghlbstk*, where would you use it?"
>
> (42–43)

The first problem with *ghlbstk* is how to pronounce it in English. We do not have words in which no letter is (or like "y" can stand for) a vowel. There are, as with any rule, exceptions. Some writers have included such unpronounceable clusters among the words they invent. Cartoonist Al Capp named that dour, luckless character who walks around with a dark cloud over his head Joe Bltzspk precisely because the name is unpronounceable. But in a way this exception proves the rule; Joe Bltszpk is a hexed character, outside society, and his name also is outside of his society's language.

Words or sounds from another language can indeed be used for humor. Jokes in dialect or a foreign language are common and puns can sometimes depend on a mispronunciation so derived. However, the vast majority of nonce words are as simple as a baby's first sounds and can serve a similar purpose, that of aiding language acquisition. Consider a sampling of Lear's nonce words: *wikky, bikky, zikky* ("Mr. and Mrs. Spikky Sparrow," 82–84) or others like Lake *Pipple Popple*, City of Tosh, Soffsky Poffsky Tree, *puffled, buffled, fluffled*, (*The History of the Seven Families of the Lake Pipple Popple*, 106–112) or the *Bong-trees* that grow on the island of the *Yonghy Bonghy Bo* (237). All of these use sound combinations very common in English.

That twentieth-century creator of nonsense who undoubtedly holds the

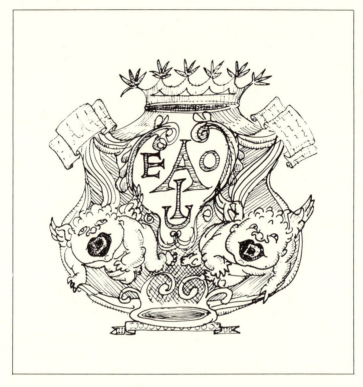

The royal coat of arms of King Azaz of Dictionopolis. Illustration by Jules Feiffer, from *The Phantom Tollbooth* by Norton Juster.

prize for new nonce words, Theodor Seuss Geisel, commonly known as Dr. Seuss, maintains a similar pattern. The one-syllable names of his animals like the Gox, the Ying, the Ish, the Gack, the Zeep, the Zed, and the Jedd, are eminently pronounceable and employ sound clusters basic to English. Seuss's *Sleep Book* yields "Biffer-Baum Birds," "Hinkle-Horn Honking Club," the "Audio-Telly-o-Tally-o-Count," the "Hoop-Soup-Snoop-Group," "Foona-Lagoona Baboona," and "Zizzer-Zoff Seeds." Such combinations, challenging initially to the eye but phonetically rather simple, are a hallmark of nonsense words. It is no coincidence that this modern master of nonsense was drawn into the challenge of creating easy-to-read books for children.

Beginning with *The Cat in the Hat*, Dr. Seuss has frequently tailored his books to the needs of children learning to cope with reading. The "I Can Read It All by Myself" Beginner Books from Random House publishers have a picture of the Cat in the Hat for logo and many of them are written by Dr. Seuss. For example, *One fish, two fish, red fish, blue fish* very inventively uses the pedagogical technique of illustrations combined with word repetition in slowly expanding contexts to allow the child reader access to the book. A simple example of this occurs in the sequence "Some are sad. / And some are glad. / And some are very, very bad. / Why are they sad / and glad and bad? / I do not know. / Go ask your Dad" (n.p.). With humor rather than monotony, Dr. Seuss has managed a simple lesson on the frequently used phoneme "ad." Expanding on the idea that "funny things are everywhere," the book moves from the fish of the title out into a zany Seussian universe that includes Yops and Zans (who open cans) and Mr. Gump's Wump ("if you like to go Bump! Bump! / Just jump on the hump of the Wump of Gump," n.p.), another simple lesson on an English phoneme, in this case "ump," a component of many words besides those Seuss chose (for example, *dump, lump, mumps, pump, rump, rumple, rumpus, sump, umpteen*).

Seuss's *Oh Say Can You Say?*, a book of nonsense tongue twisters, really puts readers through their paces. Dr. Seuss has listened closely to the language, and takes us beyond the simple initial letter alliteration of classic tongue twisters like Peter Piper. He presents us with such challenges as "A Simple Thimble or a Single Shingle" (n.p.), a nightmare combination for anyone with a lisp. Even worse is the next page's "Skipper Zipp's Clipper Ship Chip Chop Shop." He also gives us some practice in alternating voiced (*b, d, g,* and *z*) and voiceless (*p, t, k,* and *s*) sounds with phrases such as "Pete Briggs' Pink Pigs Big Pigs Pigpen." Any child who reads aloud through *Oh Say Can You Say* will have a thorough lesson in the sound system of English as well as practice in a skill important to reading, visual word recognition.

THE STRAIGHTFORWARD, PHONETIC SPELLING OF NONCE WORDS

As anyone who has tried to conquer the system of spelling in English knows it sometimes has little connection with the normal phonetic values assigned to a given letter. For this reason, English-speaking children have a great deal of difficulty learning to spell. One helpful, boundary-crossing type of language game subverts standard spelling. Represented by works like William Steig's *CDB?* and *CDC?*, this specialized form of riddling asks the reader to equate a letter with a word. The two titles are simple examples, which, decoded by the ear, ask, "See the bee?" and "See the sea?" Steig plays this game with examples that range from simple one or two syllable words (U = you, D-K = decay) to whole sentences like "D D¢ S E-Z-R N D A¢" (*CDC?*, n.p.), which translates: "The descent is easier than the ascent."

As with many forms of nonsense, children take to this strategy spontaneously. Carol Chomsky in her essay "Approaching Reading through Invented Spelling" notes instances of it. Gyles Brandreth includes "Say It With Letters" in his book *Word Games*. Like the rebus, which partially depends on such letter-sound spellings, the Say-It-With-Letters game is standard fare for children. The popularity of this type of play is further attested in movies and television shows where characters are dubbed with names spelled with letter sounds, punningly in one case, as K–9, the name for the canine robot on "Dr. Who," shows.

Seuss has long regarded the linguistic snarl of our spelling system as amusing. Long before he wrote for children, he wrote as the initial piece for a magazine series called "Dr. Seuss's Little Educational Charts," a page entitled "Ough! Ough! Or Why I Believe in Simplified Spelling," This "chart" contains three brief and nonsensical essays: "The Tough Coughs As He Ploughs the Dough," "Mr. Hough, Your Bough is in the Trough," and "Enough! Enough! I'm Through!" (in *The Tough Coughs As He Ploughs the Dough*, 57). He acknowledged the "-ough" glitch in our spelling system more subtly in *Oh Say Can You Say* with the lines "When a walrus lisps whispers /through tough rough wet whiskers" (n. p.). In *Dr. Seuss's ABC*, he makes an overt reference to spelling (a subject curiously ignored in most ABC books) with

> X is very useful
> if your name is
> Nixie Knox.
> It also comes in handy
> spelling ax
> and extra fox.
>
> (n.p.)

Seuss's more meaningful acknowledgement of the need for simplified spelling is his consistent use of phonetically simple words in his nonsense constructs. Most are one syllable, and even some others that may appear formidable at a glance (like "Biffer-Baum Birds" and "Foona-Lagoona Baboona," both from the *Sleep Book*), are easily sounded out. They are much easier to pronounce and spell than many polysyllabic words in the standard lexicon of English.

Of course, some nonsense words are intentionally difficult, intended either to mock pompous words or to convey a foreign or archaic flavor. The first verse of that most famous of nonsense poems, Lewis Carroll's "Jabberwocky," with its overload of nonce words and its old-fashioned constructions, "'Twas brillig" and "mome raths outgrabe" (*Looking-Glass*, chap. 1) was originally written (when Carroll was twenty-three) in a mock runic script as a "Stanza of Anglo-Saxon Poetry" (Martin Gardner's note in *The Annotated Alice*, 191). And Edward Lear's portmanteau words are often mocking in tone: "ombliferous" ("There was a Young Person of Crete," *Complete Nonsense*, 13), "borascible" ("There was an Old Person of Bangor," 44). The context of one such word in a passage from "The Story of Four Little Children Who Went Round the World" indicates quite clearly that a parody of pompous language is intended:

> . . . the melodious and mucilaginous sounds . . . resounding across the tumultuous tops of the transitory Titmice . . . with a serene and sickly suavity known only to the truly virtuous. The Moon was shining slobaciously . . . while her light irrigated the . . . backs of the Blue-Bottle-Flies with a peculiar and trivial splendour. (in *Complete Nonsense*, 100)

Only "slobaciously" is a nonce word, but Lear has grouped other perfectly respectable words in such a way that they lose all their dignity and most of their sense. "Tumultuous" is indeed a resounding word, but it should be paired with ocean waves or great battles, not used to describe the "tops of transitory Titmice." In another instance, the meanings of the modifiers "peculiar" and "trivial" cancel out the meaning of "splendour" and leave it truly with no sense. Taken as a whole, the passage suggests that a conglomeration of polysyllabic words may contain more sound than sense. Lear has dealt a blow to the solemnly pretentious prose of his time.

These examples are indeed more complex than the one- or two-syllable nonsense words so common in nursery rhymes, but they too serve for practice by slightly older children who are trying to come to grips with a wider vocabulary, much of which still sounds like gibberish to them. If the meaning of, for instance, "barcarole" is unknown, it sounds neither more nor less silly than "borascible." Much adult conversation is simply so much hocus pocus to children, but nonsense can serve as the counter magic that will give them the courage to unriddle the many puzzling conversations they hear. Adult and child alike, we garble or simplify words we find difficult. Children do this daily (and are often corrected for it). In the world of nonsense, this practice is permissible, and is precisely that: practice.

NONTHREATENING NONSENSE WORDS: LEARNING SOUND PATTERNS

Nonsense words enhance children's facility with both speech and writing partly because (at least in English) they tend to be more simply phonetic than many other words. Both the nursery rhyme refrains in table 1 and the following examples show this:

> Twikky wikky wikky wee,
> Wikky bikky twikky tee,
> Spikky bikky bee!
> (Lear, "Mr. and Mrs. Spikky Sparrow," 81)

> Ploffskin, Pluffskin, Pelican Jee!
> We think no Birds so happy as we!
> Plumpskin, Ploshkin, Pelican jill!
> We think so then, and we thought so still!
> (Lear, "The Pelican Chorus," 232)

Note the repetition of phonic clusters in the verses. This repetition echoes the manner in which an infant repeats individual sounds in order to learn them.

Much has been written about the initial babbling stage of the infant, which serves as practice for the sounds that form human speech, but we have located no systemic study on the later, more intellectual "babbling" which allows the young to try out words and syntax beyond their immediate ken. Nonsense words and sequences are extremely helpful in this stage. Children do not fear being laughed at for a gaffe because the whole point is experiment and laughter.

A profound relationship exists between the nonsense tradition and children's progress in speaking, reading, and writing (which of course means spelling out words). The young use nonsense constructs to experiment with a language, to learn to shape its distinctive and distinguishing sounds, to hear what carries meaning, to connect the black symbols on a white page with speech, to understand that written code well enough to decode it and reproduce it, and finally, to understand, at least intuitively, the arbitrariness of the sense-sound connection in words. And the nonsense tradition, defined broadly, as we have defined it, to include wordplay and nonce words and humor that makes intellectual boundaries visible by crossing them, aids children in all these areas. Riddles, nonsense verse, puns, palindromes, portmanteau words reveal the complexities of language, and in each of these, phonetic and phonemic considerations set the rules.

Nonsense, by its very nature, gives permission to children to experiment, to break linguistic rules, to babble nonce words if they please, and by these means to come round about to sense. Just as the recent experiments in physics have shown that ceramics, which were regarded as insulators, non-conductors of electricity, are actually superconductors—even so, nonsense turns out to be a superconductor of sense.

Baring-Gould, William S. and Ceil Baring-Gould. *The Annotated Mother Goose*. New York: World, 1972.

Bett, Henry. *The Games of Children: Their Origins and History*. London: Methuen, 1929. Detroit: Singing Tree Press, 1968.

Brandreth, Gyles. *Word Games*. New York: Harper, 1986.

Butler, Francelia. *Skipping around the World: The Ritual Nature of Folk Rhymes*. Hamden, CT: Library Professional Publications, 1988.

Carroll, Lewis. *The Annotated Alice*. Ed. Martin Gardner. New York: World, 1963; rpt. 1972.

———. *The Selected Letters of Lewis Carroll*. Ed. Morton N. Cohen. New York: Pantheon, 1982.

Chomsky, Carol. "Approaching Reading through Invented Spelling." In *Theory and Practice of Early Reading*, 2. Ed. L.B. Resnick and P.A. Weaver. Hillsdale, NJ: Lawrence Erlbaum Associates, 1979.

Cleary, Beverly. *Ramona the Pest*. Illus. L. Darling. 1968. New York: Scholastic, 1975.

Cole, Joanna and Stephanie Calmenson, eds. *The Laugh Book: A New Treasury of Humor for Children*. New York: Doubleday, 1986.

Dennis, C.J. "The Triantiwontigongolope." In *Amazing Monsters: Verses to Thrill and Chill*. Ed. Robert Fisher. London and Boston: Faber and Faber, 1982.

Dr. Seuss [Theodor Seuss Geisel], auth. and illus. *The Cat in the Hat*. New York: Random, 1957.

———. *Dr. Seuss's ABC*. New York: Random, 1960.

———. *Dr. Seuss's Sleep Book*. New York: Random, 1962.

———. *Oh Say Can You Say*. New York: Random, 1979.

———. *One fish, two fish, red fish, blue fish*. New York: Random, 1960.

———. *The Tough Coughs As He Ploughs the Dough: Early Writings and Cartoons by Dr. Seuss*. New York: Morrow, 1987.

Geller, Linda Gibson. *Wordplay and Language Learning for Children* Urbana, IL: NCTE, 1985.

Gomme, Alice Bertha. *The Traditional Games of England, Scotland, and Ireland*. 2 vols. 1895–98. New York: Dover, 1964.

Halliwell, James O. *Popular Rhymes and Nursery Tales*. London: Bodley Head, 1970; 1st edition 1842.

Juster, Norton. *The Phantom Tollbooth*. New York: Random, 1961; rpt. 1964.

Kelly, Walt. *Songs of Pogo*. New York: Simon, 1956.

Lear, Edward. *The Complete Nonsense of Edward Lear*. Ed. Hol- brook Jackson. New York: Dover, 1951.

———. *The Scroobious Pip* (completed by Ogden Nash). Illus. Nancy Ekholm Burkert. New York: Harper, 1968; rpt. 1987.

Milligan, Spike. "On the Ning Nang Nong." In *Oh What Nonsense!* Ed. William Cole. Illus. Tomi Ungerer. New York: Viking, 1966.

Nash, Walter. *The Language of Humour: Style and Technique in Comic Discourse.* White Plains, NY: Longman, 1985.

Newell, William Wells. *Games and Songs of American Children.* New York: Dover, 1963; 1st edition 1884.

Ong, Walter J. *The Interfaces of the Word.* Ithaca and London: Cornell UP, 1977.

Opie, Iona and Peter Opie. *Children's Games in Street and Play- ground.* New York: Oxford UP, 1984.

———. *I Saw Esau: Traditional Rhymes of Youth.* London: Williams and Norgate, 1947.

———. *The Lore and Language of Schoolchildren.* Oxford: Clarendon Press, 1960.

Ross, Bruce. "The Poetics of Nonsense: Echoic Abuse and Hyper- bole in Lewis Carroll's *The Hunting of the Snark.*" Paper read at a session on "Nonsense in Children's Literature" at Modern Language Association Convention, New York City, Dec. 29, 1986.

Silverstein, Shel, auth. and illus. *A Light in the Attic.* New York: Harper, 1981.

———. *Where the Sidewalk Ends.* New York: Harper, 1974.

Steig, William. *CDB?* New York: 1968.

———. *CDC?.* New York: Farrar, 1984.

Withers, Carl. *A Rocket in My Pocket: The Rhymes and Chants of Young America.* New York: Holt, 1946.

5

Said Folly to Wisdom,
  "Pray, where are we going?"
Said Wisdom to Folly,
  "There's no way of knowing."

Said Folly to Wisdom,
  "Then what shall we do?"
Said Wisdom to Folly,
  "I thought to ask you."

Tudor Jenks, in Wells, 204

Semantics and Nonsense

Words Alive with Meaning

A healthy dose of nonsense benefits the mind as well as the ear. In her study *Wordplay and Language Learning for Children*, Linda Geller states that "for the primary years . . . nonsense play represents a specific method for exploring the nature of the language system" (41). Because nonsense structures reveal how to create or subvert meaning in a given language, they can be a major aid in children's acquisition of language. According to Geller, wordplay encourages children to "focus on linguistic forms and functions . . .[and] to examine the makeup of the system through the violation of usual courses of communication" (8). Marlene Dolitsky in her study of nonsense provides a succinct list of the ways it violates the expectations of daily discourse. She holds that nonsense can disrupt (1) the expected relation usually found between a word and meaning, (2) the

63

conventional relation among words, and (3) the expected relation between the external world and the text or speech. Because of these misconnections, "meaning is emergent from the words' own interanimation" (Dolitsky, *Under the Tum-tum Tree*, 8). If discovering meaning from such interanimation of words seems too complex for childplay, consider that this is also a fairly good description of how we derive meaning from any sentence. Dolitsky means that nonsense creates a limited, self-referential world, and such a microcosm can be examined and rearranged more easily than the world at large. Children enjoy boundaries of this sort. It is one of the things they like about games. And children's love of play extends to word manipulation. It is not surprising, then, that Geller found that nonsense's "greatest champions tend to be youngsters in the five-to-seven age range, who, along with their preschool allies endlessly explore the possibilities of turning the world topsy-turvy through their appreciation of nonsensical descriptions of things" (31).

Kornei Chukovsky, the celebrated Russian scholar, writer, and educator, maintains, in his book *From Two to Five* that

> nonsense . . . not only does not interfere with the child's orientation to the world that surrounds him, but, on the contrary, strengthens in his mind a sense of the real; and . . . it is precisely in order to further the education of children in reality that such nonsense verse should be offered to them. (90)

Where some adults feel that children will lose touch with reality through nonsense, Chukovsky believes that the opposite actually happens. Children "do not for one moment believe in their [nonsense creations'] authenticity" (95). However, before the child can begin to enjoy or create wordplay, a knowledge of the true meanings of words and situations (dogs bark, cats meow) must precede the nonsense (a barking cat or meowing dog). Thus,

> to the child who plays with topsy-turvies, in an "upside-down world," this playing affords pleasure only if he does not forget for a single moment the actual juxtaposition or interrelation of things. . . . In other words, the pleasure is the greater the less he believes in the illusion created by his imagination. (100–01)

Chukovsky adds that for the child "every departure from the normal strengthens his conception of the normal. Thus he values even more highly his firm, realistic orientation" (102). More than that, topsy-turvies "raise the child's self-appreciation. And this is useful because it is essential for the child to have a high opinion of himself" (102). Think of the failures children encounter every day because of their size and their lack of knowledge of the world and how it operates, not to mention their attempts at acquiring language, and, therefore, how important each accomplishment, physical or verbal, becomes to them for their mental growth—and how comforting legitimized laughter is in the process.

Children can learn a number of language strategies through nonsense constructions: the double (or multiple) meaning of certain sound combinations, the nonliteral nature of idioms, the presence of nonce words (and therefore the need to learn the definitions of accepted words), the need for syntactical clarity, and, especially in English, the peculiar, often nonphonetic relationship between letter symbol and sound. We will explore and give examples for all of these and will also consider those nonlinguistic aspects of nonsense—incongruity and exaggeration.

PUNS

Two very fruitful types of nonsense are ambiguous words (which allow for puns) and idioms (which can be absurd when taken literally). Walter Redfern, in his book *Puns*, states that "puns illuminate the nature of language in general . . . The punster always works within limits. He cannot invent puns which are not already potential in the language" (99). He explains further that "the key movement of a pun is pivotal. The second meaning of a word or phrase rotates around the first. Or branches off of it" (23). Redfern believes that puns "make us stretch our minds and double our attention" (24). Walter Nash also explores the pun in *The Language of Humour*, where he says that "puns, like metaphors, fossilize in the very substance of the language; it is hardly possible to work the ground extensively without turning up a . . . pun. At the heart of all this wordplay seems to be a concern with two ancient and related processes: naming and riddling" (146). He also points out that the pun is often taken "for a simple thing, which it is not; a typology of punning would occupy many pages and catalogue many variants" (139), which is, of course, exactly what Walter Redfern's book does. Nash gives many examples of puns from Shakespeare and mentions that "the homophonic pun is the form above all loved and practised by nineteenth-century wits like Lamb and Hood and Carroll" (138).

Another nineteenth-century writer, known not so much for his wit as for his wisdom, but not above punning, is George MacDonald. MacDonald is more often thought of in terms of the fairy tale rather than as a creator of nonsense, but he wrote one fairy tale that Roger Lancelyn

Green, in his introduction to *The Complete Fairy Tales of George MacDonald*, calls "nearly all sheer fun" (8). The story, "The Light Princess," has the trappings of a fairy tale—a prince, princess, and evil witch—but it seems more concerned with wordplay than with magic. The evil-doer, for example, is the Princess Makemnoit (which could mean "make them" night/dark/nought/naught). Vindictive over not being invited to the christening, she pronounces a curious malediction:

> Light of spirit, by my charms,
> Light of body, every part,
> Never weary human arms—
> Only crush thy parents' heart!
>
> (15)

This spell deprives the baby princess of her gravity both physically and temperamentally.

The witch's spell results in extravagant scenes, such as the one when the servants toss the floating princess about the room like a ball or the one when the princess, grabbing a handy frog to weight herself down, inadvertently smacks the face of a page with it. In other words, "light," the very term used to describe the princess, carries a double meaning.

MacDonald plays with the word "light" at length. One conversation between the king and queen revolves around its various meanings:

> "It is good thing to be light-hearted, I am sure."
> "It is a bad thing to be light-headed," answered the queen.
> "It is a good thing to be light-handed," said the king.
> "It is a bad thing to be light-fingered," answered the queen.
> ". . . And it's a bad thing to be light-haired," screamed she.
> . . . The king hated all witticisms, and punning especially.
> And besides, he could not tell whether the queen
> meant light-*haired* or light-*heired*. (21–22)

If the king says that "the most objectional form duplicity can assume is that of punning" (21), it is because he is a bit slow at catching puns. When he requests two Chinese philosophers with the ridiculous names Hum-Drum and Kopy-Keck to cure the princess of "her *infirmity*," MacDonald notes, "The king laid stress upon the word, but failed to discover his own pun" (35). The two quacks propose cures more ridiculous than their names. But, as this is fairy tale, however humorous, it is of course a prince who cures her. This prince is allowed an unemphasized pun that may be the only sexual double entendre in Victorian children's literature. When he jumps into the lake while holding the princess, and she, for the first time in her life is impelled downward, she asks, "Is that what you call *falling in?* . . . It seemed to me like going up." The prince replies, "My feeling was certainly one of elevation too" (56).

MacDonald has said that "The Light Princess" was the favorite of his tales with his own eleven children, which suggests that the MacDonald children responded to its wit and wordplay. There is certainly enough evidence that children can both enjoy and invent rather complex verbal jokes. One of the dips that the Opies have recorded has a very sophisticated linguistic cleverness:

> Hickety pickety i sillickety
> Pompalorum jig,
> Every man who has no hair
> Generally wears a wig.
>
> (*Children's Games*, 37)

"Pompalorum" is an absolutely ingenious nonsense word in this particular context. It seems to be a portmanteau created by combining *pomade* (a perfumed hair oil) with *cockalorum* (which can mean both to brag and to be a conceited man). Whether a child invented it, we do not know, but it is children's oral culture that has kept the phrase alive.

IDIOMS AND FIGURATIVE LANGUAGE

Geller has several trenchant comments on children's interpretations of puns and certain idioms. She notes that "what contributes to an emerging sense of word-as-symbol is the discovery that many words sound the same but have different meanings" (*Wordplay*, 36) and that "literal interpretations of figurative expressions are proof of yet another important discovery about the nature of language: that it is full of words and phrases with multiple, metaphorically related meanings" (65). Such word analysis, involving metaphor and analogy, reveals the creative side of language and teaches a child that words when in use are alive and acrobatic. Geller found in her work with children that "the awareness that a single word or phrase can have multiple meanings begins to make an appearance around kindergarten age" (68). Children's authors tap this awareness. One of the most popular among them is Peggy Parish, the first of whose Amelia Bedelia series appeared in 1963. The books eventually became part of the

Greenwillow Read-Alone series and are ideal fare to tempt the child into reading by way of nonsense.

For children from five to eight Parish's series is a treasure trove. Ever since her first appearance, Amelia, a good-natured but decidedly daft maid, has been amusing a young audience with the nonsensical situations she creates through her misinterpretations. For examples, in the Rogers household for the first time, Amelia follows, to the letter, the list of duties she has been given: she changes the towels by cutting them into various shapes, puts dusting powder on the furniture, draws the drapes with pencil and paper. The hilarious results of such misunderstandings make children more aware of their language, of what it can do, and how it can misfire.

The zaniness continues throughout the series. In *Amelia Bedelia and the Surprise Shower*, Cousin Alcolu has to prune the hedge; Amelia shows him how, literally, by putting a prune on the hedge (he then does the same with the remaining prunes). When she is looking for a job, she stamps on some letters and runs a fingernail file over other papers (*Come Back, Amelia Bedelia*). In *Play Ball, Amelia Bedelia*, when told to tag a boy, she puts a real tag on his uniform instead of merely touching him, and in *Teach Us, Amelia Bedelia*, she plants light bulbs instead of flower bulbs. When Amelia is around, one silly situation follows another. Asked to take care of the baby for the day, she dutifully reads and follows her list of instructions:

> "Don't forget
> to put on Missy's bib."
> Amelia Bedelia found the bib.
> "That's plumb cute," she said.
> And Amelia Bedelia put it on.
> (*Amelia Bedelia and the Baby*, 48)

In a more recent book, *Amelia Bedelia Goes Camping*, she pitches the tent by throwing it into the bushes, and thinks that rowing boats means putting them in a row. Because the English language is such a ripe field for this kind of wordplay, the dozen or so books never have to repeat a particular phrase or expression. Because children share with Amelia Bedelia her literal-minded approach to language, often taking the meaning of a sentence for exactly what it says—not one word more or less—they take special delight in her antics. Through Amelia's nonsense, the young reader can begin to make sense out of the language, can begin to appreciate the varied levels and meanings it contains. This is also the first step towards appreciating poetry as well as prose, especially poetry with several layers of meaning.

RIDDLES AND JOKES

Riddles and jokes are two other popular forms that allow children to probe language. The many, many joke books available for children attest to the fascination they hold. Not all the humor in them is wordplay, but a high percentage is. Examples from two joke books that are in print after twenty years demonstrate this. Marguerite Kohl and Frederica Young produced *Jokes for Children* and *More Jokes for Children*. Because of a reliance on language-based jokes and because humor for juveniles tends to be less referential and topical than humor for adults, the entries do not seem dated. There are many simple puns, for example:

> Why is a river rich?
> Because the river has two banks.
>
> > (*Jokes for Children*, 39)

Some of the humor grows out of the way children disjoin combined words and discover quite other meanings:

> *Mother*: Dennis, use toothpaste on your toothbrush.
> *Dennis*: Why? My teeth aren't loose.
>
> > (*Jokes for Children*, 94)

Geller (*Wordplay*, 63) includes such instances of word boundary confusion as a major category in children's wordplay. She also explores how children enjoy and use imperfect puns, constructions "in which one similar-sounding word/phrase is humorously substituted for another" (79). She cites the popular knock-knock jokes as examples of humor based on imperfect punning, and also cites the following verse:

> Do you carrot all for me?
> My heart beets for you.
> With your turnip nose,
> And your radish face
> You are a peach.
> If we cantaloupe,
> Lettuce marry,
> Weed make a swell pear.
>
> > (80)

The lines revive memories of penny Valentine cards, and most readers will also remember less romantic examples from children's oral tradition such as: "Lettuce, turnip, and pea." Often scatalogical references appear in children's creations. "The Yellow Stream" by I. P. Daily is one of the many examples from childhood, along with limericks in a similar vein. These "originals," often passed from one generation to the next, are particularly attractive to children because of their "forbidden fruit" quality, their naughtiness.

Other riddle questions require not only a knowledge of word boundaries but also a knowledge of arithmetic: "How do you make seven even?" Answer: "Take off the *s*" (Kohl and Young, *More Jokes for Children*, 4). As Harry E. Eiss notes in the preface to his *Dictionary of Language Games, Puzzles, and Amusements*, "Mathematical play and language play often overlap (e.g. ABC words), yet these fields for the most part deal in two symbol systems" (xvi). Some jokes are based on the type of nonsense that Dolitsky described as a disjunction between the intended and perceived meaning. An example of this comes from a recent collection, Joanna Cole and Stephanie Calmenson's *The Laugh Book*: "Q: What's the best thing to put into a pie? / A: Your teeth" (8). Psychologists and educators hold that play constitutes work in childhood, that the business of the child is to learn adult roles through playful imitation. Similarly, wordplay, whether found in joke, verse, or riddle, is "wordwork." A serious investigation of language is proceeding under the laughter.

PARODIES

Children are great imitators. Lois Hood, in "Imitation in Children's Language Learning," notes that "in general, children imitate what they are in the process of learning" (10). Given examples, they can produce fascinating copies. There are examples in Nancy Larrick's collection, *Green Is Like a Meadow of Grass*, of metaphors and verses that children created after hearing Mary O'Neill's *Hailstones and Halibut Bones* and Carmen Bernos de Gasztold's *Prayers from the Ark*. One child wrote: "Gray is a feeling / like forgetting your lunch" (29). Children also enjoy listening to and creating parodies of rhymes and songs familiar to them. "Mary Had a Little Lamb" has been a favorite for parodies, with thirteen versions recorded by the Opies, and there are many more. One example that Geller gives is

> Mary had a little lamb,
> Her father shot it dead,
> It came to school with her one day
> Between two chunks of bread.

(87)

Observing that "the exploration of parody is not and never has been confined to the area of adult humor" (86), Geller cites from the many examples she collected of children's parodies of product names and TV shows, some of them, like "Sun Pissed Oranges" and "The Toilet Zone, starring Flush Gordon" (90), a bit scatalogical. Adults who think that parody is their bailiwick, a form of rhetoric beyond the grasp of children, need only return to the classroom or the pages of children's books to discover their mistake.

Verse parodies are perennial in children's literature, and a number of these will be discussed in chapter 11, "Nonsense and the Didactic Tradition." One popular writer for children, Arnold Lobel, has created parodies of familiar nursery rhymes in *Whiskers and Rhymes*. Instead of "Sing a song of six-pence," Lobel gives "Sing a song of succotash, / A Bucket full of noses" (10). "Old King Cole" is transformed into

> Old Tom, he was a merry one,
> A merry one was he.
> . . . .
> A dizzy one was he.
> He bumped his head and went to bed
> At quarter after three.
>
> (23)

Parody often conveys a darker view than the original it mocks, but in one instance Lobel's parody provides a happy reversal to a nursery rhyme. "I married a wife on Sunday" is, in the original, rather sour on life and marriage. In the version that the Baring-Goulds give, the wife's scolding increases through the week until "Dead was she on Friday; / Glad was I on Saturday night, / To bury my wife on Sunday" (*The Annotated Mother Goose*, 106, no. 131). In Lobel's version, the husband sickens but is nursed by a solicitous wife who gives him a pill and "buttered bread" so that "Full health returned on Saturday" and "When morning came on Sunday, / I gave my bride a kiss" (*Whiskers and Rhymes*, 24–25).

In *The Book of Pigericks*, Lobel created his special parody of limericks by turning the traditionally idiosyncratic characters of that verse form into pigs. The silliness of some of the lines is captured in Lobel's paintings. For instance, the verse reads

> There was a cold pig from North Stowe
> Who despised winter weather and snow.
> Sixteen coats never warmed him,
> They only deformed him,
> That frigid, cold pig from North Stowe.
>
> (15)

In the accompanying illustration, Lobel has robed the pig in countable layers of coats.

SATIRE

Children can also enjoy satire. They may miss some of the points made and hits scored against the subject of the satire, but, as Hamida Bosmajian notes, "Children are appreciative readers of satire, because of its aggression and its violation of taboos" (in *Touchstones*, 73). They can also appreciate many of the ploys of satire: size and role reversals, exaggerations, irreverence, and scatology. *Mad Magazine* would not have recently celebrated its thirty-fifth anniversary if children did not respond to this type of humor.

Not all satire is nonsense, of course, but most has at least some nonsensical elements. That premier satire by Jonathan Swift, *Gulliver's Travels*, contains impossible extremes of size, talking horses, and what may be the most humorously absurd treatment of language on record. Swift's professors (or "Projectors") of language in the grand Academy of Lagado had several mad plans for reforming language. "The first Project was to shorten Discourse by cutting Polysyllables into one, and leaving out Verbs and Participles; because in Reality all things imaginable are but Nouns" (part 3, chap. 5). This nonsensical proposal for achieving economy of language would make an excellent prompt for a lesson in grammar.

Swift also anticipated both Dadaist poetry and computer poetry with an invention by one of the "Projectors in Speculative Learning," a word machine (a sort of verbal abacus or insane word processor) which randomly turns up words and by which "Contrivance, the most ignorant Person at a reasonable charge, and with little bodily labour, may write Books in Philosophy, Poetry, Politicks, Law, Mathematicks and Theology without the least Assistance from Genius or Study" (part 3, chap. 5). Whenever the words were cranked into a new sequence, thirty-six students gleaned any "three or four Words together that might make Part of a Sentence" and recorded them. Ultimately these parts would be patched together and "literature" created. That literature would presumably be about the closest one could get to pure nonsense. The authors can attest that children love this type of language game. The Anderson children were very fond of cutting up magazine articles into individual words, shaking them in a bag and then pasting them on paper to make a Dada poem. The only editorial judgment allowed was where to end lines. As this was during the Watergate era, news stories thus garbled sometimes made quite as much sense as they had in their original form.

Northrop Frye wrote that *"Gulliver's Travels* shows us a man as a venomous rodent, man as a noisome and clumsy pachyderm, the mind of man as a bear-pit, and the body of man as a compound of filth and ferocity" (*Anatomy of Criticism*, 235). Children, who a year or two ago gleefully traded cards depicting the disgusting Garbage Pail Kids, apparently find such a vision of humankind quite as humorous as Swift did. One modern satirist who writes for children, Roald Dahl, shows up man's (and children's) foibles in *Charlie and the Chocolate Factory*. In this book the names presage the punishment inflicted on each of the nasty children who visits Willy Wonka's factory. For instance, Augustus Gloop is sucked into a chocolate-filled pipe, and Violet turns into a giant, purplish blueberry candy. The Oompah Loompahs, workers in the factory, seem a parody of a Greek chorus as they sing a satiric song after each diastrous episode. Dahl's book demonstrates how language can distort and exaggerate reality for satiric purposes.

TALL TALES

Exaggeration is the central feature of another form of writing that often contains nonsense and wordplay: the tall tale. In her book on the subject Carolyn S. Brown defines the tall tale as "a fictional story which is told in the form of personal narrative or anecdote, which challenges the listener's credulity with comic outlandishness" (*The Tall Tale in American Folklore and Literature*, 11). The nonsense in tall tales is well suited for revealing its opposite, common sense. Although tall tales contain punning, riddling, and parody or satire, they rely mainly on hyperbole, on extreme differences rather than likenesses. Using exaggeration, they reveal sense through contrast.

In their reading, children enjoy tall tales, both the traditional ones and their modern counterparts. The latter is exemplified by Judi Barrett's *Cloudy with a Chance of Meatballs*, in which Grandpa tells the two children about the unusual weather in the town of Chewandswallow where food, instead of rain and snow, comes down from the sky. "First there was a shower of juice. Then low clouds of sunnyside-up eggs moved in, followed by pieces of toast. Butter and jelly sprinkled down from the toast. And most of the time it rained milk afterward" (n.p.). It was a fine arrangement until the weather "took a turn for the worse" and the town becomes inundated with spaghetti, huge rolls, gigantic meatballs, jumbo cream cheese and jelly sandwiches and the like until the people are forced to leave (on their toast rafts with cheese-slice sails). Such books stimulate children's imagination and show them yet another way to have fun with words. As Tucker says about nonsense creations, they "have their function, in helping children to test out their knowledge of normality by making such impossible claims that even a small child will spot the difference between what can and cannot be" (*The Child and the Book*, 42).

TALL TALK AND TANGLETALK

Alvin Schwartz, who propounds a similar theory in the many books in which he has collected and written about tall tales, also makes quite clear in his various introductions and commentaries that tall tales are a highly stylized form of rhetoric. He uses an American-flavored rhetoric with many strategies. Besides the hyperbole associated with the tall tale, Schwartz deals in tongue-twisters, riddling (or, as he phrases it, "unriddling"), incongruities, and neologisms. He endorses the usefulness of all of these literary and storytelling games. Tongue-twisters are frequent in his book *A Twister of Twists, a Tangle of Tongues* and range in length from the brief "Selfish Shellfish" (20) and "Black bug's blood" (21) to a story called "Shrewd Simon Short" (50–52) which contains over three hundred words, all beginning with "s." In his introduction to the book Schwartz writes about how tongue-twisters can be used for sensible purposes:

> They have been used to train radio announcers, to test actors, to help with problems in speech, and to cure hiccups. . . . At least one opera singer sang tongue twisters as part of her daily practice. And at least one dentist used them to test his patient's speech after he installed their new false teeth. (9)

Nonsense verse and nonsense alphabets, especially the latter, have used tongue-twisters for similar purposes for centuries. The well-known "Peter Piper" is only one of many alliterative alphabets that have helped children to memorize and articulate their letters.

In *Unriddling* Schwartz points out the usefulness of riddling, nonsensical and otherwise. "It not only was fun. It was 'strengthening for the brain.' . . . It stretched your mind and sharpened your wits" (x). In his introduction he informs the reader that riddles have a long history and that history connects with childhood:

> One of the most ancient riddles we have is more than six thousand years old. It was found in the city of Babylon carved in a stone tablet that was used in a school. "What grows fat without eating?" the riddle asked the schoolchildren in those days. The answer: "A rain cloud." (x)

In another book of his, *Tomfoolery*, he includes a section on "tall talk," which he defines as "you use big words, long sentences, and large amounts of hot air to say something simple" (55). He gives the example: "My gastronomical satiety admonishes me that I have arrived at a state of deglutition inconsistent with dietetic integrity. (Translation: I've had too much to eat.)" (57). He also gives examples of tangletalk like "'Twas a moonlit day in August / The snow was falling fast" (66). His book *Flapdoodle: Pure Nonsense from American Folklore* contains more tangletalk: "The flowers were gaily singing, / The birds were in full bloom" (18); letter switches between words: "'Plums or figs?' / 'Pigs flease'" (28); doubletalk: "Grink salad with kerl dressing" (36); visual jokes, tongue-twisters, riddles, and nonsense rhymes (including parodies of "Mary had a little lamb"). All of the nonsense and wordplay here and in his other books show children the importance of such language games and often explain how children can create their own nonsense after knowing the sense of a word. Schwartz's work supports our premise that the two—sense and nonsense—cannot be separated.

Children learn more about the functioning of their language when they begin to listen to and to create nonsense. According to Nicholas Tucker in *The Child and the Book*, "the ability to understand verbal jokes . . . involves important analytic skills" (42). With some of the poems of Laura Richards, for example, a child can see how real words can become stepping-stones to nonsense, as "ice cream cone" and "begone" become "icery creamery conio" and "begonio" in her poem "Antonio." In "Eletelephoy," "elephant" and "telephone" are confused repeatedly. Children especially enjoy the latter rhyme because it gives them a chance to laugh at someone else who gets words tangled just as they do.

Other writers and illustrators have mixed sense and nonsense in varying degrees, some only in illustration and others in text; a goodly number have been able to combine the two talents. For now it is enough to realize, as Geller does, that "children explore the art of language in their word-play. . . . They hold up for view the building blocks of the system" (*Wordplay*, 95). Seeing what others have accomplished with language fosters feelings of curiosity in some children: what more can be done? what else might a particular word mean? As children gain more of an understanding of the potential of language, they begin to appreciate the many puns, riddles and the like that are dependent on wordplay. Through listening to and creating nonsense, children come to closer terms with their language. Moreover, as Elizabeth Sewell said in "Nonsense Verse and the Child," "Nonsense may prove to be one of the child's roads to Beauty" (45).

Barrett, Judi. *Cloudy with a Chance of Meatballs.* Illus. Ron Barrett. New York: Scholastic, 1976.

Bosmajian, Hamida. "Louise Fitzhugh's *Harriet the Spy*: Nonsense and Sense." *Touchstones: Reflections on the Best in Children's Literature* 1. Ed. Perry Nodelman. West Lafayette: ChLA, 1985.

Brown, Carolyn S. *The Tall Tale in American Folklore and Literature.* Knoxville: U of Tennessee P, 1987.

Chukovsky, Kornei. *From Two to Five.* Trans. Miriam Morton. Berkeley and Los Angeles: U of California P, 1963.

Cole, Joanna and Stephanie Calmenson, eds. *The Laugh Book: A New Treasury of Humor for Children.* New York: Doubleday, 1986.

Dahl, Roald. *Charlie and the Chocolate Factory.* 1964. Illus. Joseph Schindelman. New York: Bantam, 1984.

de Gasztold, Carmen Bernos. *Prayers from the Ark.* Trans. Rumer Godden. Illus. Jean Primrose. New York: Viking, 1969.

Dolitsky, Marlene. *Under the Tum-tum Tree: From Nonsense to Sense, A Study in Nonautomatic Comprehension.* Amsterdam/ Philadelphia: Benjamins, 1984.

Eiss, Harry Edwin. *Dictionary of Language Games, Puzzles, and Amusements.* New York: Greenwood, 1986.

Frye, Northrop. *Anatomy of Criticism: Four Essays.* New York: Atheneum, 1967.

Geller, Linda Gibson. *Wordplay and Language Learning for Children.* Urbana, IL: NCTE, 1985.

Green, Roger Lancelyn. "Introduction." *The Complete Fairy Tales of George MacDonald.* New York: Schocken, 1978.

Hood, Lois. "The Role of Imitation in Children's Language Learning." *Discovering Language with Children.* Ed. Gay Su Pinnell. Urbana, IL: NCTE, 1980.

Kohl, Marguerite and Frederica Young. *Jokes for Children.* Illus. Bob Patterson. New York: Hill and Wang/Farrar, 1963; rpt. 1986.

———. *More Jokes for Children.* Illus. Bob Patterson. New York: Hill and Wang/ Farrar, 1966; rpt. 1984.

Larrick, Nancy, ed. *Green Is Like a Meadow of Grass.* Illus. Kelly Oeschli. Champaign, IL: Garrard, 1968.

Lobel, Arnold. *The Book of Pigericks.* New York: Harper, 1983.

———. *Whiskers and Rhymes.* New York: Greenwillow, 1985.

MacDonald, George. *The Light Princess.* Illus. Maurice Sendak. New York: Farrar, 1969.

Nash, Walter. *The Language of Humour.* White Plains, NY: Longman, 1985.

O'Neill, Mary. *Hailstones and Halibut Bones.* Illus. Leonard Weisgard. Garden City, NY: Doubleday, 1961.

Opie, Iona and Peter. *Children's Games in Street and Playground.* New York: Oxford UP, 1984.

Parish, Peggy. *Amelia Bedelia.* Illus. Fritz Siebel. New York: Scholastic, 1963; rpt. 1969.

———. *Amelia Bedelia and the Baby.* Illus. Lynn Sweat. New York: Avon, 1981.

———. *Amelia Bedelia and the Surprise Shower.* Illus. Fritz Siebel. New York: Scholastic, 1966.

———. *Amelia Bedelia Goes Camping.* Illus. Lynn Sweat. New York: Greenwillow, 1985.

———. *Come Back, Amelia Bedelia.* Illus. Wallace Tripp. New York: Scholastic, 1971.

————. *Play Ball, Amelia Bedelia.* Illus. Wallace Tripp. New York: Scholastic, 1972.

————. *Teach Us, Amelia Bedelia.* Illus. Lynn Sweat. New York: Scholastic, 1977.

Redfern, Walter. *Puns.* London: Andre Deutsch, 1984.

Rosenheim, Edward J., Jr. *Swift and the Satirist's Art* Chicago: U of Chicago P, 1963.

Schwartz, Alvin. *Busy Bumblebees and Other Tongue Twisters.* Illus. Kathie Abrams. New York: Harper, 1982.

————. *Flapdoodle: Pure Nonsense from American Folklore.* Illus. John O'Brien. New York and Philadelphia: Lippincott, 1980.

————. *Tomfoolery: Trickery and Foolery with Words.* Illus. Glen Rounds. New York and Philadelphia: Lippincott, 1973.

————. *A Twister of Twists, a Tangler of Tongues.* Illus. Glen Rounds. New York and Philadelphia: Lippincott, 1972.

————. *Unriddling: All Sorts of Riddles to Puzzle Your Guessery, Collected from American Folklore.* Illus. Sue Truesdell. New York and Philadelphia: Lippincott, 1983.

Sewell, Elizabeth. "Nonsense Verse and the Child." *Lion and Unicorn* 4.2 (Winter 1980–81): 30–48.

Sperling, Susan Kelz. *Murfles and Wink-a-peeps: Funny Old Words for Kids.* Illus. Tom Bloom. New York: Potter, 1985.

Swift, Jonathan. *Gulliver's Travels.* Intro. Jacques Barzun. Illus. Warren Chappell. New York and Toronto: Oxford UP, 1977.

Tucker, Nicholas. *The Child and the Book: A Psychological and Literary Exploration.* New York: Cambridge UP, 1982.

Wells, Carolyn, comp. *A Nonsense Anthology.* 1902. Garden City, NY: Doubleday, n.d.

Writers whose humour relies extensively on
the manipulations of logic are often adept at
creating closed systems from which a hero-
victim can escape only by some process
of magic, some accident, or some act of the
will. . . .

Without such provisions, the humour of circular logic becomes the panic of nightmare;
only if there is an independent stance or an
escape route can we afford to laugh.

Walter Nash, The Language of Humour, *112–13*

Nonsense and Philosophy

The Underside of Thought

Why is it that philosophers so often admire and cite nonsense literature?
Shouldn't they who, like mathematicians, try to create ordered and logical
systems scorn such an absurd form of humor? Nevertheless both philosophers and mathematicians are fascinated by nonsense constructs. As
Harry E. Eiss notes, "Mathematical play and language play often overlap
. . . yet these fields for the most part deal in two separate symbol systems"
(*Dictionary of Language Games*, xvi). One Victorian philosopher-mathema-
tician, Charles Lutwidge Dodgson, alias Lewis Carroll, even wrote a great
deal of nonsense verse and fiction. As Dodgson he wrote several books on
logic and logic games; as Carroll he carried his often playful view of logic
over into the wonderland and looking-glass worlds he created. His work
gives us the answer to the question. Logic is the nexus, the connection,

between mathematics and philosophy and also between philosophy and nonsense. Nonsense writers often play with logic, deliberately using fallacious arguments, or logically valid arguments that nevertheless contradict common sense.

NONSENSE LESSONS IN LOGIC

Nonsense exchanges can be a child's first lessons in distinguishing between logic and illogic. Take, for example, the argument about intended meaning at the mad tea party in Carroll's *Alice's Adventures in Wonderland*.

> "Then you should say what you mean," the March Hare went on.
>
> "I do," Alice hastily replied; "at least—at least I mean what I say—that's the same thing you know."
>
> "Not the same thing a bit!" said the Hatter. "Why you might just as well say that 'I see what I eat' is the same thing as 'I eat what I see'!"
>
> "You might as well say," added the March Hare, "that 'I like what I get' is the same as 'I get what I like'!"
>
> "You might as well say," added the Dormouse, which seemed to be talking in its sleep, "that 'I breathe when I sleep' is the same thing as 'I sleep when I breathe'!"
>
> "It *is* the same thing with you," said the Hatter.
>
> (75–76)

Carroll has given us a light lesson in logic—the lesson that some, but not all, propositions are reversible.

Carroll seems to delight in putting invalid syllogisms in the mouths of his characters. Alice, upon finding a cake marked "EAT ME" remarks, "Well, I'll eat it . . . and if it makes me grow larger, I can reach the key; and if it makes me grow smaller, I can creep under the door: so either way I'll get into the garden" (*Wonderland*, chap. 1). Carroll, who constructed "truth tables" very like those used today in symbolic logic and mathematics, knew full well that Alice's proposition was riddled with fallacies. For one thing, the preliminary proposition (If I eat the cake, I'll grow either larger or smaller) is false on two counts. First, it contains the fallacy known as a "false dilemma" (implying only two choices when there are actually more). Alice learns this when, after eating a small amount, "she remained the same size." The author comments, "To be sure, this is what generally happens when one eats cake." Secondly, the first fallacy breeds another one, namely that when the conclusion following an "if" clause is false, it invalidates the whole proposition. Therefore, we cannot say that eating cake implies growing larger or smaller. Poor Alice commits more false reasoning with her conclusion "either way I'll get into the garden." Her first option, growing larger and obtaining the key, leaves out the necessary and contradictory condition that she must be small to fit through the little door to the garden.

Numerous authors besides Lewis Carroll have employed syllogisms in nonsense passages, but two of the most successful are L. Frank Baum and Norton Juster. Both Americans, the first of these men wrote at the turn of the century, the second in the 1960s.

Baum allowed the characters inhabiting Oz to use logic quite well on occasion to reveal a substratum of sense under a nonsense surface. For example, given the seemingly impossible task of counting to seventeen by twos, L. Frank Baum's Saw Horse, wooden head or no, reasons that if the count starts "at half of one . . . then anyone can count up to seventeen by twos" (*Marvelous Land of Oz*, 225), in other words, two one-halves, then three, five, seven, etc. In Norton Juster's *The Phantom Tollbooth*, Milo, the boy hero, breaks the logical impasse between two warring brothers—King Azaz the Unabridged, ruler of Dictionopolis, and the Mathemagician, ruler of Digitopolis—and catches the Mathemagician in a syllogistic net.

The Mathemagician insists that since Rhyme and Reason were banished from the kingdom, he and his brother Azaz have

> ". . . never agreed on anything—and we never will. . . ."
> "Never?" asked Milo. . . .
> "NEVER!" he repeated. "And if you can prove otherwise, you have my permission to go."
>
> (200–1)

Milo then very cleverly leads the Mathemagician through an argument that concludes that if each brother has sworn to disagree with whatever the other agrees with, then they are in agreement on this one point of always disagreeing. The logic is so tight that the Mathemagician has to let Milo and his friends continue on their quest to rescue the princesses Rhyme and Reason and restore peace and unity to the Kingdom of Wisdom.

There is yet another way to use logic humorously and that is using the forms of proposition and syllogism to create ridiculous connections and conclusions. A college mathematics text gives an example of a validly constructed proposition that is nevertheless a nonsensical statement: "If I am a donkey, then the moon is made of blue cheese" (Eugene D. Nichols,

37). This can indeed be turned around and stated as "The moon being made of blue cheese implies that I am a donkey." Two wrongs do not make a right, as the old saying has it, but a false hypothesis yoked to a false conclusion together make logical, if not common, sense. The very tension between a proper form and a content that lacks all propriety can heighten the humor of such nonsense.

Another instance of logical sense with no common sense occurs when Juster has the Dodecahedron (a twelve-faced man) propose what is claimed as a numerically correct (but nevertheless ridiculous) solution to a mathematical problem:

> "Why, did you know that if a beaver two feet long with a tail a foot and a half long can build a dam twelve feet high and six feet wide in two days, all you would need to build Boulder Dam is a beaver sixty- eight feet long with a fifty-one-foot tail?". . . .
>
> "That's absurd," objected Milo, whose head was spinning from all the numbers and questions.
>
> "That may be true," he acknowledged, "but its completely accurate, and as long as the answer is right, who cares if the question is wrong? If you want sense, you'll have to make it yourself."
>
> (*Phantom Tollbooth*, 175)

The sense has to come from outside the closed world of numbers. As one of the characters asks, "Where would you find a beaver that big?" (175).

Carroll also loved the absurdities that can result from mindlessly applying the logic of arithmetic to the material world. Florence Lennon in her biography of Carroll, *Victoria Through the Looking Glass*, recounts that as a tutor at Oxford he was known to set such silly problems as "If it takes ten men so many days to build a wall, how long will it take 300,000 men?" and then, any student foolish enough to calculate the answer was told, "You don't seem to have observed that the wall would go up like a flash of lightning, and that most of those men could not have got within a mile of it" (qtd. in Lennon, 279–80). Carroll asked a similar question in his introduction to *A Tangled Tale*: "If a cat can kill a rat in a minute, how long will it be killing 60,000 rats? Ah, how long indeed! My private opinion is that the rats would kill the cat."

Nonsense literature also contains existential dilemmas, epistemological puzzles, and paradoxes, the very kinds of problems that philosophers and logicians set themselves. And furthermore, philosophers and nonsense authors share an approach. Both pull the rug out from under reality, shake it a bit, and look at its underside to see how the weave of premises and conclusions about life is put together. Such inquiry may lead to intellectual discoveries or to laughter or to both at once. For not only can nonsense be philosophical, but philosophy can, on its side, be playful and humorous. In his book *Sense, Antisense, Nonsense*, Robert Champigny points out that the "purpose of a philosophic activity is ludic (playful). . . . One plays with and against some meanings of a few words. . . . A philosophical text is designed to serve as a playful partner and opponent" (11–12). And Gareth Matthews, writing on *Philosophy and the Young Child*, tells us that while "Philosophy may indeed be motivated by puzzlement . . . to show that and stop there is to suggest, quite mistakenly, that philosophy is inevitably something terribly serious. In fact, it is often play, conceptual play" (11).

Matthews argues elsewhere in his book that while philosophical inquiry does not necessarily provide answers, it often leads to yet more questions. He quotes two twentieth-century philosophers, Bertrand Russell and Ludwig Wittgenstein. Russell insists that philosophy's chief power lies in "*asking* questions which increase the interest of the world, and show the strangeness and wonder lying just below the surface" (*Problems of Philosophy*, 16), and Wittgenstein holds that the proper attitude for a philosopher is "I don't know my way about" (*Philosophical Investigation*, 49). This interrogative mode is another similarity between philosophy and nonsense humor. Both can generate queries ad infinitum.

Most philosophical problems come down to epistemology (how we are able to know), and this vital connection between the human mind and the world around it is also necessary to an understanding of how children respond to story and humor. As thinking beings, we are connected to reality through our senses and through our ability to abstract, classify, and name. The final step is to turn around and look at this process of knowing and realize that the process and its products—knowledge and language—are always relative to the observing consciousness and to the cultural forces that train that consciousness. Here is where philosophy and nonsense step in, with their nagging or waggish questions about the nature of reality and knowing and communication. Among the questions that both ask are these:

1. How can we know anything at all, and especially how can we know who we are, define ourselves and distinguish ourselves from other objects and persons?

2. Given an outside world, what are matter, time, and space and how are they related to each other?

3. How do we communicate to each other whatever it is we can know?

No one thinker nor any one school of philosophy has ever given final answers to these questions, but nonsense and philosophy have kept the questions alive. Carroll, Baum, and Juster, the children's authors cited earlier for their humorous use of syllogisms, also demonstrate how philosophical treatises and nonsense literature have other similar aims and methods. The authors broach all of these philosophical questions in their fictions.

AM I? WHO AM I? WHAT'S OUTSIDE OF ME?

To begin, how is it that we can know who we are and what is outside ourselves? Carroll, Baum, and Juster pose these questions to their readers. Alice, wandering through wonderland and looking-glass land, is frequently perplexed by the question of whether she is still the same person she was before she entered these peculiar realms. After several precipitous changes of size, she begins to wonder just who she is:

> "But if I'm not the same, the next question is, 'Who in the world am I?' Ah, *that's* the great puzzle!" And she began thinking over all the children she knew that were the same age as herself, to see if she could have been changed for any of them. (*Wonderland*, chap. 2)

Later in her adventures, her identity is questioned by a pigeon. Alice has again radically changed size from eating the growth-inducing side of a magic mushroom and has stretched out taller than the trees, her now serpentine neck at least allowing her to bend her head down among the leaves to find her hands. When she does so, an angry mother pigeon flies at her:

> "Serpent!" screamed the Pigeon.
> "I am *not* a serpent!" said Alice indignantly. . . .
> "Well! *What* are you? said the Pigeon. . . .
> "I—I'm a little girl," said Alice. . . .
> "A likely story indeed!" said the Pigeon in a tone of the deepest contempt. "I've seen a good many little girls in my time, but never *one* with such a neck as that! No, no! You're a serpent; and there's no use denying it. I suppose you"ll be telling me next that you never tasted an egg!"
> "I *have* tasted eggs, certainly," said Alice, who was a very truthful child; "but little girls eat eggs quite as much as serpents do, you know."

> "I don't believe it," said the Pigeon; "but if they do, why, then they're a kind of serpent: that's all I can say." (*Wonderland*, chap. 5)

It is indeed all that the pigeon, with its limited egocentric methods of definition, can say. The only attributes of a serpent that concern the pigeon are its stealthy and supple body (which Alice's neck now resembles) and its penchant for eating eggs (which Alice also shares). As in the ancient Socratic joke that defines human beings as featherless bipeds and therefore indistinguishable from a plucked chicken, we are forced to think about precisely what does distinguish a little girl from a serpent.

In his experiments in teaching philosophy to children, Gareth Matthews turned to children's books because he found them a rich resource for the "thought experiments" he wished to present, and he points out that L. Frank Baum is also concerned with this problem of identity. Matthews notes that the Tin Woodman, whose flesh and blood body has been replaced part by part with tin limbs, torso, and head, presents us with an ancient philosophical problem, classically called "The Ship of Theseus." This ship was replaced board by board until nothing remained of the original. The problem is when and "why then" does the ship (or Tin Woodman) become a new entity? Matthews observes that Baum has added two new elements: different material is used to replace the Tin Woodman, and the Woodman has memory of his former life and his transformations. The first new factor argues against a continuity of being: "A tin creature seems to have less claim to being a man . . . and hence less claim to being the *same* man than would a creature composed entirely of 'fleshy transplants'" (*Philosophy and the Young Child*, 60). On the other hand, Matthews informs us that "Ever since John Locke first proposed memory as a criterion for personal identity, philosophers have taken memory very seriously in discussing these matters" (60–61). Therefore the Tin Woodman's memory argues for sameness throughout the many changes.

Baum poses similar questions many times in the Oz books. In the second of the series, *The Marvelous Land of Oz*, there are two characters, Jack Pumpkinhead and the Gump, who are constructed before our eyes and brought to life with a magic powder. Nathaniel Hawthorne's wonderful story "Feathertop" haunts the creation of Pumpkinhead, and, like Hawthorne's character, Jack is a better man than many. His pumpkin head is, however, constantly falling off the wooden stake that is his neck and just saved from being smashed. If memory resides in the head, both Jack Pumpkinhead and the Tin Woodman (with a tin replacement head) are anomalies. The tin man, as any Oz fan knows, is not worried by the problem and believes he needs a new heart rather than a new set of brains. Jack's solution can best be described as organic. In a later book, *The Road to Oz*, he grows pumpkins to assure a perpetual supply of heads. His identity and classification remain ambiguous. "What are you, a man or a pumpkin?" asks the guard of the Emerald City. "Both, if you please," Jack answers (*Marvelous Land of Oz*, 66).

The Gump presents an even greater challenge. This creature is a primitive flying machine, consisting of two matching sofas, an antlered stuffed head, four large palm branches for wings, and a broom for tail. It is held together with rope and clothes lines, and, even though the Powder of Life animates it, the contraption is such a mish-mash that its Gump head, which can remember the moment in the forest before it was shot, never accepts its ungainly incarnation and asks to be dismantled after the adventure is completed. But "the antlered head [which] was again hung over the mantle-piece . . . continued to talk whenever it took a notion to do so" (*Land of Oz*, 284). Utter nonsense, of course, but as Matthews comments, one of Baum's basic themes is the investigation of "the difference between the natural and the artificial" (*Philosophy and the Young Child*, 79). And a reader who pays attention comes to realize after a number of sojourns in Oz that detachable, replaceable parts do not characterize the flesh and blood animals and people there but belong only to the things manufactured in some way. The Tin Woodman, who began as human, is an exception, but he is under a witch's curse. In general the creatures of Oz exist under a rule propounded by the Tik-tok, the mechanical man, whose master "was not a-ble to kill me, be-cause I was not a-live, and one must first live in or-der to die" (*Ozma of Oz*, 60).

When Baum wrote his Oz books early in this century, such bodily transplants and robots were fantastic, nonsensical ideas. Now, in our era of artificial hearts and joints, transplants have become more a matter of ethics than of abstract philosophy. The same holds for the questions raised by Tik Tok the Mechanical Man (who first appeared in 1907 in *Ozma of Oz*). Here the problem is whether a machine endowed with intellect can be classified as human. More than half a century later Hal, the computer "brain" of the spaceship in the novel/movie *2001* had a human enough personality for a nervous breakdown. In real life we now have talking, chess-playing computers, robots that clean house and even walk the dog. This book has come to you via a computer's memory. It would seem that both nonsense and fantasy may be prophetic of future realism. One Mother Goose rhyme from the eighteenth century goes

> What's the news of the day,
> Good neighbour, I pray?
> They say the balloon
> Is gone up to the moon!"
>
> (Baring-Goulds, 115, #147)

When written, this was nonsense in the form of hyperbole. We now know that those early attempts to sail above the earth did evolve into a moon landing.

Of course the philosophic question still remains. What are the essential and what the accidental qualities of any creature? In Juster's *The Phantom Tollbooth*, Milo's inability to know himself stems from a different problem—lack of observation. His adventures in the strange land past the tollbooth that appears in his room one afternoon do not distort his self-concept; they bestow it. Milo, who "regarded the process of seeking knowledge as the greatest waste of time" (9), begins as an anti-philosopher, dismissing what comes to him through his senses as well as what comes through reasoning.

Juster is a regular Lockean in his insistence on the primacy of the senses as a way of knowing. He emphasizes again and again that sounds and flavors and colors are good for us and that their absence impoverishes the intellect. In the divided and unhappy Kingdom of Wisdom where Milo travels after passing through the tollbooth there is a beautiful City of Reality that no one can see because "One day someone discovered that if you walked as fast as possible and looked at nothing but your shoes you would arrive at your destination much more quickly" (117), and "Because nobody cared, the city slowly began to disappear" (118). Near the end of their pilgrimage, Milo, the Watchdog, and the Humbug meet the "Senses Taker," who substitutes daydreams for the reality that is present to the senses. But the group gets past this threat, and rescues the princesses Rhyme and Reason who restore the unity and balance of art and science, of words and numbers.

Milo returns to the everyday world of his own room as a convert to philosophy, a word, that in its parts (*phil* + *sophia*), means "loving wisdom." He now realizes that "there was so much to see, and hear, and touch . . . caterpillars to watch . . . conversations to listen to in wonder . . . . books that could take you anywhere, and things to invent . . . worlds to imagine and then someday make real. . . . Everything looked new—and worth trying" (*Phantom Tollbooth*, 255–56).

Paradoxes of Time and Space

Under the guise of nonsense these three authors have presented some very central questions about how we know ourselves and the world outside us. And they also examine that outside world, considering its temporal and spatial nature. The most fascinating enigma in this dual area is that of nonreversibility, an enigma closely related to the problems of definition and identity just presented, but with an emphasis on time and change rather than on what is changed.

A classic example from Carroll's *Through the Looking-Glass* is the ability of the chess pieces to live backwards and to remember "both ways." The White Queen's finger bleeds before she cuts it; the pain and screaming also precede the accident. Alice asks kindly,

> "Have you pricked your finger?"
>
> "I haven't pricked it *yet*," the Queen said, "but I soon shall—oh, oh, oh!"
>
> "When do you expect to do it?" Alice asked, feeling very much inclined to laugh.
>
> "When I fasten my shawl again," the poor Queen groaned out: "the brooch will come undone directly."
>
> (*Looking-Glass*, chap. 5)

The game of chess does function in a closed world of reversibility. The pieces can easily be moved play by play back to their original positions, and chess players must remember forwards in the sense that they must anticipate already known, possible reactions to a move. However, as Alice's inclination to laugh suggests, the logic of a limited game world, when applied to the world at large, becomes nonsense.

In *The Marvelous Land of Oz* Baum presents a truly marvelous time puzzle. Tip has swallowed a magic pill that will grant him whatever he wishes. But it causes such a stomach cramp that Tip exclaims, "I wish I'd never swallowed that pill!" (227). The pain stops and the original three pills are in the box again. As the Woggle-Bug explains, "The wish came true, and he *didn't* swallow one of them" (227). Tip protests that nevertheless it gave him a dreadful pain.

> "Impossible!" declared the Woggle-Bug. "If you have never swallowed it, the pill can not have given you a pain. And as your wish, being granted, proves you did not swallow the pill, it is also plain that you suffered no pain."
>
> "Then it was a splendid imitation of a pain," retorted Tip angrily.
>
> (227–28)

This paradox can circle forever without any reasonable solution. We must simply shrug our shoulders and declare it ridiculous in terms of matter and time as we know them (or think we know them) in the everyday world. But although neither such pills nor such paradoxes exist outside the worlds of magic, science fiction, nonsense, and philosophy, our saying so does not stop Baum's puzzle from spinning endlessly in the world of the mind.

Professional philosophers have been driven to similar admissions of defeat. Susan Stewart, in discussing the is/is not paradox created by Epimenides the Cretan's statement that "All Cretans are liars," quotes the eminent American philosopher Alfred North Whitehead as realizing that only "nonsense" (here defined as outside the realm of logic) could provide a solution to a similar paradox (in Stewart, 29–30). Whitehead could not resolve the paradox that a category is not a member of the class it describes, except by saying that the paradox is based on a confusion of levels. But because the notion of "levels" of reality is itself a logical mental construct, a classification or category, the solution evaporates. It seems that it is only by logic-destroying ambiguity, that parent of humor and nonsense, that we can deal with such mind-teasing problems as the logical possibility and physical impossibility of classification and time reversals.

Baum's Tik-tok man would seem by his name to be an emblem of time. But, except that he is clocklike in needing to be wound up every twenty-four hours, thereby reminding us how time-bound we are, he does not inspire the philosophical questions about time that his perhaps namesake, Norton Juster's watchdog Tock, does. Tock is a pun and metaphor made visible: "a large dog with a perfectly normal head, four feet, and a tail—and the body of a loudly ticking alarm clock" (*Phantom Tollbooth*, 29). Although Tock is a rather "untimely" animal in believing that thought (a time-transcending mode) creates action (always time-bound), he takes his calling as watchdog of time seriously. He tells Milo this story:

> . . . once there was no time at all, and people found it very inconvenient. They never knew whether they were eating lunch or dinner, and they were always missing trains. So time was invented to help them keep track of the day and get places when they should. When they began to count all the time that was available what with 60 seconds in a minute and 60 minutes in an hour and 24 hours in a day and 365 days in a year, it seemed as if there was much more than could ever be used. "If there's so much of it, it couldn't be very valuable," was the general opinion, and it soon fell into disrepute. People wasted it and even gave it away. Then we were given the job of seeing that no one wasted time again. (33–34)

Tock has exaggerated his metaphysical importance. He represents clocks and the modern mania for precise schedules much more than he does the slow natural swing of cosmic time. Juster's point, however, ties in with the one he makes about a lack of sensory perception. When time is one more commodity in an inventory, the present moment loses its value. At the end of the book, Juster uses Tock for another punning metaphor when the Humbug, Milo, and the two princesses escape the falling castle in air on the soaring back of the watchdog—because "time flies" you know. The most nonsensical statement about time in the book is, however, the assurance on the sheet of instructions for the tollbooth that "if not perfectly satisfied, your wasted time will be refunded" (13). The idea that wasted time is refundable is quite as paradoxical as Baum's idea of time-cancelling wishes.

PHILOSOPHY AND LANGUAGE

The topic on which nonsense and philosophy connect most frequently, however, is not time or even identity, but the nature of human language. As we have already shown, wordplay is absolutely central to what is commonly meant by the term nonsense. The three authors we are here considering certainly have enough to say (or to play) on the subject of language.

In Carroll's writing, besides his often discussed passage where Humpty-Dumpty declares "When *I* use a word, . . . it means just what I choose it to mean" (*Looking-Glass*, chap. 6), the Alice books abound in passages centered on examining language, chiefly through wordplay. There is scarcely a page in Carroll's work that does not investigate the literal meaning of some set phrase or figuratively used word: We learn that flowers don't talk, as they do in looking-glass land because gardeners "make the beds too soft—so that the flowers are always asleep" (chap. 2), and horse flies are pictured as horses with wings metamorphized into "rocking-horse-flies" and butterflies into "bread-and-butter-flies" (chap. 3). Truly Carroll believed that "Language is worth a thousand pounds a word!" (*Looking-Glass*, chap. 3).

The Mock Turtle commits an outrageous number of imperfect puns, which in analogy with slant rhyme, might be called slant puns, culminating in "the different branches of Arithmetic—Ambition, Distraction, Uglification and Derision" (*Wonderland*, chap. 9). The White Queen not only lives backwards but is perversely literal with her language. She explains that "jam every other day" means "jam to-morrow and jam yesterday—but never jam *to-day*" because "to-day isn't any *other* day" (*Looking-Glass*, chap. 5).

Carroll plays with the syntactic as well as with the semantic quirks of

English. When the Mouse is reciting a dry and therefore "drying" history to the soaking wet animals just escaped from the pool of tears and says, "Stigand, the patriotic archbishop of Canterbury, found it advisable—," the Duck interrupts with "Found *what*?"

> "Found *it*," the Mouse replied rather crossly: "of course you know what 'it' means."
> "I know what 'it' means well enough, when I find a thing," said the Duck: "it's generally a frog or a worm. The question is, what did the archbishop find?"
>
> (*Wonderland*, chap. 3)

Carroll has zeroed in on what could be called a null set of words in English: "it," "there," and "do" as a dummy auxiliary. In many contexts these words are virtually without meaning and serve a functional, syntactic purpose that adds no content to the phrase: ("*It* is raining" or "*There* are puddles" or "*Do* you agree?"/"I agree"/"I *do* not agree"). These and other "function words" are not nonsense, nor what linguists refer to as "free morphemes" (a sound unit that is within the language system but that has no meaning attached to it). "It" and "there" and "do" are assigned abstract meanings and syntactic functions, but their meaning evaporates in certain contexts.

Frank Baum devotes less space to investigating words, but in at least one passage he makes humorously clear that language must be a mutually accepted convention before speakers can communicate. He gives us the ludicrous scene between the Scarecrow and Jack Pumpkinhead in which they erroneously believe they speak a different language and cannot at first understand each other without a translator (*Marvelous Land of Oz*, 73–79). And Baum created Mr. H. M. Woggle-Bug, T.E. (the initials standing for "Highly Magnified" and "Thoroughly Educated"). Living in the cracks in the floor of the schoolroom of Professor Nowitall, the Woggle-Bug acquired the ability to mouth such pompous phrases as "drinking thirstily of the ever-flowing fount of limpid knowledge" (*Marvelous Land of Oz*, 149). Baum pictures his other characters as horrified by such language use (or abuse), both the pomposity and the punning, but Baum himself was obviously not above making puns, as witness the name of Professor Nowitall, which is pronounced "know it all" but spelled to imply "no wit at all." Baum, however, is not as given either to as much wordplay or as minute an exploration of the ways of language as Carroll and Juster are.

The place and function of language looms large in Juster's book. And he deals with two kinds of language, natural human speech and the structured code of mathematics. These are symbolized by the two cities

"Dictionopolis" and "Digitopolis." The entire book revolves around the split and the misunderstandings between these two means of conveying information. At one point the Mathemagician has sent his brother Azaz a letter composed entirely of numbers and is hurt by the lack of a reply:

> "But maybe he doesn't understand numbers," said Milo, who found it a little difficult to read himself.
> "NONSENSE!" he [the Mathemagician] bellowed. "Everyone understands numbers. No matter what language you speak, they always mean the same thing."
>
> (*Phantom Tollbooth*, 199).

The twelve-faced Dodecahedron has already made this point to Milo, asking if all one-faced people are called Milo, because "Everything here is called exactly what it is. The triangles are called triangles, the circles are called circles" (173). Juster is encouraging us to compare the unambiguous language of mathematics, where the sign stands unequivocally for the abstract concept it names, with the extremely ambiguous language of speech, where one sign (word) can flower into multiple meanings, and one object or concept can have multiple signs. When Milo first enters the city of Dictionopolis he is greeted by five officials: the Duke of Definition, the Minister of Meaning, the Earl of Essence, the Count of Connotation, and the Undersecretary of Understanding, whose synonymous function is to offer a wealth of ways to say something. After one list of word choices, Milo suggests,

> "Wouldn't it be simpler to use just one? It would certainly make more sense."
> "Nonsense."
> "Ridiculous."
> "Fantastic.
> "Absurd." "Bosh," they chorused.
>
> (40)

They hold that "one word is as good as another—so why not use them all? . . . If one is right, then ten are ten times as right" (40). After this statement of their rather nondiscriminating philosophy of language, we are not surprised by: "'But we never choose which ones to use,' explained the earl . . . 'for as long as they mean what they mean to mean we don't care if they make sense or nonsense'" (43). Everyone is quite disconcerted, however, when the Humbug knocks over the stalls where words are sold and leaves the words all jumbled:

"Done what you've looked," angrily shouted one of the sales-
men. He meant to say, "Look what you've done," but the words
had gotten so hopelessly mixed up that no one could make any
sense at all. (58)

Just as in the language of mathematics with its formulas that must be
worked out in a certain order, a structure informs any sequence of signs
in human speech. In English especially the meaning of a word, precisely
because it may vary, relies heavily on its place in that structure. As
Marlene Dolitsky notes in her book on the comprehension of nonsense,
"While the rules of semantic relations do not apply, syntactic structure is
rigorously followed as it remains the only key to the text's meaning" (8).

Chapter 5 on "Semantics and Nonsense" demonstrated that ultimately
a great deal of sense comes from nonsense. Juster's frequent point is that
a great deal of nonsense can come from seeming sense if we are not careful
with language. He pushes the literal meanings of words to a point of
absurdity well beyond that found in Amelia Bedelia's linguistic antics.
When the earl says "as easy as falling off a log" (43), he does just that.
And if Carroll could create such strange names for the branches of
arithmetic as Ambition (= addition) and Derision (= division), Juster
goes him one better and invents some peculiar arithmetical functions,
such as "subtraction stew" which makes you hungrier as you eat it. In
fact, in the divided Kingdom of Wisdom finding nourishment is quite a
problem. At King Azaz's banquet, whatever a guest says is what is served.
Asking for a "light meal" brings a plate full of light, a "square meal"
squares. Milo's polite and empty before-dinner speech nets him a plate of
abstractions.

"I didn't know that I was going to have to eat my words," Milo
objected.
"Of course, of course, everyone here does," the king grunted.
"You should have made a tastier speech."

(88)

Juster is not just having random fun with all these absurd uses of
numbers and words. Throughout the book he is reiterating the point that
wholeness is essential. If mind and body, science and art, or mathematics
and language are divided, the human condition is diminished. By making
this point, he joins a long tradition of philosopher-thinkers, including
John Locke and Jonathan Swift, who have tried to heal the severed intellect
and senses, powers so seldom united in Western thought.

Juster, Baum, and Carroll were able to present these serious questions about the nature of existence and knowledge and language in the form of nonsense because they shared several talents: a talent for separating out accidental, superficial qualities and foregrounding them for ridicule, a talent for unbalancing the everyday equilibrium of assumptions and relationships, a talent for turning logic inside out, a talent for nosing out incongruities, and, finally, a talent for unravelling language, pulling apart the very fabric of their medium. Their young heroes and heroines move through complex but comic worlds of personified ideas to reach a state of mental independence. In negotiating the sea of nonsense, Alice, Dorothy, Tip, and Milo become child philosophers. The child reader who follows their adventures can learn that laughter and thought are closely kin and that wisdom sometimes winks.

Baring-Gould, William S. and Ceil Baring-Gould. *The Annotated Mother Goose.* New York: World, 1972.

Baum, L. Frank. *The Marvelous Land of Oz.* 1905. New York: Dover, 1969.

———. *Ozma of Oz.* 1907. New York: Dover, 1985.

———. *The Road to Oz.* 1909. Chicago: Rand, 1971.

Carroll, Lewis. *The Annotated Alice: Alice's Adventures in Wonderland & Through the Looking Glass.* Ed. and annotator Martin Gardner. New York: World, 1963; rpt. 1972.

———. Introduction to *A Tangled Tale* (published with the *Facsimile Alice*). London: Macmillan, 1886.

Champigny, Robert. *Sense, Antisense, Nonsense.* Gainesville: U of Florida P, 1986.

Dolitsky, Marlene. *Under the Tumtum Tree: From Nonsense to Sense, A Study in Nonautomatic Comprehension* Amsterdam: Benjamins, 1984.

Eiss, Harry Edwin. *Dictionary of Language Games, Puzzles, and Amusements.* New York and Westport, CT: Greenwood, 1986.

Juster, Norton. *The Phantom Tollbooth.* New York: Random, 1961; rpt. 1964.

Lennon, Florence. *Victoria through the Looking Glass: The Life of Lewis Carroll.* New York: Simon, 1945.

Matthews, Gareth B. *Dialogues with Children.* Cambridge: Harvard UP, 1984.

———. *Philosophy and the Young Child.* Cambridge: Harvard UP, 1980.

Nash, Walter. *The Language of Humour: Style and Technique in Comic Discourse.* White Plains, NY: Longman, 1985.

Nichols, Eugene D. *College Mathematics for General Education.* New York: Holt, 1970.

Stewart, Susan. *Nonsense: Aspects of Intertextuality in Folklore and Literature.* Baltimore: Johns Hopkins UP, 1979.

Together with the power of speech, the mathematical gift, the gripping thumb, the ability to make tools, humour is a specifying characteristic of humanity. For many of us, it is more than an amiable decoration on life; it is a complex piece of equipment for living, a mode of attack and a line of defence, a method of raising questions and arguments, a protest against the inequality of the struggle to live, a way of atonement and reconciliation, a treaty with all that is wilful, impaired, beyond our control.

Walter Nash, The Language of Humour *1*

Psychological Aspects

of Nonsense Literature for Children

by Leo Schneiderman

As children we perceive the social world around us as constituting the natural order of things. With experience we discover the cream of jest; namely, that we live in accordance with arbitrary conventions. But for the child—as for Alexander Pope in his *Essay on Man*—everything is as it should be. This is because it is difficult, in the absence of experience, to imagine a plurality of worlds or a realm of unrealized possibilities. It is the heretical mission of nonsense literature to teach the young that the world constructed by their elders is an artificial thing. Nonsense literature uses the spirit of playfulness to rearrange the familiar world. It thereby reveals that the rules we live by are not inevitable, nor do they exist on a purely objective plane and apart from human intentions. In this way nonsense literature, with its experiments in absurdity, is the antidote to literal-mindedness and a remedy for excessive concreteness. No doubt literal-minded, officious adults were once children who were made to accept as reality the world of appearances and conventional lies. Nonsense literature, by expanding the imagination, may free the child to contemplate an enlarged universe of possibilities. This act of liberation contributes to the development of flexibility, a capacity for humor, and a sense of proportion.

THE DIFFERENCE BETWEEN NONSENSE AND FANTASY

But nonsense literature is not to be confused with the realm of the mythical. Fairy tales and folk narratives are qualitatively different from nonsense literature insofar as they are the literary or folkloric residue of archaic rituals and beliefs. As I have argued elsewhere (Schneiderman, 125–58), many fairy tales, if not most, appear to be allegories of initiation rites for adolescent boys and girls. In these tales, the novice has to prove himself or herself by undergoing trials and tribulations imposed by disguised taskmasters acting as parent surrogates. Initiation rites and their narrative survivals refer to actual and symbolic rites of passage for the individual child and serve as mechanisms of social incorporation for the group. When the little protagonist of the fairy tale has duly surmounted all obstacles, overcome his or her willful nature, and undergone instruction in the mysteries, i. e., adult expectations, a "problem" has been solved. In other words, an impulsive child, at the mercy of selfish wishes and infantile fears, has been transformed into a disciplined and duty-bound adult.

In nonsense literature—Dr. Seuss' *Cat in the Hat*, for example—quite another problem is posed and then resolved. The issue at hand is how to affirm for the young child the legitimacy of self-assertive drives, while providing reassurance that parental nurturence and love will not be withdrawn as a punishment. A thoroughly modern intent underlies nonsense literature, although it is not unrelated to parodies and satirical songs composed in honor of "Mother Folly" in the Middle Ages with the imprimatur of civil and ecclesiastical authorities (Wright, 207–13). Nonsense literature addresses itself to the child's need to cope with the terrors created by his own inexperience and barely suppressed emotions of jealously and rage, particularly in relation to siblings and parents. These fears pose a threat to the child's security insofar as the capacity for control is not well developed and the danger of acting out is ever-present, with dire consequences that the child can hardly imagine. Although fairy tales also deal with fears generated by the child's aggressive feelings, often objectified in the form of giants and ogres, they promise safety through conformity via obedience, patience, courage, and sometimes resourcefulness. Adherence to these norms of behavior promises not only mastery of the child's tumultuous inner world, but success, as well, in meeting the challenge of the external world. Nonsense literature tells the child that as wild and destructive as his or her fantasies may be, they can be rendered harmless with the help of humor and mental agility, rather than magical helpers in the form of fairy godmothers or enchanted animals.

Nonsense as Permission

One cannot imagine nonsense literature apart from the spirit of carnival. It belongs to the sphere of permitted license, in which, for a limited time, everything is turned upside down. Nonsense literature belongs also to the sphere of irreverence and does not hesitate to ridicule even demigods such as Polyphemus, Poseidon's son, whom Lucian in his *Dialogues* (61–63) derides as an uncouth shepherd whose singing resembles the braying of an ass. In nonsense literature, all adults roar like an ass, all men are mad hatters, and all women are modeled after Lewis Carroll's Queen of Hearts. It must not be supposed that Carroll, an ordained minister, was a critic of society; he belongs rather with those conservatives, like Jonathan Swift, who see humanity as living in a fallen state and therefore capable of every folly. Whether or not it comments on the nature of society, nonsense literature confirms the child's perception of grownups as inexplicably irritable, unreasonable, unfair, and entirely incomprehensible.

Nonsense as a Violence Vaccine

Moreover, adults are perceived as capable of violence, a penchant seen in much nonsense literature. The following refrain provides an example:

> Send us the beef first, good Mrs. Bond,
> And get us some ducks dressed out of the pond,
> Cry, Dilly, dilly, dilly, dilly, come to be killed,
> For you must be stuffed and my customers filled!
>
> (Opie, 91)

The following rhyme, apparently derived from an old oral tradition, is equally threatening:

I went to the toad that lies under the wall,
I charmed him out, and he came at my call;
I scratched out the eyes of the owl before,
I tore the bat's wing: what could you have more?

(Opie, 407)

Although adults are often presented as violence-prone in nonsense literature, attempts are made to convince the juvenile reader that the danger is
not real. Lewis Carroll, for example, casts adults as mere playing cards,
officious little animals acting like humans, or grotesque creatures of some
sort. He seems to be saying to his youthful readers: "These grumpy,
insulting, and somewhat scary grownups need not be taken seriously
because they are silly and quite harmless." In addition, as Martha
Wolfenstein observes: "The joker does not intend to carry out any
damaging action: he is only joking" (*Children's Humor*, 29–30). The message conveyed by nonsense literature is that violent figures conjured up
by the imagination are not a threat, just as one's destructive impulses are
harmless. Of course, it may not be obvious to a child that a writer is
joking. For example, Edward Lear's *History of the Seven Families of Lake
Pipple-Popple* describes how the young offspring of various adult birds and
animals perish miserably because of their disobedience, and how the
parents, out of grief, destroy themselves, as well. Although Lear's account
is highly amusing from an adult standpoint, especially because of his
clever choice of words, a child might be upset by all the fighting and
destruction that occur in the story. The mass suicide of the adult birds
and animals could be especially disturbing to young children, with their
not uncommon fears of abandonment. One might also mention, as a
possible source of anxiety, the Mother Goose rhyme in which a blackbird
pecks off a maid's nose, which, in some later versions, happily, is restored
by a little wren (Baring-Goulds, 26–27). Nonsense literature, then, sends
a conflicting message to the young reader; namely, that dangerous possibilities exist in the world, but that through cleverness, particularly verbal
ingenuity, disaster can be averted. Perhaps the most important implication
of the message is that dangerous *thoughts* can be neutralized by verbal
humor, often involving mock-logical, esthetically satisfying "solutions" to
absurd or menacing situations. In the following pages I propose to
examine how nonsense literature contributes to the intellectual, linguistic,
and emotional development of children precisely because of its willingness
to confront the uncanny with the power of reason expressed through
humor.

NONSENSE AND THE IMAGINATION

The growth of imagination is an important dimension of intellectual development in children. Nonsense literature shapes the imagination in a distinctive way, not to be confused with the effects of science fiction, adventure stories, or fairy tales. Nonsense literature deals in improbabilities, whereas science fiction and kindred genres deal in possibilities, once certain assumptions are granted. Improbabilities are closer to the child's worst fears than the kinds of scenarios that unfold in other forms of literature designed for children. I say this because the "uncanny" events and predicaments that characterize nonsense literature, most notably in the work of Lewis Carroll and, more recently, in the writings and illustrations of Maurice Sendak, can be referred to the innermost layers of the child's psyche. Nonsense literature unlocks the very wellspring of the imagination, a region of half-forgotten memories, distorted perceptions, and frightening emotions that are more closely related to the child's personal history than the images associated with science fiction or fairy tales. Whereas the latter involve culturally patterned fantasies, nonsense literature deals with the idiosyncratic. It fosters a type of imagination that owes little to traditional sources, such as the rituals and myths of the collectivity as reflected in fairy tales, or the group paranoia that visualizes extraterrestrial beings as monstrous "aliens." Exposure to nonsense literature informs the child that it is safe to explore forbidden regions of the mind, but that it is necessary to arm oneself with wit and a sense of the ridiculous. The child who would otherwise be afraid to trust his or her imagination is helped to see that it is safe to indulge in fantasy, providing one remains in control by means of clever wordplay and feats of logic.

A brief look at Baum's *Dorothy and the Wizard in Oz* provides interesting examples of how the reader's imagination is stimulated by improbable situations that are not allowed to get out of control. In the opening pages of the book, for example, the author describes Dorothy and her boy companion falling through a crack in the earth's surface created by an earthquake. At first the children, seated in their horse and buggy, descend to the bowels of the earth at an alarming rate and seem to be in danger of being dashed to pieces when they hit bottom. Baum, however, saves the situation by indicating that the children's headlong fall is slowed to a gradual descent when the top of the buggy fills with air "like a parachute or an umbrella filled with wind" (9), permitting a safe landing in the midst of a city filled with glass houses. Still later, Dorothy, her boy companion Zeb, and the Wizard are prisoners of a race of people called the wooden Gargoyles. Securing sets of wooden wings used by the Gargoyles to fly through the air and fastening the wings to their horse and buggy, the prisoners make their escape. Again, Baum demonstrates the force of logic by causing the Wizard to frighten off the pursuing Gargoyles by setting fire to the wooden wings once the fugitives have landed in a safe place. The Wizard reasons that wooden people will not dare approach a raging bonfire. It could be argued that adventure stories also depict heroes in perilous situations which they surmount by hitting upon imaginative solutions. But nonsense literature imposes an additional burden on the imagination, demanding nothing less than the higher sophistry—solutions based on ingenious arguments and verbal gymnastics. This is not to suggest that nonsense literature ignores the imagistic dimensions of the imagination in favor of symbolic thinking. After all, Tenniel's illustrations for *Alice in Wonderland*, Shepard's artwork for *Winnie-the-Pooh*, Dr. Seuss's illustrations for his own books, and Sendak's graphic productions are hardly less memorable than their associated texts. Nonsense literature stimulates the imagination in many ways, but it relies on verbal dexterity more than any other modality in order to resolve problematic situations. Intellectual development in children is heavily dependent on the acquisition of verbal skills, especially the kinds of skills that cannot be mastered through rote learning. Nonsense literature provides the inspiration to use words in an innovative way, whether in novel rhymes—the more absurd the better—or to "figure out" the verbal formula that will bring together the seemingly disparate parts of a problem.

NONSENSE AND THE FLEXIBLE MIND

In addition to furthering intellectual growth by stimulating the imagination—above all, the power of the mind to evoke striking images associated with novel word combinations—nonsense literature encourages *flexibility*. It prepares the mind to shift back and forth between the real and the unreal, between the reasonable and the outrageous, and between meaning and the absence of meaning. A mind that has been so prepared is perforce capable of responding in a resilient manner to life's many contingencies. It is difficult to imagine a rigid, doctrinaire person tolerating nonsense in any form, for nonsense implies that what is manifestly solid and incontrovertible can be rendered ambiguous when shown in a certain light. The rigid person demands certainty to shore up a precarious security system; the flexible person can confront life resourcefully because of not being a prisoner of a set of desperately held, arbitrary assumptions or nonrational beliefs. The experience of reading nonsense literature inoculates the child against narrow-mindedness by educating the youngster to modify or abandon successive frames of reference as they become untenable owing to inappropriateness. Here we see a preparation for life consisting of learning the difference between situations that can be salvaged through flexible perseverance and situations that must be written off as a lost cause. It is a question of learning to recognize when it is time to move beyond old, ingrained habits and failed strategies.

NONSENSE AND PROBLEM SOLVING

The child who has acquired a flexible mind has also gained a *problem-solving* set; that is, a tendency to look for answers and solutions where others might be tempted to give up, or might even fail to detect the existence of a problem. As Martha Wolfenstein has indicated, the popularity of joking riddles among children is understandable as an attempt to provide clever, albeit nonsensical answers to seemingly unknowable questions (*Children's Humor*, 99–157). By posing a baffling riddle to another child, a youngster gains reassurance that life's mysteries, still inpenetrable because of inexperience, may yet be made to yield their secrets. Children's riddles are the analogue, then, of real problems that the child will have to solve, but these problems do not come with ready-made answers. Even so, nonsense literature prepares the child to consider a variety of bold initiatives in coping with the unknown. The opening scene of *Through the Looking Glass*, for, example, shows Alice wondering what it would be like to be on the other side of the mirror that hangs over the mantel piece. She then imagines that she has passed over to the other side and fantasizes how she would appear to someone looking into the mirror and seeing her on the other side: "Oh, what fun it'll be, when they see me through the glass in here, and can't get at me!" Alice is not engaging in idle curiosity; she is exploring ways of placing herself beyond the reach of others.

The nonsense world is also the world of untested hypotheses and untried strategies for dealing with people and situations. Unlike the archaic world view embodied in fairy tales, in which obstacles can be overcome mainly with the help of fetishes and magical creatures, the basic assumption underlying nonsense literature is that barriers can be surmounted by means of ingenuity. Nor are its absurd characters and situations immune to logical analysis. When Alice finds, for example, that she cannot read the "Jabberwocky," she reasons that the poem is in a looking-glass book and concludes: "And, if I hold it up to a glass, the words will all go the right way again" (*Looking Glass*, chap. 1). In everyday life, problematic situations are often perceived as too complex to resolve, or even as "impossible." The child who has learned to enjoy reading about outlandish situations will not feel threatened by the unfamiliar, but will look for a way out of an impasse. By the same token, nonsense literature teaches the child that some situations are inherently absurd and that some problems are pseudoproblems, and therefore call for nonsolutions, albeit expressed in an amusing manner in keeping with the silliness of the problem. These nonsolutions or nonexplanations fill the pages of Carroll and Lear and other masters of the genre; they sharpen the reader's ability to recognize the irrational way people respond to equally ridiculous nonproblems. This is a valuable lesson when one considers the vast amount of time and energy that humanity has expended in the effort to solve problems that have existed only in the minds of necromancers and witch doctors of one sort or another.

Nonsense: A Litmus Test for Literal-Mindedness

A special intellectual benefit to be derived from reading nonsense literature is the insight a child gains into how *concrete* and literal-minded people can be. Nonsense literature demonstrates that the concrete world of appearances is not to be taken literally, and that the penalty for literal-mindedness is a reductio ad absurdum. For example, in Carroll's *Sylvie and Bruno Concluded* (614), Mein Herr explains that in his country humans are unsinkable because they have become lighter than water, thanks to artificial selection. However, he concludes in the next breath that despite their ability to float on water, his countrymen are apt to drown on land whenever their underground theaters are flooded up to the ceiling in order to extinguish fires that break out not infrequently. Carroll goes on to show how a literal application of the principle of artificial selection by Mein Herr and his fellow countrymen has enabled them to produce walking sticks that can walk by themselves and cotton-wool that is lighter than air.

True literal-mindedness, unlike the feigned literal-mindedness of comics, is incompatible with lightheartedness. Nonsense literature plays with the concreteness of things, revealing the folly of literal-mindedness and dramatizing the ambiguity that surrounds ordinary people, objects and events. Examples include the scenes in *Alice in Wonderland* in which Alice becomes tiny and then becomes large, or the many scenes in which inanimate objects come to life, or creatures change their shape. The reader is given to understand that concrete reality is ephemeral and subject to modification not only by the vicissitudes of time and circumstance, but by the exercise of imagination. One can claim that nonsense literature has the capacity to discover the hidden essence of things or to define their abstract meaning. Its strength lies in its ability to surprise the reader by replacing familiar terms of discourse and objects of perception with nonsensical equivalents. The result is to suggest that the concrete world of appearances is not to be taken too seriously because it does not exhaust the logical possibilities, however fanciful. By transcending the concrete meanings of objects and events, nonsense literature signifies that these meanings point to something beyond themselves and can serve as a point of departure for further exploration. Nonsense literature informs the reader that it is not necessary to remain in bondage to conventional meanings or customary interpretations, and that it is permissible to wonder if things can ever be different.

Is there any danger, then, that by reading *The Wizard of Oz* or *The Cat in the Hat* a child may become confused as to what is concretely real and what is unreal and can never happen in the real world? I do not think so. On the contrary, I believe that nonsense literature prepares the mind to grasp the ironic and paradoxical nature of what adults call "reality." Dictionaries define irony as incongruity between what might be expected and what actually happens. On the basis of limited experience, the child expects people to perform the actions that he or she has witnessed in the past. What actually happens, as the child observes with growing maturity, is substantively different in many ways from what the child expects. Thus, the love and kindness expressed by the child's parents are not necessarily reflected in the behavior of strangers, nor is the loyalty of childhood friends necessarily the same as the alliances formed during one's adult years, particularly in the workplace and the marketplace. By teaching children the limits of literal-minded perception, nonsense literature paves the way for redefining the boundaries of reality with indicators that point to truths that are too often hidden by concrete appearances.

Nonsense and the Nature of Language

The ability to go beyond the concreteness of things by rearranging meanings and shapes playfully, as in nonsense literature, helps the child develop insight into the arbitrary nature of words and symbols. In his book *The Language and Thought of the Child*, Jean Piaget has demonstrated how the young child believes that the names of objects inhere in the objects themselves. This primitive mode of thinking is only a few steps away from the conventional adult's tendency to think that familiar social, economic, and political arrangements reflect something inherent in human nature. When Jonathan Swift causes Gulliver to enter a world in which horses are superior to men, he shows how arbitrary is the assumption that humans are more noble than other creatures. Similarly, Carroll places Alice in a garden with flowers that not only can talk, but do not hesitate to ridicule Alice for looking "faded" and having "untidy petals." The words we use in everyday speech not only carry arbitrary meanings, but they reflect unspoken values. We have to hear them from the mouths of horses or some other unlikely source before we recognize their arbitrariness and the arrogance they often imply.

In this regard, the parodic side of nonsense literature is especially valuable in alerting the young reader to the artificiality of language. By listening to a parody of a familiar rhyme, for example, the child begins to understand that words that sound alike can have very different meanings. The contents of a parody may be nonsensical, or they may make as much sense as the original words, but it is a revelation to realize that such transformations can be made with impunity. The very idea that one can tinker with language and deliberately make changes in a time-honored text was beyond the comprehension of the ancient scribes, who took great pains never to alter a single word in any text, especially in sacred ones. The fear of making textual alterations cannot be attributed exclusively to the sentiment of religious awe. It is necessary to acknowledge the awful "tyranny of words," to use Stuart Chase's apt phrase. The transmission of language from one generation to the next involves the communication of an entire world view, as Benjamin Whorf has consistently argued (and as the title of his selected works, *Language, Thought, and Reality* suggests). This world view contains a code for representing the external world and the interior life, as well. This code is received as a given, as if it has existed unchanged from the beginning of time. Nor is it prudent for the child to misuse this linguistic code. To the extent that language serves an instrumental (as well as expressive) purpose from the very start of a child's life, its misuse would prevent the child from conveying urgent needs to caretakers.

Nonsense literature gives the child "permission" to deviate from customary linguistic formulas and to be flippant and irreverent about language. It dares to be outrageous without using offensive words; it dares to be childish and does not pretend in the least to be edifying. Nonsense literature invites the child to take liberties with language and to play games with it, while removing that sense of guilt that comes with laying profane hands on something sacred. The child who has been moved to laughter by nonsense literature is not likely to be awed by language or be deceived by charlatans, who know that they can evoke in others whatever emotions they want merely by uttering certain charged words. Nonsense literature instructs the child to be the master of words, rather than their servant, and ultimately, their victim. The child who does not absorb this lesson will never discover how much nonsense is embedded in so-called serious literature, or in everyday speech. Because, by and large, words mean what the dead ancestors wanted them to mean, language itself is in perpetual danger of becoming stale, of deadening rather than vivifying. Nonsense literature puts life back into words and enables the writer to add richness and variety to the language. The child who reads nonsense literature finds that language is not a dead letter, but a set of flexible rules for generating new language. Pity the society whose academicians have fixed the rules of language for all time! Its children may never learn to sing their own song.

NONSENSE: SEEING AND HEARING FRESHLY

The innovative function of nonsense literature contributes not only to the intellectual and linguistic resources of the child, but stimulates visual and auditory imagery as well. Lewis Carroll has given us a wealth of fresh imagery and delightful neologisms. James Joyce has shown, as is well known, that the invention of new words need not be confined to nonsense literature for children. But to read *Ulysses* or *Finnegans Wake* is to recognize at once that Joyce's neologisms are qualitatively different from Carroll's inventions. Joyce evokes familiar imagery by means of unfamiliar words that he has constructed artfully, often out of several languages. Carroll suggests unfamiliar visual images (with the indispensable help of Tenniel) by means of words that sound familiar, but are also artificial. Joyce's word-pictures represent an urban world that every adult is familiar with in a general way; Carroll's visual imagery refers to a universe that has never existed. He has transformed familiar objects (rabbits, playing cards, turtles, etc.) magically by placing them in novel contexts, altering their shapes, or giving them unexpected powers. Nonsense literature creates visual images that have the power to delight children because of their novelty. Joyce's experimental writings, by contrast, are intended for adults who are prepared by the author to look more closely at a world they already know, but which they wish to see described with fresh nuances of meaning and with hitherto neglected sensory images.

If one grants the validity of this distinction, it is reasonable to conclude that nonsense literature is ideally suited to the linguistic needs of children because it adds to their limited store of auditory images. Such literature also opens the door to experimentation with sound, unlike ordinary language and literature, which provide the child with a set of "correct" sounds and arrangements of sounds. Nonsense words reinstate the child's innate capacity to make new sound combinations spontaneously. More importantly, nonsense literature legitimizes the child's natural affinity for making novel, self-stimulating sounds. Although humans are not the only creatures that produce sounds spontaneously, they are the only creatures who can freely choose from a repertoire of sounds and arbitrarily assign meaning or non-meaning to certain sound combinations. This capacity for improvisation is too often stultified by parental emphasis on standardized speech and the fear that the child will not outgrow infantile speech patterns. Learning to play with the sound of words is analogous to learning a second language, except that there is greater freedom to invent. In both instances, the child learns that there is more than one way to communicate a given meaning, and that words are not only arbitrary sounds, but can assume hitherto unsuspected forms. Finding that it is gratifying to master new sounds is akin to the discovery that even sounds that have no meaning can be evocative and pleasurable in their own right. Carroll's nonsense words, for example, carry their own half-mysterious, half-familiar associations: "Twas brillig, and the slithy toves / Did gyre and gimble in the wabe: / All mimsy were the borogoves / And the mome raths outgrabe" ("Jabberwocky," *Looking Glass*, chap. 1).

It must not be supposed that the sound of nonsense words is entirely random. Although standard words are arbitrary sounds (except for ono-matopoeic words), deliberate distortions of these words by nonsense writers—and inventive children—seem to imitate the rhythms and sounds of everyday speech. There is a lawfulness to sound play that enables children to approach the outer boundaries of their native tongue and to intuit its distinctive phonetic patterns, and, in a broader sense, its peculiar genius. Parody is especially suited to highlighting the unconscious structure of a language and the psychology of the people who use it. The psychological intention behind the sound pattern we call language is laid bare when one exaggerates the way words sound, or, better yet, makes up nonsense words and phrases that sound like the real thing. It is only necessary to imagine someone imitating an American, a Britisher, a Frenchman, or a German while using nonsense words to apprehend the theatricality of language, its posturing and pretence—and its human frailty. It is good for a child to see that language can be stretched this way, because it leaves no doubt that even behind the most portentous words there is concealed a human being and not an oracle. As Dorothy found in *The Wizard of Oz*, behind the impressive talking head is a small man from Omaha who is not really a wizard.

NONSENSE AND SUBCONSCIOUS FEARS

Nonsense literature is humorous by definition. For the small child surrounded by authority figures, the nonsensical is the ideal equalizer, permitting tension-reduction through humor, especially humor of the grotesque or exaggerated type. The pioneer of this kind of humor is Edward Lear whose nonsense verse and prose is closer to a young child's need system than Carroll's sophisticated humor. Lear's humor appeals to the most archaic layers of the personality:

> O My aged Uncle Arly!
> Sitting on a heap of barley
> Thro' the silent hours of night,—
> Close beside a leafy thicket:—
> On his nose there was a Cricket,—
> In his hat a Railway-Ticket;—
> (But his shoes were far too tight.)
>
> (*Complete Nonsense*, 275)

The effect of nonsense humor is to reassure the child that his or her anxieties can be overcome. The young child's anxieties center on the fear of abandonment, fear of bodily harm, and fear of parental anger or even retaliation for hostile wishes toward family members. There is also a fear of the unknown. Nonsense humor works in several ways to address these fears. For example, it describes potentially troublesome situations and then reverses their expected consequences in a funny, magical way. Or else, nonsense humor starts with innocuous situations, proceeds to create a worst-possible scenario of disorder in the manner of Dr. Seuss, and produces a swift and reassuring resolution that is as humorous as it is absurd. These transformations of reality tell the child that all's well that ends well and that vexing situations are often inherently funny. Still another message, subversive and eye-opening, is carried by nonsense literature; namely, that there is a resemblance between silly, nonsensical solutions to frustrating situations and adult "realistic" solutions to problems. In other words, the humor in nonsense literature caricatures the serious, adult-dominated world of reality. Illustrations of this tendency are seen in nonsense fantasies that mimic fairy tales and nonsense lyrics that are a mimesis of serious poetry. Nonsense tales and ballads about people and creatures that are killed or mutilated are caricatures of blood-and-thunder adventure tales. Nonsensical drawings, Edward Lear-style, are so crude as to be parodies of cartoons—caricatures of caricatures.

NONSENSE AND THE SHIP OF (ADULT) FOOLS

By providing a burlesque of adult society, nonsense literature takes liberties with the reality principle and suggests that the spirit of playfulness points to a deeper and more abiding reality. Like all comedy, nonsense humor furnishes a commentary on humanity's Lilliputian pretensions. The child who laughs at the ridiculous posturings of adults in the context of nonsense literature gains a valuable perspective on life, including a sense of proportion and a set of implied standards of candor and honesty. The ambience of nonsense literature is not unlike that of Mardi Gras, in which "fools" and masquers change place with authority figures and make a mockery of everything sacred. As Ernst Kris puts it: "It is precisely this incongruity of form and content which is so often demonstrated; thus parody devaluates the content, travesty the form" (175). Nonsense literature, which seeks to deride conventional form and content alike, shortens the distance between the sublime and the ridiculous. It enables the young reader to see that society's conventions, slightly exaggerated and distorted, are grotesque when they are not silly. Kris uses the metaphor of "unmasking" to describe the effect of caricature. The child reads "The Valiant Little Tailor," whose hero's prowess consists of swatting many flies at a single blow, and the absurdity of the tailor's vanity helps him or her to develop an all-purpose folly detector. The process of learning to distance oneself from life's pompous asses is liberating in the highest degree at the same time that it is disillusioning. But the true idealist is one who can persevere in pursuit of goals without illusion and despite knowledge of human frailty. The comic sense allows us to laugh at those who hide behind conventional masks, certain in the knowledge that any fool or scoundrel can don the same disguise. The child who has been allowed to read nonsense literature will be the first to cry out that the emperor is naked, and far from being shocked or turning into a cynic, will smile and try to imagine how the emperor would look if he were clothed in virtue.

It is but a short step from the recognition that the emperor is naked to the hostile thought that he would look better in a jester's conical hat and bells. Nonsense literature helps the child release tension and hostility because it is a medium for conveying ridicule, and in a more general sense, fulfilling interdicted wishes. The child's resentments cannot always be made known with impunity. Often, destructive impulses, including death wishes directed at others, have to be expressed indirectly through the child's unconscious use of symbolism. Symbolism of this kind corresponds in many ways to the artful distortions and disguises of the caricaturist, the composer of nonsense verses and limericks, and the fantasist. Symbol-formation seems to follow the same rules in expressing the comic spirit as in the articulation of the childish wish. In both instances, the world of everyday reality is magically transformed in conformity with powerful unconscious motivations. Presumably, the adult author of nonsense literature remains more-or-less in control of his hostile feelings, whereas the child who is amused at the former's antic inventions is much more under the influence of his half-acknowledged aggressive drives. These emotions, which are controlled only by the expenditure of great psychic energy, are released harmlessly when the child finds himself in the presence of a literary merry-andrew. The latter performs on the verbal plane those mocking and defiant acts that the child wishes to carry out behaviorally. This accomplishes his hostile ends so cleverly that retribution is avoided, as illustrated by Dr. Seuss's *Cat in the Hat* series.

The writer of nonsense literature, like the caricaturist, shows people in a ridiculous light by exaggerating their salient traits. Even such a gentle writer as L. Frank Baum depicts his Wizard of Oz as fraudulent and given to bombast and absurd pretensions. Beneath a veneer of innocent fun and wordplay, nonsense literature serves as a means for vicarious acting-out and retribution. It is similar to the stylized taunting songs and counter-songs used by the Tiv tribesmen of Nigeria to settle disputes between individuals or families (Bohannan). These singing contests, known as "drumming the scandal," were intended to mobilize public opinion on one side or the other of a dispute. As is true of nonsense rhymes of a derogatory nature, such airing of grievances succeeds in raising ridicule to the level of popular art. For the child, learning to express opposition by verbal means is an advance over direct physical action, negativism, or repression. When in addition, the verbal means employed are clever and witty, the child has taken an important step toward mature behavior. The hostile content of much nonsense literature has a constructive side to it and is not an invitation to the child to be defiant or disrespectful. It is the child who is lacking in verbal resources who is most likely to show rude, poorly socialized behavior, including violence.

It would seem, then, that nonsense literature contributes to the civilizing process and contains a larger measure of "sense" and sensibility than is apparent at first glance. Such literature, paradoxically, also sensitizes the child to the real world, which, by implication, exists in contradistinction to the topsy-turvy world of nonsense literature. It would be an error to suppose that the child who reads, say, Vachel Lindsay's *Springfield Town is Butterfly Town* or John Ciardi's *You Read to Me, I'll Read to You*, is unfamiliar with the workaday world of school, sports competition, and sibling rivalry. Nonsense literature affirms the perdurability and solidity of the real world by lampooning it. Caricature, ridicule, and absurd fantasy are the tribute that the author and readers pay to the reality principle, knowing that to play with words so as to hold the mirror up to human vanity is not to question the existence of the real world, but rather to criticize it. Let it be said of the writers of children's nonsense literature that their criticism of life is gentle and without rancor; it is not meant to turn the actual world upside down or even to set it right, but to show that it leans too much to the side of folly.

Baring-Gould, William S. and Ceil Baring-Gould. *The Annotated Mother Goose.* New York: World, 1972.

Bohannon, Paul. *Justice and Judgment among the Tiv.* London: Oxford UP, 1957.

Carroll, Lewis. *The Complete Works of Lewis Carroll.* New York: Modern Library, n.d.

Ciardi, John. *You Read to Me, I'll Read to You.* Philadelphia: Lippincott, 1962.

Kris, Ernst. *Psychoanalytic Explorations in Art.* New York: Schocken, 1964.

Lear, Edward. *The Complete Nonsense of Edward Lear.* Ed. Holbrook Jackson. New York: Dover, 1951.

Lindsay, Vachel. *Springfield Town is Butterfly Town.* Kent, OH: Kent State UP, 1969.

Lucian's Dialogues. Trans. Howard Williams. London: George Bell, 1903.

Nash, Walter. *The Language of Humour: Style and Technique in Comic Discourse.* White Plains, NY: Longman, 1985.

Opie, Iona and Peter Opie, eds. *The Oxford Dictionary of Nursery Rhymes.* Oxford: Oxford UP, 1952.

Piaget, Jean. *The Language and Thought of the Child.* New York: NAL, 1959.

Schneiderman, Leo. *The Psychology of Myth, Folklore and Religion.* Chicago: Nelson-Hall, 1981.

Whorf, Benjamin Lee. *Language, Thought, and Reality: Selected Writings.* Ed. John B. Carroll. Cambridge, MA: Technology Press, MIT, 1956.

Wolfenstein, Martha. *Children's Humor: A Psychological Analysis.* Glencoe, IL: Free Press, 1954.

Wright, Thomas. *A History of Caricature and Grotesque in Literature and Art.* London: Virtue Brothers, 1865.

Part III | ALL KINDS OF NONSENSE

"What were you trying to do? Make sense out of things? Bring order?"

Edward Albee, The Zoo Story, *22*

"Sesame Street" as Theater of the Absurd

by Blair Whitney

One major goal of the Children's Literature Association is to encourage the serious study of children's literature as literature, as a legitimate branch of the humanities. The literary skill and philosophical maturity of children's literature is not difficult to demonstrate when one is studying the work of C. S. Lewis or E. B. White, but it is somewhat harder to make a case for children's literature when one is dealing with the popular forms experienced by most children. Children's television, for example, provides the proof for Newton Minow's "vast wasteland" thesis. The frenetic, violent cartoons and inane comedies are totally devoid of merit. One exception, however, is "Sesame Street", produced by the Children's Television Workshop.

Perhaps the best program for children ever presented, "Sesame Street" uses the dramatic techniques, literary conventions, and philosophical arguments of the "theater of the absurd." The plays of Sartre, Camus, Beckett, Ionesco, Albee, and others were once the epitome of avant-garde theater. A generation later, their ideas are now familiar to millions of children in the United States and Europe. What was once a drama for sophisticated intellectuals is now a tool for teaching their children, and the children of the poor and uneducated as well.

OSCAR THE GROUCH AS EXISTENTIALIST

To demonstrate this remarkable phenomenon quickly, one can ask any child about Oscar the Grouch. Oscar, he will tell you, is a large, green furry character who lives in a garbage can. In a deep gravelly voice, Oscar sings his theme song, "I Love Trash."

> Oh, I love trash!
> Anything dirty or dingy or dusty.
> Anything rotten or ragged or rusty.
> Yes, I love trash.
>
> I have here a sneaker that's tattered and worn.
> It's all full of holes and the laces are torn. . .
> I love it because it's trash.
> (Jeffrey Moss "I Love Trash" in *The Songs of
> "Sesame Street"*)

Oscar is a perfect representative of Albert Camus's metaphysical rebel. The ordinary world, Oscar believes, has all the wrong values, so he boldly asserts his own instead. In Camus's words,

> He attacks a shattered world to make it whole. He confronts the injustice at large in the world with his own principles of justice. Thus all he originally wants is to resolve this contradiction and establish a reign of justice, if he can, or of injustice if he is driven to the end of his tether. Meanwhile he denounces the contradiction. (*The Rebel*, 29)

One day, for example, the residents of "Sesame Street" awake to find that a strong wind has blown over garbage cans and scattered trash all over their clean doorsteps. They set to work immediately to clean up the mess, while Oscar howls in agonized protest. For one brief, shining moment the real world has lived up to his vision of it.

The existentialism of Camus and Sartre provides the philosophical outlook of many "absurd" plays. Oscar is the direct heir of Nag and Nell, Hamm's parents in Samuel Beckett's *Endgame*, who have lost their legs and live out their lives firmly rooted in two ashbins. Like Oscar, they have a contrary view of the world. Nell, for instance, asserts that "Nothing is funnier than unhappiness" (*Endgame*, 29). The play's characters are a good demonstration of the fundamental principles of the theater of the absurd, principles that Edward Albee states succinctly in his essay "Which Theatre Is the Absurd One?"

> The Theatre of the Absurd is an absorption-in-art of certain existentialist and post-existentialist philosophical concepts having to do, in the main, with man's attempt to make sense for himself out of his senseless position in a world which makes no sense— which makes no sense because the moral, religious, political, and social structures man has erected to "illusion" himself have collapsed. (170)

Thus, if the playwright believes that the proper metaphor for the world around him is a garbage can, he puts his characters into real garbage cans as a way of making concrete sense of what he sees.

"Sesame Street" is also concerned with making sense out of the world and tries to educate by demonstrating such absurdities as Oscar in his garbage can. On "Sesame Street," however, sweet, pleasant, rational adults like Susan, Gordon, Bob, and Mr. Hooper are around to explain and comfort. The absurd playwrights do not allow their audiences any such solace. According to Martin Esslin, chief scholar of the genre, the theater of the absurd attempts to make modern man "face up to the human condition as it really is, to free him from illusions that are bound to cause constant maladjustment and disappointment" (*The Theatre of the Absurd*, 316). Sesame Street is a clean and happy place, but 125th Street in Harlem is not. It may be that Oscar is the one who sees more truly.

THE LANGUAGE OF THE ABSURD

Another common concern of both "Sesame Street" and the theater of the absurd is with the nature of language. Both use language games to instruct and amuse, and both experiment with language, test its limits, and explore its absurdities. Eugene Ionesco, a Rumanian who lives in Paris and writes in French, wrote his first play, *The Bald Soprano*, while he was trying to learn English from the absurd sentences in a typical primer.

He did not learn English, but he learned some startling truths. In a series of conversations between the primer's Mr. and Mrs. Smith about their children, their servant Mary, and their friends the Martins, he discovered that "starting from basic axioms, they build more complex truths" (Esslin, 87). These "truths" include such important statements as "The country is quieter than the big city." From this escalating succession of cliches, Ionesco constructed a marvelous comedy, which he believed was not a comedy at all but a "tragedy of language."

The Bald Soprano begins with comforting formulas:

> There, it's nine o'clock. We've drunk the soup, and eaten the fish and chips, and the English salad. The children have drunk English water. We've eaten well this evening. That's because we live in the suburbs of London and because our name is Smith. (Ionesco, 9)

These comforting bromides break down under pressure, however, and by the end of the play the language reverts to its original elements. The characters begin to scream.

Mr. Smith.	The pope elopes! The pope's got no horoscope. The horoscope's bespoke.
Mrs. Martin.	Bazaar, Balzac, bazooka!
Mr. Martin.	Bizarre, beaux-arts, brassiere!
Mr. Smith.	A, e, i, o, u, a, e, i, o, u, a, e, i, o, u, i!
Mrs. Martin.	B, c, d, f, g, l, m, n, p, r, s, t, v, w, x, y, z!

(Ionesco 41)

Of course this sort of thing happens all the time on "Sesame Street," only the process is reversed. *The Bald Soprano*, an absurd anti-play, moves from integration to disintegration. On "Sesame Street," children go through the normal process of learning to build words from letters, except for the most absurd character on the program, Big Bird, a giant, yellow, stork-like dodo, who cannot understand. As a result, he is left out of the rational world. He expresses his problem in a song that is a perfect expression of what Ionesco means when he speaks of the tragedy of language, which is only funny to those onlookers not caught up in it. Big Bird sings,

ABCDEFGHIJKLMNOPQRSTUVWXYZ
It's the most remarkable word I've ever seen.

ABCDEFGHIJKLMNOPQRSTUVWXYZ
I wish I knew exactly what I mean.
It starts out like an A-word,
As anyone can see,
But somewhere in the middle
It gets awfully QR to me.

ABCDEFGHIJKLMNOPQRSTUVWXYZ
If I ever find out just what this word can mean,
I'll be the smartest bird the world has ever seen.
(Joe Roposo and Jon Stone, "ABC——DEFGH,"
The Songs of Sesame Street)

Children laugh at poor big Bird, and adults laugh at the Smiths and Martins of *The Bald Soprano*, thus proving that tragedy and comedy are not too far apart.

THE VAUDEVILLE ELEMENT

One of the best-known absurd plays is Beckett's *Waiting for Godot*, in which two tramps named Vladimir and Estragon (or Didi and Gogo) wait for a Mr. Godot, who never comes. While waiting, they talk to one another in the language of vaudeville or the music hall. The play contains a good deal of slapstick humor, along with its densely symbolic philosophical commentary. In fact, exvaudevillian Bert Lahr had his last success in *Godot*. Beckett uses comic pratfalls symbolically, according to one critic, because the play contains "no fewer than forty-five stage directions indicating that one of the characters leaves the upright position, which symbolizes the dignity of man (Esslin, 15). "Sesame Street's" answer to Vladimir and Estragon is the comedy team of Ernie and Bert, two more of Jim Henson's marvelous Muppets, who also use slapstick routines for quite sophisticated educational purposes. To see these similarities, one can compare these two brief excerpts:

> *Estragon:* (*violently*) I'm hungry.
> *Vladimir:* Do you want a carrot?
> *Estragon:* Is that all there is?
> *Vladimir:* I might have some turnips.
> *Estragon:* Give me a carrot. (VLADIMIR *rummages in his pockets, takes out a turnip and gives it to* ESTRAGON *who takes a bite out of it. Angrily*). It's a turnip!

> *Vladimir:* Oh pardon! I could have sworn it was a carrot.
>
> *(Godot*, 14)

Bert: Wake up, Ernie. You're supposed to learn something.

Ernie: I did learn something. I learned that you won't let me take a nap.

Bert: (*holds up a number 5*) Don't be funny. What's this I'm holding up?

Ernie: Uh . . . a banana cream pie?

Bert: No, you meatball! Guess again.

Ernie: I know! It's a chocolate cream pie!

Bert: (*holds up chocolate cream pie*) Look, birdbrain. If this number 5 is a chocolate cream pie, then what's this in my other hand.

Ernie: It's a number 5. (Bert *hits* Ernie *in face with pie, then exits*). I knew what it really was . . . but who wants to get hit with a number 5? Yum.

(Jeffrey Moss et al., *The Sesame Street Storybook*)

Such similarities may not be the result of any direct attempt on the part of the Children's Television Workshop to introduce children to the theater of the absurd, but just a reflection of their common roots. Children's literature has always dealt with the absurd—Esslin (230) points to *Alice in Wonderland* as a good example—and the format of "Sesame Street" uses the two most absurd theatrical forms, the animated cartoon and the television commercial. Both cartoon and commercial try to lift the viewer out of his ordinary existence and transport him in to wonderland where, for instance, a little furry creature, pursued by some larger enemy (cat, dog, or wolf) races up a tree and runs out on a limb. The villainous animal whips out a saw from his invisible pocket and cuts through the limb. But the limb remains suspended in space while the tree crashes, smashing the bad guy. In commercials, vegetables tap dance gaily, and lifesize cold germs hold a convention inside a giant nose. "Sesame Street" uses the commercial technique to "sell" learning. "Today "Sesame Street" is brought to you by the Number Three and the Letter J." The program also uses animated cartoons to illustrate basic verbal and mathematical concepts.

GAMES AND PLAY

In short, "Sesame Street" tries always to emphasize the element of play:

> Somebody come and play.
> Somebody come and play today!
> Somebody come and smile the smiles,
> And sing the songs,
> It won't take long.
> Somebody come and play today.
>
> (Jeffrey Moss, "Somebody Come and Play" in *The Songs of Sesame Street*)

This same element of play is present in most absurd drama, even when in plays that take a very morose view of the world. In Edward Albee's *Who's Afraid of Virginia Woolf* (the title is itself a pun on a children's song), the four characters spend the entire play in an elaborate game called Get the Guests. At the end of the play, George and Martha begin to sum up their lives together in this passage.

> *George:* Oh, it's a real fun game, Martha.
> *Martha:* (*pleading*). No more games.
> *George:* (*quietly triumphant*). One more, Martha. One more game and then beddie-bye. Everybody pack up his tools and baggage and stuff and go home. . . .
>
> (206–07)

The title of Beckett's *Endgame* refers to a chess term, and suggests that the characters are now at the end of a special sort of game. The action begins when Hamm speaks this condensed, yet powerful line, "Me—to play" (*Endgame*, 2). Likewise, Max Frisch's *Biedermann and the Firebugs* is subtitled "a learning-play without a lesson." "Sesame Street" is a learning play *with* a lesson.

The spirit of play that characterizes the theater of the absurd is perhaps the most striking difference between it and conventional realistic drama, which is always serious, even in comedies. That a playwright could "play" with such serious philosophical notions may have amazed and confused audiences in the 1950s, when most of these plays first appeared, but the same theories of drama have now been adapted by children's television. An audience of off-Broadway theater-goers may simply have failed to realize that what they were seeing was not really avant-garde at all. In fact, Samuel Beckett, Eugene Ionesco, Edward Albee, and the others were often simply engaging in their own particular brand of play. The theater of the absurd and "Sesame Street" are successful examples of performing art because they share a knowledge that play should be serious business and serious business should be play. For this reason, they are seldom dull, and their nonsense makes sense. We live in an absurd world in which the logical and the rational are daily overturned. The absurd playwrights of the 1950s realized this, and now "Sesame Street" is helping the world's children towards the same realization.

Albee, Edward. *The American Dream and The Zoo Story: Two Plays by Edward Albee.* New York: NAL, 1961.
———. "Which Theatre is the Absurd One?" *American Playwrights on Drama.* Ed. Horst Frenz. New York: Hill and Wang, 1965.
———. *Who's Afraid of Virginia Woolf?* New York: Atheneum, 1963.
Beckett, Samuel. *Endgame.* New York: Grove, 1958.
———. *Waiting for Godot.* New York: Grove, 1954.
Camus, Albert. *The Rebel.* Trans. Anthony Bower. Harmondsworth Middlesex, England: Penguin, 1971.
Esslin, Martin. *The Theatre of the Absurd.* New York: Doubleday, 1961.
Frisch, Max. *Biedermann and the Firebugs.* New York: Methuen, 1962.
Ionesco, Eugene. *Four Plays by Eugene Ionesco.* Trans. Donald M. Allen. New York: Grove, 1958.
Moss, Jeffrey et al. *The Sesame Street Storybook.* New York: Children's Television Workshop, 1971.
Raposo, Joe and Jon Stone. *The Songs of Sesame Street.* New York: Columbia Records, 1970.

But the Snark is at hand, let me tell you again!
　　'Tis your glorious duty to seek it!

To seek it with thimbles, to seek it with care;
　　To pursue it with forks and hope;
To threaten its life with a railway-share;
　　To charm it with smiles and soap.

Lewis Carroll, "Fit the Fourth,"
The Hunting of the Snark, *lines 27–32*

Nonsense Verse and Its Appeal

Jordan Brotman, in his essay, "A Late Wanderer in Oz," observed that the child has a "sense of words as things" (167). Perhaps that is why children delight in manipulating words in their own play and love to hear the nonsense created by others. This is especially true of nonsense poetry with its added appeal of strong rhythms and rhyme patterns. The infant, to whom most words are nonsense, responds to the sound of a parent's voice, perhaps accompanied by actions (patty-cake, knee-bouncing, toe or nose-tweaking) that please the child and give it more contact with the parent. The infant or toddler being rocked to sleep to the accompaniment of a nursery lullaby enjoys the triple pleasures of song, motion, and loving closeness. It is no wonder that a child reared with nursery rhymes will have a continued love of the genre. Such a child will also have the security to appreciate the topsy-turvy humor so frequent in nursery rhymes.

There are adults who believe that children need realism, not nonsense and fairy tales, during their formative years when they are learning about their language and the world around them. Others hold that nonsense helps children come to terms with reality. As we have already noted, Kornei Chukovsky, called "the dean of Russian children's writers" by his translator, Miriam Morton (*From Two to Five*, xii), vehemently defends nonsense. He believes that a child's recognition of nonsense comes from his understanding of the real world, for "the more aware the child is of the correct relationship of things, which he violates in his play, the more comical does that violation seem to him" (99). Moreover, nonsense verses are regarded by children precisely as nonsense. "They do not for one moment believe in their authenticity" (95), Chukovksy claims and says, "hardly has the child comprehended with certainty which objects go together and which do not, when he begins to listen happily to verses of absurdity" (96). Chukovsky concludes by stating that "it is high time to promote these 'nonsense' verses into the category of educationally valuable and perceptive works of poetry which contribute to the strengthening in the child's mind of the correct understanding of reality" (113). Linda Geller's book *Wordplay and Language Learning*, so valuable for this present study of nonsense, is a much needed attempt to follow Chukovsky's advice and integrate nonsense verse and related forms into the grade school curriculum.

Nonsense Verse: A Bagful of Tricks for All Ages

As with nonsense in general, the definition of nonsense verse varies. Myra Cohn Livingston makes perhaps too fine a distinction between nonsense verse and humorous verse using inversion, whimsical exaggeration, wordplay, and parody. She holds, for instance, that the anonymous verse beginning "'Tis midnight and the setting sun / Is slowly rising in the west" is not nonsense, "but rather a self-contained (albeit inverted) world dependent upon our recognition of certain physical laws" ("Nonsense Verse: The Complete Escape," 128–29). We are closer to Chukovsky's view. As we have argued, such inversions do rightfully belong to the genre, in fact are a central mechanism for creating nonsense. Whimsical exaggeration that distorts rather than inverts the world also has its place, as do wordplay and tampering with poetic conventions. As Rebecca Lukens writes, in her chapter "From Rhyme to Poetry," "nonsense plays upon our delight in the illogical and the incongruous, upon our pleasure in words cleverly used or misused, upon some secret yearning to see the immutable laws overturned" (*A Critical Handbook*, 182). Major nonsense anthologists, like Carolyn Wells, Roger Lancelyn Green, and William Cole, include in their collections poems with all of these elements. The important distinction is the one that Wells made in her introduction to *A Nonsense Anthology* (1902) on the need "to discriminate between nonsense of integral merit and simple chaff" (15).

Classic nonsense verses like those in the Mother Goose collections and Lear's and Carroll's rhymes, although the most famous examples of the genre, scarcely exhaust it. Modern authors have produced a wealth of nonsense verse for a variety of ages. One popular writer for young children who are beginning to explore beyond nursery rhymes is N. M. Bodeker. In *Let's Marry Said the Cherry and Other Nonsense Poems* he reveals his pleasure in many types of wordplay. Like Ogden Nash and Laura Richards, he will sometimes distort words and rhymes. He plays with both sound and meaning in verses like "Booteries and Fluteries and Flatteries and Things." In "Gluk" Bodeker has chosen actual place names of foreign cities (Gdansk, Lvov, Zagreb, etc.) that will sound like nonsense to American children. In "If I Were an Elephant" he plays with what linguists call a bound morpheme (a legitimate sound unit in the language that carries meaning only when joined with certain other units):

> If I were a radish
> I would love my ish.
> You don't know what an ish is?
> It's what that radish had
> to have,
> because without it
> it would only be a rad.

>   (16)

His verses are also full of nonsense situations. In "Miss Bitter" the baby-sitter performs her job literally and actually sits on the baby, a pun very accessible to twentieth-century children; Shel Silverstein uses it with his sitter Mrs. McTwitter (*A Light in the Attic*, 16). Bodeker further capitalizes on modern tastes when, in "Mr. Docer," he has not only "drawers full / of jam and porridge" but even "peanut butter / wrapped in socks" (28), an image sure to cause giggles. Accompanying all the verbal fun are nonsensical pen and ink illustrations. For example, for "The Lark in Sark" a bird is drawn with teeth and crying "WOOFF" (10). Bodeker's other collections of nonsense, notably *It's Raining Said John Twaining*, equally popular with children, have such lines as "Me and I and You / sailed a wooden shoe" (n.p.) and "Little Miss Price / rode with her mice / over the ice." This book is also full of silly situations, like catching "a trout with applesauce." Bodeker enjoys and uses a full repertoire of nonsense tricks in his verse.

Animals that do not actually belong to the species of nonsense creatures but who behave in an absurdly unanimal-like manner have long been a favorite with nonsense writers—and with children who read their work. Hilaire Belloc wrote *The Bad Child's Book of Beasts* (1896) and *More Beasts for Worse Children* (1897) in both of which the human children and adults are more likely to appear beastly than the animals do. John Gardner created *A Child's Bestiary* (with added poems by Lucy Gardner and Eugene Rudzewicz). Birds are included in this bestiary, among them the cockatoo who "is widely known / For talking on the telephone / And also (wretched, thoughtless bird) / For hanging up without a word" (15). Gardner's lizard "longs to be a dinosaur" (36). Several of the poems are similar to those of Ogden Nash, but without Nash's elan or level of nonsense. Gardner's lines "If somebody offers you a Bear, bow low / And say no" (7), seem common sense prose compared to Ogden Nash's solution to the bear problem in "The Adventures of Isabel":

> Isabel met an enormous bear,
> Isabel, Isabel, didn't care;
>
> . . . .
> The bear said, Isabel, glad to meet you,
> How do, Isabel, now I'll eat you!
> Isabel, Isabel, didn't worry,
> Isabel didn't scream or scurry.
> She washed her hands and she straightened her hair up,
> Then Isabel quietly ate the bear up.
>
> (In *The Random House Book of Poetry*)

Gardner indeed has incongruities, like the phone-using cockatoo, but Nash, with the role reversal of bear and girl, seems farther into nonsense territory.

John Ciardi, whose collections of poetry have been popular with adults and school-age children, is another writer who runs the gamut of nonsense in his verse. He can create subtle nonsense, complete with a literary allusion, as in "Lobster Music" where "His traps were made of fiddle strings. / And every lobster that caught / Played him a tune" but in the boiling pot the only song they heard was "Bubble, Bubble, Toil and Trouble" (*The Man Who Sang the Sillies*, 35). He plays with the idea of mismating, so common in nonsense literature, as when, in "Sylvester," the hero's marriage proposal reaches a Lady Kangaroo by mistake. She accepts, much to his dismay, "—And how do you think it all turned out? / —I only wish I knew!" (21). Ciardi also has out and out nonsense animals. In his collection *The Reason for a Pelican* there is a Bugle-Billed Bazoo, a Saginsack, who "has Radio Horns / And Aerials for ears" (28), and a Brobinyak from the "Land of the Pshaw and the "Psham" (16). The last example also demonstrates Ciardi's love of wordplay, and the same collection includes a great deal of alliteration with names like Samuel Silvernose Slipperyside and Lucifer Leverett Lighteningbug.

In *The Man Who Sang the Sillies* he has fun with nonsense words as well as with nonsense animals. His "SHREEK is a shiverous beast" with a "boomerous laugh" ("Please, Johnny!" 57). And in "As I Was Picking a Bobble-Bud" he takes us to a "bangle-thicket" where a "Crow with a voice the color of mud" announces "The Needles are bringing prickle-cakes, / And all the Threads are fishing" (17), as delightful a pair of nonsense lines as can be found.

The poems of another famous poet for adults are beginning to make an appearance in books intended for children: E. E. Cummings. As can be seen in *Hist Whist and other Poems for Children*, he experimented with words in a way that appeals to the child. The collection contains twenty poems, sixteen of which, as George J. Firmage the editor says on the jacket flap, appeared earlier "in a privately printed edition . . . entitled *16 Poemes Enfantins* in January 1962." The often anthologized "in just- / spring" is included, as is "little tree," now also out singly in an illustrated edition. Many poems are about animals and nature, most with the peculiar syntax and divisions or combinations of words that Cummings is known for:

> if a cheerfulest Elephantangelchild should sit
> (holding a red candle over his head
> by a finger of trunk, and singing out of a red
> book) on a proud round cloud in a white high night
> (Poem 16, n.p.)

In "O the sun comes up-up-up in the opening" wordplay takes the form of inventive onomatopoeia with lines like "the grintgrunt wugglewiggle / champychumpchomps yes" (Poem 1). Poem 18 gives a good example of the way Cummings transcends word classes in his poetry:

> blossoming are people
>
> nimbler than Really
> go whirling into gaily
> . . . .
> when is now and which is Who
>
> and i am you are i am we

Many of the poems have the alliteration that children love—"maggie and milly and molly and may" (Poem 4). Cummings may well be this century's master of lyric nonsense, and while individual poems of his have found their way into children's books, collections devoted to those of Cummings's poems that are accessible to children are a welcome addition to the field. Another picture-poetry book, *in Just- / spring* was published in 1988.

Another book of verses that contains a variety of nonsensical fare is William Jay Smith's *Mr. Smith and Other Nonsense*. In one poem called "The Floor and the Ceiling," which is reminiscent of Lear's "The Table and the Chair," Smith pictures an impossible scene in which:

> The Floor bought the Ceiling an ostrich-plumed hat,
> And they dined upon drippings of bacon fat,
> Diced artichoke hearts and cottage cheese
> And hundreds of other such delicacies.
>
> (18)

Another similar poem by Smith, "The Antimacassar and the Ottoman," begins fancifully enough as the Antimacassar asks the Ottoman to fly away with him to Turkistan, but the last stanza brings both the objects and the reader out of the airy realm of nonsense and down to earth:

> But an Ottoman, it cannot fly,
> And an Antimacassar—who knows why?—
> Is pinned to permanence to a chair.
> So when morning came, they both were there.
>
> (21)

Also included in the collection are limericks and a section on nonsense birds, the "Pinhead Peacock," "Hoopskirted Heron," and "Wallflower Warbler" among them. The book concludes with Smith's parody of Edward Lear's "Self-Portrait of the Laureate of Nonsense":

> How rewarding to know Mr. Smith,
> Whose writings at random appear!
> Some think him a joy to be with,
> While others do not, it is clear.
>
> (60)

This tribute in the form of imitation is not surprising, considering how many echoes of Lear there are in Smith's verses. He is probably best appreciated by those children who are already familiar with Edward Lear's work.

A much-loved writer of humorous and nonsensical verse is Jack Prelutsky. One of his books, *The Queen of Eene*, contains fourteen ridiculous rhymes. In the title poem, "The Queen of Eene is such a goose / she brushed her teeth with onion juice" (8). "Pumberly Pott's Unpredictable Niece" eats her uncle's new car piece by piece—carburetor, muffler, the works (10–11). "Adelaide" has a different digestive quirk: "the more she ate, the less she weighed" (12). Prelutsky seems to be especially fond of unusual appetites. "Gretchen in the Kitchen" begins, "I start with quarts of curdled mud" (30), and her witchy recipe gets worse as the verse progresses:

> Then deep into my reeking vat
> I toss a tongue of pickled rat,
> some salted spiders (half a pound),
> two candied eyeballs, sweet and round.

> (30)

In "Four Foolish Ladies" the ladies are "chewing on basketballs, swallowing soap" (22), and in yet another gustatory poem "Uncle Bungle" ate yeast and "a large shoe-polish pie," died and "still shines and rises in the east" (32). Prelutsky's inventive nonsense food may have something to do with his popularity with children, for whom eating and refusing to eat are major activities.

In Prelutsky's *The Queen of Eene* there are also ridiculous situations galore, as in the case of "Mister Gaffe" whose "talking's all reversed, / he begins with what should finish. / and he ends with what comes first" (14). Other characters are incongruously odd. In "Poor Old Penelope" we read that "a pumpkin has started to grow from her nose" (16), and she has two pigeons on her earlobes. Her reaction to these odd appendages is even stranger than they are: "I'd hoped for a goose / and a dear little duck" (16). "Aunt Samantha" has a rhinoceros on her head, and "The Pancake Collector" has pancakes on the ceiling, in his pockets, mittens, and everywhere. All of these absurdities are accompanied by comical, wonderfully expressive black and white illustrations by Victoria Chess, which are perfectly suited to Prelutsky's wit.

Prelutsky also wrote *Zoo Doings: Animal Poems*, a compilation of his animal poems from three other collections: *A Gopher in the Garden*, *Toucans Two*, and *The Pack Rat's Day*. These poems are filled with zestful nonsense language. Children will be tickled by the alliteration, "The Giggling, Gaggling Gaggle of Geese" (36–37), the rhythm and repetition in "The Wallaby":

> The wallaby, the wallaby
> defies the laws of gravity
> and leaps as high as we can see;
> the willy wally wallaby."

(33)

Another example occurs in "Don't Ever Seize a Weasel By the Tail": "Yes
the weasel wheezes easily; / the weasel freezes easily" (26–27). Children
will also enjoy the made-up words in "The Yak":

> Sniggildy-snaggildy, sniggildy-snag,
> the yak is all covered with shiggildy-shag;
> he walks a ziggildy-zaggildy-zag,
> sniggildy-snaggildy, sniggildy-snag.

(22)

The book ends with a tongue-twister: "In the zoo do view the zebu" (78).

A large collection of Prelutsky poems, *The New Kid on the Block*,
comically illustrated by James Stevenson, contains more zany examples of
the range of his nonsense. He creates bizarre flavors like that in "Jellyfish
Stew": "You're soggy, you're smelly, / you taste like shampoo" (8) or
"Bleezer's Ice Cream" with flavors like "Cocoa Mocha Macaroni / Tapioca
Smoked Baloney / Checkerberry Cheddar Chew / Chicken Cherry Honey-
dew" (48). These have the sound of the silly product names that children
invent. Prelutsky includes more of his unusual characters such as "Eu-
phonica Jarre" with a "voice that's bizarre" (26) and the Bloders (who also
fit into the strange-eating-habits category): "You are bound to go to
pieces / when you dine on TNT" ("The Bloders Are Exploding," 37). He
continues to challenge the young reader with both sensible (though
uncommon) words like *declaim, quibble, cantankerous, banter, haggle* ("Never
Mince Words with a Shark," 89) and nonce words like those in "The
Mangle and the Munn" (88). The book is fine fare for children and adults
who like to laugh.

In a more recent collection, *Ride a Purple Pelican*, Prelutsky has taken
actual places, silly characters, and incongruous actions and objects and
blended them into alliterative nursery rhymes. A sampling of these yields
"Grandma Bear from Delaware / rocked in a rickety rocking chair" (36),
"Grandfather Gander flew over the land, / he flew to Rhode Island and
sat in the sand" (26), and "Timble Tamble Turkey / lived in Santa Fe" (48).
Other rhymes without placenames have plenty of nonsense in the sound
and situations:

> Jillicky Jollicky Jellicky Jee,
> three little cooks in a coconut tree.
>
> (38)

The heavy dactylic meter of "Jillicky" is repeated in several other verses ("Rumpitty Tumptitty" and "Hinnikin Minnikin"), but there are anapests and other meters as well to give variety to the rhymes. Garth Williams's bright expressive paintings add to the book's charm. Throughout Jack Prelutsky's many collections of verse there are spritely examples of nonsense. His popularity with his young audience is easy to understand.

Shel Silverstein is another children's poet with a large following, although he is not as solidly in the nonsense tradition as Prelutsky. Myra Cohn Livingston, who, as mentioned, defines nonsense more strictly than we do, says of Silverstein's *Where the Sidewalk Ends* that it is "hilariously funny and witty but more in the realm of wild imagination or illusion than nonsense" ("Nonsense Verse: The Complete Escape" 134). This is true of much of his verse, but a respectable portion of it, in both *Where the Sidewalk Ends* and *A Light in the Attic*, deals with the inversions and incongruities that we identify with nonsense. He has, for example, a number of nonsense creatures (see chap. 10). As with many nonsense author-illustrators, elements from Lear's work appear in both his verse and drawings. The poem "Upstairs" is a good example of this. The verse informs us that

> There's a family of wrens who live upstairs,
> Upstairs, upstairs, upstairs,
> Inside my hat, all cozy in
> My hair, my hair, my hair.
>
> (*Sidewalk*, 60)

The illustration for the poem shows a distressed, moustached man whose tall top hat has four wrens poking beak and head out of holes and the ripped top. This is similar in subject and tone to the limerick and accompanying illustration of Lear's head poem in his first collection *A Book of Nonsense* (1846):

> There was an Old Man with a beard,
> Who said, "It is just as I feared!—
> Two Owls and a Hen, four Larks and a Wren,
> Have all built their nests in my beard!"
>
> (*Complete Nonsense*, 3)

UPSTAIRS

There's a family of wrens who live upstairs,
Upstairs, upstairs, upstairs,
Inside my hat, all cozy in
My hair, my hair, my hair.
I've moved a dozen times and still
They're there, they're there, they're there.
I'd like to get away from them,
But where, but where, but where?
This hat just isn't big enough
To share, to share, to share.
But now I see you're bored and you
Don't care, don't care, don't care
'Bout the wrens who live inside
My hair, my hair, my hair.

Another of Silverstein's poems solidly in the nonsense tradition is "If the World Was Crazy." It is filled with the same type of reversals that Warren Wooden noted in John Taylor's early nonsense poem. The poem's narrator claims that "If the world was crazy," he would eat such things as "roasted ice cream or a bicycle pie," "a nice notebook salad," and "an omelet of hats"; he would wear "a tie of eclair, / Some marshmallow earmuffs, some licorice shoes"; he would do things like call boys "Suzy" and girls "Harry" or "walk on the ocean and swim in my shoe" (*Where the Sidewalk Ends*, 146). Siverstein's work also has more subtle examples of this type of nonsense whose absurdity consists in crossing categorical boundaries. In "Shadow Wash" a woman decides it is time to wash her shadow:

> And so today I peeled it off
> The wall where it was leaning
> And stuck it in the washtub
> With the clothes.

(113)

In "Poemsicle" he merges categories by questioning the power of the suffix "-sicle":

> If you add sicle to your pop,
> Would he become a Popsicle?
> Would a mop become a mopsicle?
> . . . .

(Above:) Illustration by Edward Lear from "There Was an Old Man with a Beard." *(Left:)* From *Where the Sidewalk Ends*, written and illustrated by Shel Silverstein.

> Heysicle, I can't stopsicle.
> Ohsicle mysicle willsicle Isicle
> Havesicle tosicle talksicle
> Likesicle thissicle foreversicle—?
>
> (*Light in the Attic*, 133)

Here he has invented an even sillier nonsense language than Pig Latin (if that is possible) and simultaneously provided a brief lesson in the ways syllables and words combine in English.

But Silverstein's poem that speaks to the absolute center of what nonsense finally means is the meditation in "Reflection," where a child, observing himself mirrored upside down in the water subdues his laughter:

> For maybe in another world
> Another time
> Another town,
> Maybe HE is right side up
> And I am upside down.
>
> (*Light in the Attic*, 29)

Reading through Shel Silverstein's verse provides a good survey of what is concrete humor, what is mere whimsy, and what is nonsense.

Silverstein seems to have a kindred soul in Dennis Lee, a Canadian author of nonsense verse, not yet well known in the United States. The title of one of his most popular books is, in itself, a contradiction in terms: *Garbage Delight*. His rhymes are full of alliteration: "Paddle addle through the puddle, / Pump the pedal till it's dark" (33) and letter reversals: "The Big Molice Pan and the Bertie Dumb" (54) or "Booing gubble chum." There are also tongue-twisters:

> Quintin's sittin' hittin' Griffin,
> Griffin's hittin' Quintin too.
> If Quintin's quittin' hittin' Griffin,
> What will Griffin sit 'n' do?
>
> (11)

There are intriguing titles for children, such as "Suzy Grew a Moustache," "Smelly Fred," "I Eat Kids Yum Yum!," "The Tiniest Man in the Washing Machine," and "Goofus." His "Bath Song" is sheer silliness:

> A biscuit, a basket, a bath in a hat,
> An elephant stuck in a tub,
> Seize her, and squeeze her, and see if she's fat,
> And give her a rub-a-dub-dub.
>
> (12)

Dennis Lee also wrote *Wiggle to the Laundromat*, an over-sized book with dramatic black and white illustrations by Charles Pachter for the fourteen poems. Again Lee includes a tongue-twister, this time with a name-place pun:

> Some day I'll go to Winnipeg
> To win a peg-leg pig.
> But will a peg-leg winner win
> The Piglet's ill-got wig?
>
> (n.p.)

Lee uses alliteration ("Willoughby Wallaby Woo") and Indian names that sound strange to English-speakers (Temagami, Temiskaming, Missinabi). He also echoes street rhymes in "Street Song": "Step on a crack / Or you can't come back" and in the title poem "Wiggle to the Laundromat": "Skip to Casa Loma / And you can't catch me." Dennis Lee's nonsense verse deserves more recognition in this country than it has yet received.

PROSE WRITERS TURNED VERSIFIERS

Other writers, more known for their prose than for nonsense verse, occasionally turn to this form. Ellen Raskin is one such writer. Well known for her children's stories, she is, nevertheless the author of *Twenty-two, Twenty-three*, a collection of crazy rhymes with illustrations of animals wearing outlandish clothing. These illustrations cleverly use color to set off the animals featured in a particular verse; the background characters are pictured in black and white. Typical of the verses are "'You are naked, madam,' said the ram in the tam" (11) or "owl in the cowl, / . . .yak in the sack" (12), or "asses in glasses" (18). Among the many lines are two well-known borrowed ones, "ape in a cape / the cat in the hat" (22). As the story progresses, the illustrations become more crowded and more bizarre. A capital letter *M*, sometimes upside down, is displayed with rope and streamers adding new letters to it, until at the end it spells out "Merry"; the animals spell out "New Year" with strange postures and clothes. "Happy Christmas from page Twenty-two" is also at the end.

The traditional positions of "Happy" and "Merry" have been transposed, a simple but convention-breaking device. Ellen Raskin's sojourn into the territory of children's nonsense verse produced some happy results.

The porter Gruffanuff from *The Rose and the Ring*, written and illustrated by W. M. Thackeray.

Roald Dahl is another writer more thought of in connection with prose than with verse, but he has a fine time with *Dirty Beasts*, a book of nine rhymes best read or given to older children since most of the beasts encountered make a meal of people. In one, the mispronunciation (according to the British Dahl) of "aunt" makes the poor woman prey to an anteater. Dahl is in a long tradition of British satirists who occasionally used nonsense sequences either for sheer fun or to make a point. Jonathan Swift is perhaps the most famous, but others, like William Makepeace Thackeray also dabbled in nonsense. For adults he wrote an absurd verse version of the story of Goethe's sentimental hero young Werther who kills himself for love:

> Charlotte, having seen his body
> Borne before her on a shutter,
> Like a well-conducted person,
> Went on cutting bread and butter.
>
> (In Wells, *Nonsense Anthology* 201)

And in his delightful fairy-tale parody *The Rose and the Ring*, the headings on facing pages create a rhyming and a sometimes ridiculous running commentary on the story: "Ah, I fear, King Valorosa, / That your conduct is but so-so!" (12–13).

Many other books and writers could be included in this section. Peter and Iona Opie, for instance, have written volumes on children's nursery rhymes, games and, language that lovers of nonsense should delve into. Ogden Nash added a number of books to the field for the enjoyment of adults and children alike. Spike Milligan, unfortunately found primarily in anthologies in the United States, is a nonsense writer worth pursuing. A favorite, "On the Ning Nang Nong," is well known. Milligan also wrote:

You must never bathe in an Irish Stew
It's a most illogical thing to do
But should you persist against my reasoning
Don't fail to add the appropriate seasoning.

X. J. Kennedy, the well-known poet and anthologist, has created an unusual assortment of children in *Brats*. There is

Stephanie, that little stinker,
Skinny-dipped in fabric shrinker.
We will find her yet, we hope,
Once we buy a microscope.

(7)

Most of Kennedy's rhymes are humorous without being nonsensical, although a number of them might be classed with those nonsense poems that parody moralistic and didactic verse for children.

A few more examples of nonsense versifiers will suffice. Carl Withers and Alta Jablow produced *Rainbow in the Morning*, a collection of counting rhymes, skipping rhymes, limericks, tongue-twisters, riddles, and just plain nonsense, as in

An owl and an eel and a frying pan
All went to call on a the soft soap man,
But the soft soap man, he wasn't in.
He'd gone for a ride on his rolling pin.

(n.p.)

They include the familiar classics "How many miles to Babylon," "How much wood would a woodchuck chuck," and "Fuzzy Wuzzy." A section of nonsense jingles has plenty of alliteration: "a flea and a fly in a flue" and "round and round the rugged rock / the ragged Rascal Ran." Children find the following hilarious:

A bullfrog sat on a downy nest,
And hatched out goslings three.
Two were turkeys with slenders legs,
And one was a bumble bee."

Wally the Wordworm by Clifton Fadiman, has a worm who introduces children to long and short words in an entertaining fashion: he eats the words. For example, midway through Wally's safari in the dictionary:

From *Wally the Wordworm* by Clifton Fadiman, illustrated by Lisa Atherton.

He decided he needed a little food to pick up his spirits. Quickly and deftly, he swallowd a very small word indeed, and also a small lizard [an eft]. A few pages later he came to ESCALATOR. The "up" and "down" of it sounded ticklish so he ate ESCALATOR, too, and the EFT got a free ride. (34)

Very funny watercolor sketches by Lisa Atherton illustrate what is happening.

Nonsense Alphabets: A Special Kind of Verse

It could be argued that alphabet books are the quintessential type of children's literature. From horn books to "Sesame Street" alphabets that use some gimmick to entice children into learning their letters have been produced in abundance, many of them in verse.

Among the classics are John Newbery's *Giles Gingerbread Boy*, with its game of forming the letter with gingerbread dough, and the anonymous *Peter Piper's Practical Principles of Plain and Perfect Pronunciation*, which, aside from the famous jingle for the letter P, contains such delightful rhymes as

> Oliver Oglethrope ogled an Owl and Oyster:
> Did Oliver Oglethrope ogle an Owl and Oyster?
> If Oliver Oglethrope ogled an Owl and Oyster,
> Where are the Owl and Oyster Oliver Oglethrope ogled?
>
> (in de Vries, *Flowers of Delight*, 83)

Lear contributed a number of nonsense alphabets, three in *Nonsense Songs, Stories, Botany and Alphabets* (1871), one in *More Nonsense, Pictures, Rhymes, Botany, Etc.* (1872), and one in *Laughable Lyrics* (1877). The verses in the first alphabet in *Nonsense Songs* are the least nonsensical, though with some internal contradictions in attitude, as in

F was a fish,   N was a net,
Who was caught in a net,   and   Which was thrown in the sea
But he got out again,   to Catch fish for dinner
And is quite alive yet.   for you and for me.
       f!   n!
Lively young Fish!   Nice little Net!
(*Complete Nonsense*, 132)   (134)

Note that Lear, like many abcedarians, cleverly works in both the upper and lower case letters. The second alphabet included in the 1871 *Nonsense Songs* is more characteristic of the playfulness that made Lear famous:

> f
> F was once a little fish
> Fishy
> Wishy
> Squishy
> Fishy
> In a dishy
> Little Fish!
>
> (*Complete Nonsense*, 139)

The third example from 1871 returns, however, to the "nice little" formula. The 1872 alphabet is by far the silliest. Here for F we get

The Fizziggious Fish
who always walked about upon stilts
because he had no legs.

(Complete Nonsense, 139)

By 1877, Lear has returned to an edible fish:

F was a little Fish.
  Cook in the river took it,
Papa said, 'Cook! Cook! bring a dish!
And Cook! be quick and cook it!

(Complete Nonsense, 264)

Since Lear's time, literally thousands of alphabet books have been published. Gillian Avery has done extensive research on both earlier and later alphabets, and recently Patricia L. Roberts has published an annotated bibliography, *Alphabet Books as a Key to Language Patterns*, that is an excellent resource for books in this genre that are currently available. In

The Fizziggious Fish from
"Twenty-Six Nonsense Rhymes
and Pictures," written and
illustrated by Edward Lear.

her introduction, Roberts maintains that alphabet books, with their patterns of sound and letter shapes are valuable to children in many ways: these "Patterns provide a foundation for oral responses . . . provide relationships in language learning . . . provide a foundation for reading . . . help begin the process of reading . . . [and] provide a foundation for writing" (2–4). Some fifty of the examples Roberts includes are in the nonsense tradition, and these are included in our general bibliography of primary sources. Among them are books by many of the authors and illustrators we mention in conjunction with other types of nonsense: Mitsumasa Anno and Theodor Geisel, who has produced alphabets under his famous pseudonym, Dr. Seuss, and his less well-known one, Theo Le Seig (with a tall-tale language ABC). Joseph Low, X. J. Kennedy, Steven Kellogg, Peggy Parish, and John Ciardi have animal alphabets. Anita Lobel creates human figures out of products in *On Market Street*, Jeffrey Moss gives us *Oscar the Grouch's Alphabet of Trash*, and Hilaire Belloc's contribution is *A Moral Alphabet in Words of from One to Seven Syllables*. In Crockett Johnson's *Harold's ABC*, the familiar purple crayon transfoms letters into means of transportation. Famous examples like Walter Crane's *An Absurd ABC*, Maurice Sendak's *Alligators All Around*, *Hilary Knight's ABC*, Fritz Eichenberg's *Ape in a Cape*, and, of course, *Peter Piper* are also listed and described in Roberts's book. Less well-known books worth noting are numerous. Among them is Beau Gardner's *Have You Ever Seen?*, which features such incongruous combinations as "an inchworm on iceskates" (Roberts, 50). Every imaginable type of nonsense seems to have found its way into some alphabet book or other. Lilian Obligado gives us *Faint Frogs Feeling Feverish and Other Terrifyingly Tantalizing Tongue Twisters*. In Dennis Nolan's *Alphabrutes* green monsters make noises like "Aargh," "Blurp," and "Cackle" in alphabetical order. Ann Bishop produced *A Riddle-iculous Rid-alphabet Book*. In Maureen McGinn's *I Used to Be an Artichoke*, an artichoke metamorphizes from A to Z. Peggy Kahn gives us neologisms such as "snuzzle," "a hug given by a Wuzzle" (Roberts, 196) in *The Wuzzles' Alphabet Book*, and Scott Corbett wrote *The Mysterious Zetabet*, a backwards alphabet set in Zyxland.

Two rather eminent examples that Roberts does not include in her bibliography demonstrate the dark side of some comtemporary nonsense humor. These are Chris Van Allsburg's *Z Was Zapped*, in which objects disintegrate or fall apart in various surprising fashions, and Edward Gorey's *The Gashlycrumb Tinies*. This gruesome account, in alphabetically ordered couplets, of the unhappy end of twenty-six ill-fated children is a favorite with many young people, who are not deterred by such lines as

> E is for ERNEST who choked on a peach
> F is for FANNY sucked dry by a leech
>
> (*Amphigorey*, n.p.)

The examples given are convincing proof that, whether the humor is dark or light, alphabet books are a major source of nonsense.

Returning to nonsense verse in general, one final book worth mentioning is Joseph Low's *There Was a Wise Crow*. In this book (as in Chris Van Allsburg's *The Z Was Zapped*) the child must turn the page to complete the rhyme and find out what the action is. For example, one rhyming triplet reads "There was a small man / Who sat in a pan / [Turn the page.] And waved a fine fan" (n.p.) Children's anticipation is heightened by this format, and their imaginative thinking encouraged as they try to envision what silliness might come next.

Other famous creators of nonsense verse, for example, Dr. Seuss and Maurice Sendak, known for their illustrations as well as their writing, are discussed in other chapters of this book. Unfortunately, there is not possibly space enough in a one-volume study to give more than a sampling of the vast number of nonsense collections that are available. Our bibliography mentions many more, although it too must be selective.

Rebecca Lukens points out in her *Critical Handbook* that "children thrive on nonsense. They make up and invent words, or make illogical comparisons. . . . They repeat nonsense words in series, just for the pleasure of tasting and hearing their sounds. . . . Like nursery rhymes, nonsense leads to poetry" (182). And, according to Joyce Thomas, like other forms of nonsense, "nonsense verse is necessarily confined by the sensible restraints of language" ("'There Was an Old Man . . .': The Sense of Nonsense Verse," 119). She continues, "even where the words are unknown, nonsense entities, they exist beside known, sense words . . . [for] nonsense is play—but it is playing with our known world and known language, language we use to define, frame and control that world" (120–21). As such, sense and nonsense are inextricably intertwined, all to the benefit of children. Nonsense verse permits them to delight in their language and its infinite possibilities, encouraging them to explore both poetry and language further, enticing them with its rhythms and sounds to seek out new experiences. Such favorable reactions to a genre are reason enough to expand its use with children and to elevate it as a subject worthy of study and approbation.

Note: Alphabet books by the authors mentioned in this chapter are marked (ABC) after the entry.

Anno, Mitsumasa. *Anno's Alphabet: An Adventure in Imagination.* New York: Crowell, 1975. (ABC)
——— and Masaichiro Anno. *Anno's Magical ABC: An Anamorphic Alphabet.* New York: Philomel/Putnam, 1981. (ABC)
Belloc, Hilaire. *A Moral Alphabet: In Words of from One to Seven Syllables.* Illus. Basil T. Blackwood. London: E. Arnold, 1899. London: Duckworth, 1973. Chelmsford, England: Tindal Press, 1974. (ABC)
Bishop, Ann. *A Riddle-iculous Rid-alphabet Book.* Illus. Jerry Warshaw. Chicago: Whitmore, 1979. (ABC)
Bodeker, N. M. *It's Raining Said John Twaining: Danish Nursery Rhymes* New York: Atheneum, 1973.
———. *Let's Marry Said the Cherry and Other Nonsense Poems.* New York: Atheneum, 1974.

Brotman, Jordan. "A Late Wanderer in Oz." In *Only Connect: Readings on Children's Literature*. Eds. Sheila Egoff et al. New York: Oxford UP, 1969, 1980. 156–69.

Chukovsky, Kornei. *From Two to Five*. Trans. Miriam Morton. Berkeley and Los Angeles: U of California P, 1963.

Ciardi, John. *The Man Who Sang the Sillies*. Illus. Edward Gorey. Philadelphia and New York: Lippincott, 1961.

———. *The Reason for the Pelican*. Illus. Madeleine Gekiere. Philadelphia and New York: Lippincott, 1959.

———. *You Read to Me, I'll Read to You*. Illus. Edward Gorey. Philadelphia and New York: Lippincott, 1962.

Corbett, Scott. *The Mysterious Zetabet*. Illus. Jon McIntosh. Boston: Atlantic/Little, 1979. (ABC)

Crane, Walter, auth. and illus. *An Alphabet of Old Friends and the Absurd ABC*. New York: Metropolitan Museum of Art, 1981. (ABC)

Cummings, E. E. *Hist Whist and Other Poems for Children*. Ed. George J. Firmage. Illus. David Calsada. New York: Liveright, 1983.

———. *Little Tree*. New York: Crown, 1987.

———. *in Just- spring*. Illus. Heidi Goennel. Boston: Little, 1988.

Dahl, Roald. *Dirty Beasts*. Illus. Rosemary Fawcett. New York: Farrar, 1983.

De Vries, Leonard, ed. *Flowers of Delight: An Agreeable Garland of Prose and Poetry: 1765–1830*. New York: Pantheon, 1965.

Dr. Seuss. *Dr. Seuss's ABC*. New York: Beginner/Random, 1960. (ABC)

Eichinberg, Fritz, auth. and illus. *Ape in a Cape: An Alphabet of Odd Animals*. New York: Harcourt, 1952. (ABC)

Fadiman, Clifton. *Wally the Wordworm*. Illus. Lisa Atherton. Owings Mills, MD: Stemmer House, 1983; 1st edition, 1964.

Gardner, Beau, auth. and illus. *Have You Ever Seen. . . ? An ABC Book*. New York: Dodd, 1986. (ABC)

Gardner, John. *A Child's Bestiary*. With Lucy Gardner and Eugene Rudzewicz. Illus. Lucy, Joel, Joan, and John Gardner. New York: Knopf, 1977.

Geller, Linda Gibson. *Wordplay and Language Learning for Children*. Urbana, IL: NCTE, 1985.

Gorey, Edward. *The Gashlycrumb Tinies*. In *The Vinegar Works*. New York: Simon, 1963. In *Amphigorey: Fifteen Books by Edward Gorey*. New York: Perigee/Putnam, 1981. (ABC)

Johnson, Crockett. *Harold's ABC*. New York: Harper, 1963. (ABC)

Kahn, Peggy. *The Wuzzle's Alphabet Book*. Illus. Bobbi Barto. New York: Random, 1986. (ABC)

Kellogg, Steven. *Aster Aardvark's Alphabet Adventures*. New York: Morrow, 1987. (ABC)

Kennedy, X. J. *Brats*. Illus. James Watts. New York: Atheneum, 1986.

———. *Did Adam Name the Vinegaroon?* Boston: Godine, 1982. (ABC)

Knight, Hilary. *Hilary Knight's ABC*. Illus. New York: Golden Press, 1961. (ABC)

Le Seig, Theo [pseudonym for Dr. Seuss]. *Hooper Humperdink . . . Not Him!* Illus. Charles E. Martin. New York: Random, 1976. (ABC)

Lee, Dennis. *Alligator Pie*. Illus. Frank Newfield. Toronto: Macmillan of Canada, 1974.

———. *Garbage Delight*. Illus. Frank Newfield. Boston: Houghton, 1987.

————. *Wiggle to the Laundromat.* Illus. Charles Pachter. Toronto-Chicago: New Press, 1970. Rpt. 1975.

Livingston, Myra Cohn. "Nonsense Verse: The Complete Escape." *Celebrating Children's Books.* Eds. Betsy Hearne and Marilyn Kaye. New York: Lothrop, 1981. 122–39.

Lobel, Arnold, auth. and illus. *On Market Street.* Illus. Anita Lobel. New York: Greenwillow, 1981; Scholastic, 1985. (ABC)

Low, Joseph, ed. and illus. *Adam's Book of Odd Creatures.* New York: Atheneum, 1962. (ABC)

————. *There Was a Wise Crow.* Chicago: Follett, 1969.

Lukens, Rebecca. *A Critical Handbook of Children's Literature.* Glenview, IL: Scott, Foresman, 1976; 2nd edition 1982.

McGinn, Maureen. *I Used to Be an Artichoke.* Illus. Anita Norman. St. Louis: Concordia, 1973. (ABC)

Nash Ogden. "The Adventures of Isabel." *The Random House Book of Poetry.* Comp. Jack Prelutsky. Illus. Arnold Lobel. New York: Random, 1983.

Moss, Jeffrey. *Oscar-the-Grouch's Alphabet of Trash.* Illus Sal Murdocca. Racine, WI: Western, 1977. (ABC)

Newbery, John. *The Renowned History of Giles Gingerbread Boy: A Little Boy Who Lived upon Learning.* London: Newbery, c. 1765. (ABC)

Nolan, Dennis, auth. and illus. *Alphabrutes.* Englewood Cliffs, NJ: Prentice, 1977. (ABC)

Obligado, Lilian, auth. and illus. *Faint Frogs Feeling Feverish and Other Terrifyingly Tantalizing Tongue Twisters.* New York: Viking, 1983. (ABC)

Parish, Peggy. *A Beastly Circus.* Illus. Peter Parnall. New York: Simon, 1969. (ABC)

Peter Piper's Practical Principles of Plain and Perfect Pronunciation. London: J. Harris, 1813, 1820, rpt. in De Vries. (ABC)

Prelutsky, Jack. *A Gopher in the Garden.* Illus. Robert Leydenfrost. New York: Macmillan, 1967.

————. *The New Kid on the Block.* Illus. James Stevenson. New York: Greenwillow, 1984.

————. *The Pack Rat's Day.* Illus. Margaret Bly Graham. New York: Macmillan, 1974.

————. *The Queen of Eene.* Illus. Victoria Chess. New York: Greenwillow, 1978.

————. *Ride a Purple Pelican.* Illus. Garth Williams. New York: Greenwillow, 1986.

————. *Toucans Two.* Illus. Jose Aruego. New York: Macmillan, 1970. Printed in England as *Zoo Doings and Other Poems.* London: Hamilton, 1971.

————. *Zoo Doings: Animal Poems.* Illus. Paul O. Zelinsky. New York: Greenwillow, 1973.

Raskin, Ellen. *Twenty-two, Twenty-three.* New York: Macmillan, 1976.

Roberts, Patricia L. *Alphabet Books as as a Key to Language Patterns: An Annotated Action Bibliography.* Hamden, CT: Library Professional Publications, 1987.

Silverstein, Shel, author-illus. *A Light in the Attic.* New York: Harper, 1981.

————. *Where the Sidewalk Ends.* New York: Harper, 1974.

Smith, William Jay. *Mr. Smith and Other Nonsense.* Illus. Don Bolognese. New York: Delacorte, 1968.

Thackeray, W. M. *The Rose and the Ring, or, The History of Prince Giglio and Prince*

Bulbo: A Fireside Pantomime for Great and Small Children. Baltimore: Penguin, 1972; 1st edition 1855.

Thomas, Joyce. "'There Was an Old Man . . .': The Sense of Nonsense Verse." *ChLAQ* 10: 3 (Fall 1985): 119–22.

Van Allsburg, Chris. *The Z Was Zapped*. Boston: Houghton, 1987. (ABC)

Wells, Carolyn, comp. *A Nonsense Anthology*. 1902. Garden City, NY: Doubleday, n.d.

Withers, Carl and Alta Jablow. *Rainbow in the Morning*. Illus. Abner Graboff. New York: Abelard, 1955. Eau Claire, WI: Hale, 1961.

In the course of his word hunt Wally met a number of imaginary creatures.
CENTAUR (which is only half an animal) and CHIMERA (which is really three animals).
Also the ROC, the UNICORN, the PHOENIX, and the CHESHIRE CAT.
"It's a funny thing," thought Wally, "these animals aren't alive. They live only in the Dictionary and the imagination. Yet they'll still be alive in those two places thousands of years from now, when lots of real animals may have died out entirely. . . ."

Clifton Fadiman, Wally the Wordworm, *31*

Nonsense Creatures

Types of Nonsense Creatures

How do you know a nonsense creature when you meet one? This genus nonsensicus has the largest, most wildly diverse number of species on earth. Therefore, identifying and then classifying a nonsense creature is difficult. Among the problems is that some kinds exist in large numbers (Itch-a-pods, griffins, and Mewlips) while other kinds have only one known member of the class (the Cheshire Cat, the Dong with a Luminous Nose, and the Minotaur).

There are, however, some clues. If you find a creature that

> is part human and part animal
> or part animal and part inanimate object
> or part all three
> or talks and/or wears clothes though not human
> or exists in an absurdly inappropriate environment
> or acts in an impossible manner
> (and has a name that makes you laugh)

then you have probably found a *creatus nonsensicus*. Depending on the definition used, nonsense creatures may include everything from the talking animals of fable, through the beasts (early and late) of each age's myth, to toy animals and androids.

There are levels of nonsense creatures. Margaret Blount, in her book *Animal Land*, laments that it is "extremely difficult to make up a convincing new animal. The best most science-fiction writers and others do is to add up pieces of old ones, as in the game of head, body and legs" (289n). The best specimens, however, are conglomerates with memorable names who exist out of proper place and speak or act in a ridiculous manner (the Quangle Wangle, the Collapsible Frink, the Woggle-Bug). The second level have venerable histories or ancestries (the dragon, the Chimaera, the Cockatrix, the fox of fable and Reynard cycle), and the third and fourth levels include, respectively, talking, clothed animals, and toys. And then there are unique creatures who, like the Cheshire Cat, make the list by the grin of their teeth.

In his book *Poetry of Nonsense*, Emile Cammaerts sums up the historical connection between nonsense in general and nonsense creatures: "Nonsense steps in gradually, first through the animal story, then through the confusions of all classes and values, finally through the creation of such wild images that they defy classification" (25–26; qtd. in Stewart, 67). The history of the nonsense tradition confirms this. In ancient times both myths and fables combined characteristics from different species. The mythical creatures increased in number and in bizarre traits in the medieval bestiaries. Similarly, the ancient fables, with their anthropomorphic animals acting the roles of trickster and fool, evolved into the beast epic, as for example, in the stories of Reynard the fox or Anansi the spider.

In other words, the ability to imagine species that do not exist is apparently as old as our race. Such amalgamated creatures as the Sphinx (with human head and lion body) or mermen and mermaids (half human, half fish) can be traced in folktales and art as far back as we have records. Surviving folkart and legend like those of the Eskimos continue to blend the human form with seals or bears or birds. Of course these strange invented beasts serve purposes other than humor. Springing from ancient totemic rituals, as symbols they can still speak to us powerfully of our connection with the forces of nature and the forces of our own emotions. But even so, the unicorn, the gryphon (or griffin), the phoenix, the dragon, and other fabulous beasts have been co-opted by the nursery and exist in a somewhat tamed form in many books for children, and they are the first type of nonsense creature to consider.

Mythical Beasts in the Nursery

The initially threatening or frightening appearance of such creatures is usually shown up as a facade. For instance, when the Queen of Hearts leaves Alice alone with the Gryphon, the child observes its eagle's beak and claws, its lion's body and does "not quite like the look of the creature" (*Wonderland*, chap. 9). But the Gryphon and his friend the Mock Turtle (which, as John Tenniel depicts it with a cow's head, tail, and hind hooves protruding from a tortoise body, is a marvelous parody of a mythical beast) prove among the most sympathetic of the characters Alice meets. Another example, the Phoenix in E. Nesbit's *The Phoenix and the Carpet* is more like a cantankerous fairy godfather than a venerable emblem. Dennis Lee reduces Bigfoot to a nursery denizen who protects the child narrator (*Garbage Delight*). And although the dragons of J. R. R. Tolkien and Ursula LeGuin retain their fire, the dragon enters the pages of children's literature at the peril of becoming either ridiculous, like Shel Silverstein's Dragon of Grindly Grun who weeps because his over-hot breath overcooks the damsels that he prefers medium rare (*A Light in the Attic*, 33),or of becoming a meek, unwilling aggressor like the worm in Kenneth Grahame's *The Reluctant Dragon*, or susceptible to laughter, like the one in John Gardner's story "Dragon, Dragon." In the popular song by Peter, Paul, and Mary, this once fire-breathing terror is reduced to a child-loving playmate and dubbed "Puff." Like the magic foxes, deer, and bears who help fairy-tale characters, the monsters of classical myth, when they appear in storybooks, usually aid rather than threaten the child characters, are often given humorous characteristics, and may exist side by side with more recently invented creatures intended as nonsensical from their inception.

There is yet another reason for considering such awesome beings as centaurs and the sphinx as nonsense creatures. They share with nonsense constructs the ability to cross the boundaries that order information (in their case species boundaries) and thereby call into question the whole classification system of human knowledge. Susan Stewart has astutely analyzed this aspect of nonsense: "Nonsense bares the ideological nature of common sense, showing common sense's precarious situation—rooted in culture and not in nature" (49). She notes that "Any system of classification comes built with leaks and anomalies" (60) and that nonsense and irony allow us to escape through these gaps, to move from one class or category to another, and, as in the case of many nonsense creatures, combine cateories (several species mixed in one animal) or invert them (animal to human, human to animal). She finds that this "method of making nonsense, the inversion of animal and human categories, is perhaps the most prevalent of all proper not [is-is not] inversions" (66).

ANIMALS ALL MIXED UP

Nonsense literature relies heavily on these mixed areas of reality. In one of her poems, Nancy Willard brings much of what we are discussing here succinctly and symbollically together. In "The Wise Cow Makes *Way*, *Room*, and *Believe*," her very title, by taking the three idiomatic phrases ("make way," "make room," and "make believe") and compressing the three nouns into the compound object of the one verb "makes," creates such semantic tension that the various meanings of the words burst this confinement. How many possible definitions are there of "to make"? Is "making room" anything like "making cake"? Willard has used a typical ploy of nonsense writing and crossed grammatical boundaries. And the title serves as a warning of what is to come. For example, in two lines in the poem, "*Believe* shall be a boat / having both feet and fins" (*William Blake's Inn*, 30), Willard merges the classes of animal, fish, object, and abstract thought.

Such crossovers can happen, of course, among many cateteries. In stories, inanimate objects may be endowed with feelings or the ability to move. Examples of this occur in Aesop's tale of the brass and china jars who were respectively vain and modest and in many of Hans Christian Andersen's stories, where scissors, darning needles, street lamps, and Christmas trees are given human emotions and histories. The extreme form of reacting, self-propelling normally immobile objects can be found in this century's animated cartoons. Such a totally animate universe, though dismissed or understood as metaphorical in adult thought, has enormous appeal for the child, and explains the enduring popularity of works like Margaret Wise Brown's *Goodnight Moon* in which the child finds it quite proper to speak to objects, although such behavior draws smiles from adults.

From *Franklin Stein*,
written and illustrat-
ed by Ellen Raskin.

INDUSTRIAL ANIMALS

A new dimension, a new set of possible confusions and combinations, was added by the scientific and industrial revolutions. The scientific revolution of the sixteenth and seventeenth centuries called into question the validity of much traditional knowledge and of the testimony of our senses—how and what we know. The weirder inhabitants of the medieval bestiaries were dismissed both scientifically and symbolically. An educated person was less likely to fear the glance of the basilisk or to believe seriously that bear cubs were born shapeless and had to be licked into form. (See Beryl Rowland's *Animals with Human Faces* and *Birds with Human Souls* for a scholarly and lively account of the beliefs recorded in medieval bestiaries.) Depending on perspective, either the new theories or the old explanations of the nature of the physical world seemed to be nonsense.

The industrial revolution added another possible component to nonsense creatures—mechanical animation. Equipment had previously relied on a seen force (hand or water or work animal) to move it. Now engines whose workings might be hidden from the eye supplied the force. This blurred the line between the functions and capabilities of machines and of people and created the possibility of hybrids that straddled that line. A major new mythical beast joined the list when Mary Shelley's fictional scientist Frankenstein sewed together his monster. Though he was never granted a mate, Frankenstein's monster has numerous progeny, like L. Frank Baum's Tin Man, *Star Wars'* R–2–D–2, or the countless robots and androids that inhabit the world of children's television. By the time authors were deliberately creating nonsense verse and fiction for children, they had a diverse cast of improbable mongrels for characters. And, because those who write nonsense, will, by the very nature of their work, seek new ways to mix and match the parts of the universe, these authors created many more ridiculous and impossible creatures.

NONSENSE CREATURES PROPER

The proliferation of nonsense creatures coincides with the growth of children's literature. The beasts of fables, mythical animals, and talking toys do indeed have niches in this pantheon of nonsense, but nonsense creatures proper consist of that strange medley of hybrid beasts created over the last century or so, and members of this group have many traits in common: a silly origin or ridiculous name, outlandish appearance, and foolish behavior. They turn up where you would least expect them and are either acted upon outrageously or perform actions that would be futile in the everyday world. Their physical characteristics, although not neatly divided into halves or thirds, like those of the beasts of classical mythology, are drawn from any number of people, animals, or things.

Examples of silly origins are the Mock Turtle ("the thing Mock Turtle soup is made from," *Wonderland*, chap. 9), Kipling's "Stickly-Prickly Hedgehog" and "Slow-Solid Tortoise" who melded into an Armadillo (*Just So Stories*, 53), the "Hoop-Soup-Snoop-Group," so named because, while engaging in collective sleepwalking "a-la-hoop," the group gets hungry and "Stops hooping and does some quick snooping for soup" (*Dr. Seuss's Sleep Book*, n.p.).

This last, the Hoop-Soup-Snoop-Group, also meets another criterion for nonsense creatures—a silly name. Although Walter Nash argues that there is no such thing as a humorous sound simply as sound, he concedes that meaning and context can together produce a humorous effect. Nonsense names need to be peculiar enough to provoke laughter. Take, for example (to pull a name out of a hat, so to speak), Lear's Quangle-Wangle. The names achieve their humor also by incongruous combinations (Lear's Dong with the luminous nose), overuse of alliteration (Seuss's Biffer Baum Birds, *Sleep Book*), or by being a mere part of a standard English word (Seuss's Ish, *One fish, two fish*, or his Offt who sleep aloft, *Sleep Book*).

Nonsense creatures live in very strange settings or else they turn up somewhere completely inappropriate (and by doing so make ordinary places strange). They live in nowhere worlds like Carroll's Wonderland or Looking-Glass Land, Baum's Oz, Willard's Cythera, Dahl's giant peach turned planet, Sendak's outside over there, or Juster's Dictionopolis. Shel Silverstein gives numerous examples of incongruous combinations of

The Centerpede from *How Beastly!* by Jane Yolen, illustrated by James Marshall.

creature and place: in *Where the Sidewalk Ends*, a crocodile sits in a dentist's chair, the dentist crouching on its lower jaw while working (66–67). In *A Light in the Attic* a boy uses a rhinoceros horn (with the rhinoceros attached) to write his theme (156). Jack Prelutsky places a "middle-sized rhinoceros" squarely on the head of a Aunt Samantha (*The Queen of Eene*, 24). One nonsense menagerie was permanently removed from any environment when they did not make it into Noah's ark. Or so Countee Cullen's "co-author" Christopher Cat claims in the book *The Lost Zoo*.

And in their various peculiar settings, nonsense creatures wear and eat and do the most preposterous things. Silverstein pictures a hippo with slatted wings strapped to it (*Light*, 88–89), a walrus with braces on its tusks (*Light*, 103), and a camel with a brassiere on its humps (*Light*, 166–670). Jenny, the sealyham terrier in Sendak's *Higgledy-Piggledy Pop* acts out the rhyme literally and swallows a mop (fortunately made of salami), the Mad Hatter bites a piece out of his teacup (*Wonderland*, chap. 11), and similarly, Edward Gorey's Doubtful Guest eats part of his plate (*Amphigorey*, n.p.). But Spike Milligan's Gofongo has the most outlandish eating habits of all:

> The Gofongo, when he likes,
> Swallows jam and rusty bikes,
> Orange pips and treacle
> Pudding boiled in glue.
>
> He loves chips with rusty nails
> And can swallow *iron rails*.
> That is why they cannot
> Keep one in a zoo.
>
> <div align="right">(in Fisher <i>Amazing Monsters</i>, 55)</div>

The nongustatory antics of nonsense creatures are also unusual. Lear's "Fizzgiggious Fish / . . .always walked upon stilts" (*Complete Nonsense*, 111), Carroll's obliging flamingos serve as live mallets for the Queen of Hearts' croquet game (*Wonderland*, chap. 8). But the top contenders for silly behavior are Dr. Seuss's creatures. They do such nonsensical things as read with their eyes shut, think up Glunks, play Ring the Gack, and oil orange owls.

The physical and personality traits of nonsense creatures are diverse and therefore difficult to categorize. However, a few common types can be noted. There is the gentle type, sometimes furry or hairy, and with either a worried expression or a perpetual silly grin that proclaims harm to no one but possibly itself. "The Dong with the Luminous Nose" and the "Pobble Who Had No Toes" fit this category, as do many of Dr. Seuss's creations. Shel Silverstein's "Flying Festoon" who "will fly to the outmost tip of the moon. . . . / Just as soon as he learns how to fly" (*Where the Sidewalk Ends*, 80) is a good example. Harmless and ineffectual, either acted upon or performing actions that would be futile in the real world, these nonsense creatures descend from the fools of fable and folklore. The other common type of nonsense creature, descended from mythical beasts, is superficially threatening, but its fierceness is undercut by the hyperbole of its appearance or actions; it is a parody of a monster.

Maurice Sendak's Wild Things come immediately to mind, as do Carroll's Bandersnatch, James Whitcomb Riley's "lugubrious Whing-Whang," James Reeves's Snitterjipe and Bogus-Boo, Spike Milligan's Bongaloo, and Edward Gorey's Wuggly Ump.

This latter class of nonsense creatures brings us round full circle to the ancient origins of imaginary beasts. Just as centaurs and harpies or the Minotaur and the Sphinx give us ways of dealing metaphorically with inexplicable forces, so also do their zany descendents. They take the child into a fanciful universe where failure and danger can be faced with humor. They are patchwork beings whose very grotesqueness serves to remind us that "there are more things in heaven and earth than are dreamt of in our philosophy." The humorous diversity of nonsense creatures can best speak for itself in the glossary with which we end this chapter.

An Incomplete Glossary of Nonsense Beasticles and Birdles
(Which readers are instructed to finish for themselves)

(A brief description and author or historical source are given.)

Aardwort	J. Yolen. Four-legged fungus.
Amphisbaena	Ancient Myth. A two-headed lizard. (Rowland)
Attery Squash	Lear. Lived in the Quangle Wangle's hat.
Auitzotl	New World Myth. Black, lizard-like with a hand at the end of its tail.
Baboopine	T. Hood. Prey of the Chinchayak.
Bandersnatch	Carroll. A frumious beast.
Barbazzoop (Wild)	S. Silverstein. Not described, but kidnaps children and sells them to Ragged Hats.
Basilisk	Ancient Myth. A lizard with a deadly glance and fiery breath.
Biffer-Baum Birds	Dr. Seuss. Round-bodied, prehensile digits on both feet and wings, build nightly nest of sticks and bricks.
Big Bird	J. Henson. Friendly, yellow, stork-like dodo who lives on Sesame Street and frequents parades.
Bigfoot	New World Myth. Large creature, somewhere between a bear and an ape.
Biscuit Buffalo	Lear. Not described.
Bisky Bat	Lear. Lived in the Quangle Wangle's hat.
Bogus-Boo	J. Reeves. Your nightmare creature and mine.
Bongaloo	S. Milligan. Seen only on a "dark sunny night."
Booba	S. Corbet. A scaled, round creature with vestigial arms, runs upright and is silent.

Borogove

Carroll. A Jabberwocky animal, "a thin shabby- looking bird with its feathers sticking out all around—something like a live mop."

Boss-Woss

Lear. A bright blue crustacean who lures young fish to muddy death.

Buffalant

T. Hood. Not described

Bunyip

Australian myth. A water monster.

Bustard

Dr. Seuss. A Fluffy bird "who only eats custard with sauce made of mustard."

Camelotamus

T. Hood. "Lean and Gaunt."

Centaur

Ancient Myth. A hunter, half-horse, half-man.

Centerpede

J. Yolen. A single-footed, many-pawed creature that stands on the dinner table and eats after everyone leaves.

Chat-Huant

New World Myth. Half cat, half owl.

Cheshire Cat

Carroll. A self-admitted mad animal with the ability to appear and disappear either all at once or bit by bit.

Chimaera

Ancient Myth. A triple combination of lion's head, goat's body, and serpent's tail. (Homer)

Chugg

Dr. Seuss. Bean-shooting bug.

Chippendale Mupp

Dr. Seuss. A fang-toothed fuzzy with tail so long a bite at night wakes it in 8 hours.

Cockatrix

Medieval Bestiary. Serpent with deadly glance, hatched from a cock's egg.

Collapsible Frink

Dr. Seuss. Creature with very long rope-like neck, arms, and legs that go limp and collapse when it rests.

Crocoghau

T. Hood. Lives in the Stagnolent Lake.

Dinkey-Bird

E. Field. Sits in an amfalula tree and sings false promises to the young.

Dong with a Luminous Nose

Lear. A love-lorn musician, encased in tin with tin lantern shaped like a warming pan tied to his nose.

Double-Tail Dog

S. Silverstein. A tail at each end, costs nothing to feed, "very, very good at sitting down," but must be walked often.

Double-Headed Hoodwinkus

C. Cullen. A creature too mixed up to enter Noah's ark.

Doubtful Guest

E. Gorey. Cross between a crow, a seal, and Woody Allen, wears sneakers and scarf.

Doze

J. Reeves. A small cousin of the Abominable Snowman, "damp, despised, and aimless."

Dragon of Grindly Grun	S. Silverstein. Firebreath too hot and overcooks damsels.
Dragon	Ancient Myth. A winged, fire-breathing, serpent, representing evil or protecting power depending on the culture. (Rowland)
Dromedaraffe	T. Hood. "Spottified."
Elephant-Cat	Dr. Seuss. An Elephant-Cat
Exactly-Watt	S. Silverstein. Large, soft, egg-shaped creature, no arms, sad eyes and derby hat, pulled on a chain by a Meehoo (which see).
Fiffer-feffer-feff	Dr. Seuss. Four-tufted fuzzy.
Fimble Fowl	Lear. Has a corkscrew leg and came to the Crumpetty Tree of the Quangle Wangle.
Fizzgiggious Fish	Lear. Stilt-walking fish.
Fizza-ma-Wizza-ma-dill	Dr. Seuss. World's biggest bird, has animal head, soft feet, eats pine trees.
Flustard	Dr. Seuss. Beast "who eats only mustard with sauce made of custard."
Frankenstein's Monster	M. Shelley. Sewed together from various parts, given to philosophizing and strangling.
Franklin Stein's Monster	E. Raskin. Modern child-built monster with mop and coffee pot for head, Venitian blinds for wing-arms, potato masher for right hand and garden rasp for right hand.
Foona-Lagoona-Baboona	Dr. Seuss. Yellow, pink, and white blissful-looking primates.
Gink	S. Silverstein. Long, big-toothed lizard, so quick-digesting that swallowed children come out the other end intact.
Glotz	Dr. Seuss. Goat-like, shaggy with black spots (see Klotz).
Glurpy Slurpy Skakagrall	S. Silverstein. "Three thousand pounds and nine feet tall" and fanged.
Glunk	Dr. Seuss. A "greenish / Not too cleanish" monster, makes expensive long-distance call, difficult to "un-thunk."
Gofongo	S. Milligan. A fish with "singing knees" and mixed political sympathies.
Gooloo	S. Silverstein. Footless bird that lays its eggs while flying.
Goops	Gelett Burgess. Unmannerly creatures who blandly break all the rules of etiquette.
Gou-Gou	New World Myth. Androgynous giant beast.

Gox	Dr. Seuss. Generic Seuss, wears boxing gloves.
Griffin (Gryphon)	Ancient Myth. Lion's body, eagle's head and wings.
Grinch	Dr. Seuss. Mountain-dwelling, Scrooge-like creature.
Gump	L.F. Baum. Antlered head, two-sofaed body, brown tail, palm leaf wings; flies and carries Oz characters.
Ha-Ha-Ha	C. Cullen. Humorous cynic, refused to board Noah's ark and now extinct.
Harpy	Ancient Myth. Vulture-bodied with head and breast of a woman.
Hipporhinosticow	S. Milligan. Self-explanatory, wears yellow cow socks.
Houyhnhnm	J. Swift. Intelligent, speaking horses who despise and subject Yahoos.
Iota	Dr. Seuss. Long-necked fuzzy with wild blue hair from the "Far Western part / Of Southeast North Dakota."
Ish	Dr. Seuss. Generic Seuss, can swish and wish.
Jabberwock	Carroll. Strong jaws and claws and flaming eyes, whiffles and burbles, a manxome foe.
Jedd	Dr. Seuss. Small red animal that grows pom poms on its head to make a bed.
Joat	Dr. Seuss. Dog-shaped, long-necked, cow-footed, squirrel-skinned, goat-voiced animal.
Jott	Dr. Seuss. Circus bug, can juggle 22 question marks, 44 commas, and 1 dot.
Jubjub	Carroll. A bird, inhabits the territory of the Jabberwock and Bandersnatch.
Kalidah	L.F. Baum. Oz creature, bear body, tiger head.
Kangaroad	S. Silverstein. A projected progeny of a kangaroo and toad, which never existed because of a dispute over the name (see Toadaroo).
Klotz	Dr. Seuss. Goat-like, shaggy with black dots (see Glotz).
Lamia	Ancient Myth. A shape-changing female, a threat to men and infants.
Lapalake	C. Cullen. Tried to drink up all the water of Noah's flood, became bloated and was punctured by a swordfish.
Liodillo	T. Hood. Roars loudly.
Lorax	Dr. Seuss. A voracious Once-ler who eats up Triffula Trees.

Loup-Garou	New World Myth. Human turned wolf.
Lunk	Dr. Seuss. Generic Seuss creature with a ruff blue fur, lives in the "Wilds of Nantucket."
Manticore	Ancient Myth. A man-headed lion.
Manitou	New World Myth. Human body, goat head, lynx ears, could be both good and evil.
Marrog	R.C. Scriven. From Mars, brass body, extra appendages, purple hair, blue eyes, lives in the back of class rooms.
Maquizcoatl	New World Myth. Snake with a head on both ends.
Meehoo	S. Silverstein. A creature with one foot, no body, a head with arms; perpetrates knock- knocks and has an Exactly-Watt (which see) on a chain.
Mewlips	Tolkien. Greedy, ghoulish, anxiety-closet monsters.
Minotaur	Ancient Myth. A bull-headed monster who defeated intruders in his labyrinth.
Mock Turtle	Carroll. Calf head, tail, and hind legs; turtle body and flippers; what mock turtle soup is made of.
Mouldiwarp	E. Nesbit. A moralistic, short-tempered little animal.
Mulligatawny	Dr. Seuss. Scraggle-footed beast of burden from the Desert of Zind.
Nupiter Piffkin	Lear. Not described.
Obsk	Dr. Seuss. "A sort of a kind of a Thing-a-Bobsk."
Octopie	J. Yolen. A many-legged dessert.
Offt	Dr. Seuss. Balloon-like fuzzy with two-puffed tail, "weighs minus one pound."
Ookpik	D. Lee. A creature that is entirely and completely made of hair.
Peccarbok	T. Hood. Whistles whiningly.
Pegasus	Ancient Myth. Winged horse.
Phoenix	Ancient Myth. A bird that consumes itself with fire every five hundred years and resurrects itself.
Piguana	J. Yolen. Warty lizard tail but looks like a pig and tastes like a newt.
Pobble	Lear. A humanoid who loses both his toes and his red flannel while swimming the channel.
Proo	Dr. Seuss. Small, startled creature whose double head tufts droop to form a heart.

Psammead	E. Nesbit. An ancient, grouchy but kindly sand-fairy with a round furry spider body, bat ear, eyes on stalks, a wish granter.
Pushmi-pullyu	H. Lofting. A gentle animal so polite he has a mouth at both ends so he need never talk with his mouth full of food.
Quangle-Wangle	Lear. A stick-like creature, rather like a praying mantis, ships as cook for the 4 children, is feared by the cats of Lake Pipple Popple, and later hid under a hat 102 feet wide.
Questing Beast	Medieval Bestiaries (and Mallory and T.H. White). A fast-running, long and slinky creature made of various heraldic animals and forever questing.
Quetzalcoatl	New World Myth. A colorful serpent-bird, the incarnation of the Aztec creator god.
Razor-Tooth Sline	S. Silverstein. Enormous bird with ears and teeth; drops in on families for dinner.
Satyr	Ancient Myth. Lustful creature with a man's head and torso and goat's hindquarters.
Saw Horse	L.F. Baum. Log body, stick legs, bark ears, knot-hole eyes, animated by powder of life.
Scroobious Pip	Lear. Pan figure with ears and hind quarters of a deer, scaly fish tale, paws of a predator, white owl head adorned with round glasses, feathered goat beard, gazelle horns and insect antennae.
Seeze Pyder	Lear. Large, boat-eating fish.
Shreek	J. Ciardi. "A shiverous beast. . .as loud as a boy-and-a-half."
Siren	Ancient Myth. Combination of woman's head and breast, birds feathers and claws, fish's tail; lured men; often confused with mermaid.
Skank	J. Yolen. "A tense ancestor of the skunk."
Skrelling	New World Myth. Pygmy-sized, covered with hair, fierce fighters.
Slithergadee	S. Silverstein. A sneaky, slimy sea creature.
Slumming	J. Yolen. Rabbit-like creatures who hold paws to jump in dumps.
Snitterjipe	J. Reeves. A luminous, bewhiskered, bad-breathed monster who frightens apple-snitchers.
Snumm	Dr. Seuss. Drum-tummied circus animal.

Spangled Pandemonium	P. Brown. Describe it yourself.
Sphinx	Ancient Myth. Human head with lion's body, a riddle giver.
Squilililigee	C. Cullen. A shy creature so teased about its name it refused to enter Noah's ark.
Stoop	S. Corbet. Large-eyed, four-footed beast "that looks at everything but never touches."
Sweetums	J. Henson. Large, hairy Muppet, eats anything.
Taughtus	J. Yolen. A "Bahston Beast" who lectures.
Thwerll	Dr. Seuss. Large sad bug with thread-like, snarled up legs.
Tigeroceros	T. Hood. Calf of a tiger and rhinoceros.
Tik-Tok	L.F. Baum. A round-bodied robot made to last a thousand years.
Tin Woodman	L.F. Baum. Once human, but replaced part by part with tin, lives in Oz.
Toadal	J. Thurber. "A blob of glup. . .It makes a sound like rabbits screaming" and gloms "evildoers having done less evil than they could."
Toadaroo	S. Silverstein. Projected progeny of a toad and kangaroo, which never exists because of a dispute over the name (see Kangaroad).
Tock	N. Juster. A guardian of time, a canine with a watch for body.
Toop	S. Corbet. Rabbit-like animal that obligingly trims the grass in gardens.
Tropical Turnspits	Lear. Not described, but inhabit the narrow sea where the four children are stalled among the already cooked soles covered with shrimp sauce.
Uglies	G. MacDonald. Nightmare but ultimately lovable creatures.
Ugstabuggle	P. Wesley-Smith. Nightmare creature of afternoon naps.
Unicorn	Ancient Myth. Horselike with one long horn, fond of virgins.
Uniped	New World Myth. Fast-hopping, one-legged bowsmen who shot at Norse and French explorers.
Vampire	European Folklore. Human turned to bat or wolf, lives on human blood.
Watchbird	M. Leaf. A beaked, beady-eyed bird who watches all bad behavior on the part of children.

Wendigo	O. Nash. A gulping, slithery, tentacled beast with blubbery lips and an appetite.
Wheelers	L.F. Baum. Humanoids with wheels for hands and feet.
Whing-Whang	J. W. Riley. A lugubrious monster who lives in lonely swamps.
Woggle-Bug	L.F. Baum. H. [Highly] M. [Magnified] Woggle-Bug, T. [Thoroughly] E. [Educated], given to pompous language and puns.
Wuggly Ump	E. Gorey. Sharp-toothed cross between a dog and a dragon, has "nasty little willful eyes," eats umbrellas, gunny sacks, brass doorknobs, and children.
Wump	Dr. Seuss. Camel-like with one to seven humps and four to eight legs.
Wyvern	C. Connell. A tasty, dragon-like animal, now extinct.
Yahoo	J. Swift. Baboon-like, of vulgar tastes and disgusting habits; live in Houyhnhnm's Land.
Ying	Dr. Seuss. Generic Seuss, sings in showers.
Yop	Dr. Seuss. Blue, triple festooned, finger-hopping bug.
Zans	Dr. Seuss. Large, hooved, its antler opens cans.
Zed	Dr. Seuss. Small, yellow, one fast-growing hair on its head.
Zedonk	Dr. Seuss. The offspring of a zebra and donkey.
Zeep	Dr. Seuss. Very large, gentle, furry pet with a long, thin, pink-tufted tail.

SOME POST-ALPHABETICAL ANIMALS FROM *On Beyond Zebra* BY DR. SEUSS

Yuzz-a-ma-Tuzz	Mountain-tall, blue-eyed fuzzy.
Umbus	Ninety-eight uddered, sort of cow.
Fuddle-dee-Duddle	Fancy bird with long tail that takes six bearers to keep it out of "muddle-dee-puddles.
Glikker	Blue bug that juggles cinnamon or cucumber seeds.
Sneedle	A "ferocious mos-keedle."
Quandary	Symmetrical sea animal with no right side up.
Thnadner	Melancholy, fuzzy with the wrong shadow.

Floob-Boober-Bab-Boober-Bub	Aquatic, blubbery, surface-floating cross of ball, fish, and squid, used as stepping stones.
Itch-a-pods	Small, scampering, fearful, never- roosting generic Seuss creatures.
Yekko	Howling, doglike, lives in grottoes, loves echoes.
Vroom	Extraterrestial, broom-shaped, sweep with each other.
High Gargel-orum	Giant, generic Seuss, people porters.

Aesop. *Aesop's Fables*. Retold by Blanche Winter. Illus. New York: Airmont, 1965.

Andersen, Hans Christian. *The Complete Fairy Tales and Stories*. Trans. Erik C. Haugaard. Garden City, NY: Anchor/Doubleday, 1983.

Baum, L. Frank. *The Marvelous Land of Oz*. Illus. John R. Neill. New York: Dover, 1969.

————. *Ozma of Oz*. Illus. John R. Neill. New York: Dover, 1985.

————. *The Wizard of Oz*. Illus. W. W. Denslow. Chicago: Rand, 1956.

Blount, Margaret. *Animal Land: The Creatures of Children's Fiction*. New York: Avon, 1974.

Brown, Margaret Wise. *Goodnight Moon*. Illus. Clement Hurd. New York: Harper, 1947, Rpt. 1975.

Cammaerts, Emile. *The Poetry of Nonsense*. New York: Dutton, 1925.

Carroll, Lewis. *The Annotated Alice: Alice's Adventures in Won- land & Through the Looking Glass*. Ed. and annotator Martin Gardner. Illus. John Tenniel. New York: World, 1972.

Ciardi, John. *The Man Who Sang the Sillies*. Philadelphia: Lippincott, 1961.

Corbet, Sybil. *Animal Land Where There are No People*. London, 1897.

Cullen, Countee and Christopher Cat. *The Lost Zoo*. Illus. Joseph Low. Toronto: Ryerson Press, 1940. Rpt. 1968.

Dahl, Roald. *James and the Giant Peach*. New York: Knopf, 1961.

Dr. Seuss [Theodor Seuss Geisel]. *Dr. Seuss's Sleep Book*. New York: Beginner/Random, 1960.

————. *I Can Lick Thirty Tigers Today and Other Stories*. New York: Random, 1969.

————. *I Can Read with My Eyes Shut*. New York: Beginner/Random, 1978.

————. *If I Ran the Circus*. New York: Random, 1956.

————. *If I Ran the Zoo*. Beginner Books. New York: Random, 1950.

————. *Oh Say Can You Say*. New York: Beginner/Random, 1979.

————. *On Beyond Zebra*. New York: Random, 1955.

————. *One fish two fish red fish blue fish*. New York: Beginner/Random, 1960.

Fadiman, Clifton. *Wally the Wordworm*. 1964. Illus. Lisa Atherton. Owings Mills, MD: Stemmer, 1983.

Fisher, Robert, ed. *Amazing Monsters: Verses to Thrill and Chill*. Illus. Rowena Allen. London and Boston: Faber, 1982.

Gardner, John. *Dragon, Dragon and Other Tales*. Illus. Charles Shields. New York: Knopf, 1975.

Gorey, Edward. *Amphigorey*. New York: Putnam, 1972.

Grahame, Kenneth. *The Reluctant Dragon*. Illus. E. H. Shepard. New York: Holiday House, 1938. First published in *Dream Days*. London: John Lane, 1898.

Hamilton, Mary. *A New World Bestiary*. Illus. Kim LaFave. Vancouver and Toronto: Douglas & McIntyre, 1985.

Juster, Norton. *The Phantom Tollbooth*. Illus. Jules Feiffer. New York: Random, 1961; Rpt. 1964.

Kipling, Rudyard. *Just So Stories*. 1902. New York: Airmont, 1966

Lear, Edward. The Complete Nonsense of Edward Lear. *Ed. Holbrook Jackson. New York: Dover, 1951.*

————. The Scroobious Pip. *Illus. Carol Newsom. New York: Lothrop, 1983.*

Lee, Dennis. Garbage Delight. *Illus. Frank Newfield. Boston: Houghton, 1978.*

————. Wiggle to the Laundromat. *Illus. Charles Pachter. Toronto and Chicago: New Press, 1970.*

Lofting, Hugh. The Story of Dr. Doolittle. *1920. New York: Yearling/Dell, 1976.*

Nash, Walter. The Language of Humour: Style and Technique in Comic Discourse. *White Plains, NY: Longman, 1985.*

Nesbit, E. Five Children and It. *1902. New York: Viking/ Penguin, 1985.*

————. The Phoenix and the Carpet. *1904. New York: Viking/ Penguin, 1984.*

————. The Story of the Amulet. *1906. New York: Viking/ Penguin, 1985.*

Prelutsky, Jack. The Queen of Eene. *Illus. Victoria Chess. New York: Morrow/ Greenwillow, 1978.*

Raskin, Ellen. Franklin Stein. New York: Atheneum, 1972.

Rees, Ennis. Lions and Lobsters and Foxes and Frogs: Fables from Aesop. *Illus. Edward Gorey. Reading, MA: Addison-Wesley/Young Scott Books, 1977.*

Rowland, Beryl. *Animals with Human Faces*. Knoxville: U of Tennessee P, 1975.

————. *Birds with Human Souls*. Knoxville: U of Tennessee P, 1978.

Sendak, Maurice. *Higglety Pigglety Pop! or There Must Be More to Life*. New York: Harper, 1967.

————. *Outside Over There*. New York: Harper, 1981.

Silverstein, Shel. *A Light in the Attic*. New York: Harper, 1981.

————. *Where the Sidewalk Ends*. New York: Harper, 1974.

Stewart, Susan. *Nonsense: Aspects of Intertextuality in Folklore and Literature*. Baltimore: Johns Hopkins UP, 1979.

Swift, Jonathan. *Gulliver's Travels*. 1726. Toronto and New York: Oxford UP, 1977.

Thurber, James. *The 13 Clocks*. New York: Simon, 1950.

Willard, Nancy. *Sailing to Cythera and Other Anatole Stories*. Illus. David Mc Phail. New York: Harcourt, 1974.

————. *A Visit to William Blake's Inn: Poems for Innocent and Experienced Travelers*. Illus. Alice and Martin Provensen. San Diego: Harcourt, 1981.

Yolen, Jane. *Dragon Night and Other Lullabies*. Illus. Demi. New York: Methuen, 1980.

————. *How Beastly! A Menagerie of Nonsense Poems*. Illus. James Marshall. New York and Cleveland: Collins, 1980.

11

Nonsense and the Didactic Tradition

Nonsense that Moralizes, Nonsense that Mocks

Nonsense literature is related to the didactic tradition for children in two
ways: some nonsense hides a moral under its humor and some satirizes or
parodies a moralistic didactic work. Because political and social satire
require a knowledge of events beyond the experience of virtually all
children, satire in children's literature tends to limit itself to the concerns
of family and school and frequently uses a parody of the literature that is
known to the young as its vehicle. The parodies can be of individual
poems, as when Lewis Carroll turned the theologian Isaac Watt's verse
"Against Idleness and Mischief" into amoral absurdity by transforming
lines like "How doth the little busy bee / Improve each shining hour" into
"How doth the little crocodile / Improve his shining tail" (*Wonderland*,
chap. 2). Parodies can also be of a particular type of literature, and the

majority of nonsense parodies are of cautionary verse and didactic tales in general.

To begin with the category mentioned first, humor-coated morals, two verse examples of didactic nonsense are Heinrich Hoffman's "The Story of the Man that went out Shooting" and Arnold Adoff's *The Cabbages Are Chasing The Rabbits*. In the first a well-accoutred hunter (whose fittings include some needed spectacles) goes out to shoot a rabbit. Meanwhile, "The hare sits snug in leaves and grass, / And laughs to see the green man pass" (*Struwwelpeter*, 16). The hare turns the tables on the hunter by stealing his glasses and gun while he sleeps, then, when he wakes, chasing him and shooting at him as he falls down a well. This reversal of hunter and hunted has a curious twist in the final lines. We learn that although the hare's shot missed the hunter, it did knock cup and saucer from his wife's hand, and

> There lived close by the cottage there
> The hare's own child, the little hare;
> and while she stood upon her toes,
> The coffee fell and burned her nose.
> "Oh dear! she cried, with spoon in hand,
> "Such fun I do not understand."
>
> (18)

Under the seeming nonsense, Hoffman has put together as complex a bit of anti-gun propaganda as one could wish for.

Hoffman's parodic nonsense was written in 1844 and first published in 1847. About one hundred and forty years later, a book that could be called a delayed spin-off was published. (Adoff has stated, however, that he did not have the Hoffman poem in mind when writing his book.) Adoff's *The Cabbages Are Chasing The Rabbits* is dedicated by the author to "All Great Vegetables I Know And Love" (copyright page). It features a more extreme, and therefore more nonsensical, transposition of the accepted hierarchy of creatures: cabbages chase rabbits; rabbits chase dogs; dogs turn on the hunters; the hunters abandon their guns to chase the trees, which, a refrain repeats, "Are Flying Quietly Away" and chasing their leaves. Then, on the concluding pages, "The Sun Comes Out To Stay / And Shines A Good Morning" on all these creatures and on "All Fair Fowl And Warms The Wiggling Worms Of May. . . . / It Was A Special Kind Of A Morning / It Was A Special Kind Of A Day" (n.p.). In an interesting reversal of E.E. Cummings lower case preference, Adoff has capitalized the first letter of every word in the text, creating an egalitarian aristocracy among words. His topsy-turvy world has a utopian atmosphere that matches that in the old folk song "The Land of Cock-ayne." In an article in *The Lion and the Unicorn*, Adoff has said, "If there is a force behind my work for young people, it is this force for change" (10). In *The Cabbages are Chasing the Rabbits* he has enlisted nonsense on the side of that force.

Nonsense written with a moral or lesson in mind also includes fables (which by their very nature have a moral). Many of Dr. Seuss's stories are in this tradition. His Grinch is a latter-day Scrooge whose initial meaness and final conversion teaches children the loneliness of greed. Seuss's Sneetches teach tolerance. Even the delightfully silly *Green Eggs and Ham* is basically a lesson in the necessity to expand food preferences, a much needed lesson for the majority of middle-class children. And of course there is the openly defined pedagogical motive in the Dr. Seuss "I Can Read It All by Myself Beginner Books": to teach children to read.

But besides these rather specific lessons, there is throughout Seuss's work an underlying message that can be summed up as—Keep your eyes and ears open; the world is a fascinating place. In *To Think I Saw It on Mulberry Street*, *One fish two fish*, his zoo and circus books, *I Can Read with My Eyes Shut*, *Oh the Thinks You Can Think*, and *On Beyond Zebra*, to name some of the best examples, an exuberance pervades. Geisel conveys a very positive moralism that asks the child to reach out to adventure and challenge and diversity. And Theodor Seuss Geisel, the man, provides a model that matches his Seussian creations. His eye, ear, spirit, and sense of humor seem as lively in many recent works as they were when he first penned cartoons as a college student some sixty years ago. He has followed the advice that the Cat in the Hat gives in *I Can Read with My Eyes Shut*:

> But it's bad for my hat
> and makes my eyebrows
> get red hot.
> So—
> reading with my eyes shut
> I don't do an awful lot.

(n.p.)

After this early warning, the reader is told near the end of the book:

> There are so many things
> You can learn about.
> But—you'll miss
> the best things
> if you keep
> your eyes shut.

If all moralistic and didactic books came in this Seussian flavor, there would be little need for the parodies that mock the confining stuffiness of so much of the genre.

One special class of books that straddles the border of didactic and nonsense literature is the humorous manners book. Some of these are sugarcoated lessons in good behavior, others make fun of them. Gelett Burgess's Goops and Munro Leaf's Watchbirds taught the parents and grandparents of the present generation the do's and don'ts of polite conduct: how to eat neatly, how not to hoard toys or throw tantrums. More recently Helen Oxenbury and Fay Maschler wrote *A Child's Book of Manners*, which, while amusing in both its verses and illustrations, is intended to teach sensible manners and morals. For example, the second poem admonishes

> A pet is not a moving toy
> You tire of at your leisure;
> For every owner, girl or boy,
> There's work as well as pleasure.

(n.p.)

On table manners, they write

> Try to keep the food you eat
> Off your clothes and off your seat,
> On your plate and fork and knife.
> This holds true throughout your life.

(n.p.)

Munro Leaf, whose famous *Story of Ferdinand*, is a gentle moral tale about a pacifist bull, also wrote *The Watchbirds* and *Manners Can Be Fun*, and what could be called a linguistic manners book, *Grammar Can Be Fun*. His simple, stick-people illustrations have nonsense elements like those pictured for the Wobbly Necks who "shout UH-HUH and UN-UN then wiggle and wiggle and wiggle" (6), but the text, for all its light-heartedness, is promoting standard formal English.

Nonsense is more frequently called to the task of parodying manners books. Sesyle Joslin's two books, *What Do You Say, Dear* and *What Do You Do, Dear*, both illustrated by Maurice Sendak, fall into this category. In *What Do You Say, Dear*, the recommended responses are pristinely proper: "Thank you very much," "No, thank you," "May I please be excused," and "I'm sorry," to list a few, but the situations that prompt these polite replies are quite outside the realm of everyday manners. For example,

THIS IS A WATCHBIRD WATCHING **YOU**

THIS IS A WATCHBIRD WATCHING A BUTTER-IN

THIS IS A BUTTER-IN

bumping into a crocodile while downtown shopping is what elicits the "Excuse me." And an even sillier situation occurs when

> You are flying around in your airplane and
> you remember that the Duchess said, "Do
> drop in for tea sometime."
> So you do, only it makes a rather large hole
> in her roof.
>
> What do you say, dear?
> [Next page]
> I'm sorry.

(n.p.)

The disparity between the actions and the language subverts the lesson in mannerly speech. In such a hazardous universe, propriety appears weak and out of place. In *What Do You Do, Dear* the incongruity is between potentially violent action and polite behavior as counteraction. The polite behavior is shown as sometimes ludicrously inappropriate, as when a boy kidnapped while reading in the library is advised to exit quietly (it is a library after all). Another absurd example is

> You are at the North Pole, sitting in your
> igloo eating a bit of blubber, when in
> comes a huge lady polar bear wearing a
> white fur coat.
>
> What do you do, dear?
> [Next page]
> Help her off with her coat.
>
> (n.p.)

And the crowning foolishness reads

> You are a circus acrobat walking on the high
> tight wire and you happen to meet a lady
> tightrope walker coming from the opposite
> direction.
>
> What do you do, dear?
> [Next page]
> Step aside and let the lady pass.
>
> (n.p.)

The young gentleman of course falls off in doing so. This last lesson has a metaphoric value and implies that etiquette is a tightrope sometimes perilous to negotiate, and must be applied with good common sense.

Many individual poems mock overstrict adherence to decorum by imagining role reversals or exaggerated consequences. An example of the first is Pamela Espeland and Marilyn Waniek's poem "When I Grow Up." The narrator claims that

> I'll never wash between my toes,
>
> And when I eat
> In a restaurant
> And feel like it, I'll blow my nose.
>
> (*The Cat Walked through the Casserole*, n.p.)

Another of their rebellious characters would "make my mom take baths all the time," "give the principal spankings," and "make all the farmers eat spinach." Espeland and Waniek have tapped the spontaneous nonsense wishes of the child who is rebelling against an adult code. Most children, while they are still in the never never time and space of the very young, say to a parent, "When I am big and you are little, I'll. . . ."

From *Robert Francis Weatherbee* by Munro Leaf.

A folk rhyme included in William Cole's anthology *Beastly Boys and Ghastly Girls* (1964) catches the spirit of childish role reversal wishes:

> Johnny went to church one day,
> He climbed up in the steeple;
> He took his shoes and stockings off
> And threw them at the people.
>
> (24)

Cole also includes instances of exaggerated consequences for unmannerly or greedy behavior. Overeating, for example, leads to exploding (F. Gwynne Evans, "Little Thomas," 45–47), falling through the floor (Leroy F. Jackson, "Jolly Jake and Butter Bill," 55–57), and being mistaken for a ball (Katherine Pyle, "The Sweet Tooth," 57–61).

The truest vein of nonsense related to the didactic tradition is that which dismisses overly pious moralism through exaggeration or through parody. In these there is an adult perspective, but the adult is absolving the child for various misdemeanors. As Cole says in his introductory poem,

> For it isn't normal to always be good—
> I don't think you'd want to, and don't think you should;
> Just as food tastes better with a shake of salt,
> A small bit of mischief is hardly a fault.
>
> (n.p.)

Cole has numerous examples of the type of exaggeration that can lighten the seriousness of some common admonition. The child told "Not to be a crybaby" is more likely to be provoked to laughter than to further tears by the anonymous poem about a boy who howled and cried so long and often that his "mouth grew so big that—alack!— / It was only a mouth with a border of Jack" (in Cole, 37).

Hilaire Belloc, whose various volumes of mock cautionary verse collected in *Hilaire Belloc's Cautionary Verses* are preeminent among this type of nonsense, invented a number of sinister punishments whose seriousness contrasts with the triviality of the misdeed that caused them. In their *Child's Book of Manners*, Oxenbury and Maschler admonish lightly

> Doors have handles.
> Doors have jambs.
> What doors should never have
> Are slams.
>
> (n.p.)

When Belloc takes on this childhood fault, he creates "Rebecca, Who slammed Doors for Fun and Perished Miserably" (59–63). Rebecca "would deliberately go / And Slam the door like Billy-Ho!" (60). Until one day

> It happened that a Marble Bust
> Of Abraham was standing just
> Above the Door this little Lamb
> Had carefully prepared to Slam,
> And Down it came! It knocked her flat!
>
> (61)

At her funeral the children attending hear a sermon that

> Mentioned her Virtues, it is true,
> But dwelt upon her Vices too,
> And showed the Dreadful End of One
> Who goes and slams the door for Fun.
>
> (63)

Belloc's sly antididacticism covers a range of social and moral gaffes and, in total, comments on the culture of his age.

A maxim like "Be kind to animals" is knocked into the world of nonsense by poems like A. E. Housman's "Inhuman Henry, or, Cruelty to Fabulous Animals" (in Cole, 25–27). It recounts the terrible fate of a boy who was unkind to unicorns and ends up eaten by the lion he lets loose on them. Destruction by lions is a very popular punishment in mock cautionary tales. Improbable as it seems, lions were one of the dangers that English and American children were warned against in the nineteenth century. William Darton's *The Third Chapter of Accidents and Remarkable Events: containing caution and instruction for children*, which was published in 1807, contains a section entitled "Feed and treat a Lion well" that tells a horror story of a servant decapitated by a lion (in de Vries, 211). Hilaire Belloc's lead poem in his *Cautionary Tales for Children* is "Jim, Who ran away from his Nurse, and was eaten by a Lion." As in all of Belloc's humorous cautionary verses, the wit is quiet but sharp. The poem ends with Jim's bereaved but "self-controlled" father asking all children to "attend / To James' miserable end, / And always keep a-hold of Nurse / For fear of finding something worse" (*Hilaire Belloc's Cautionary Verses*, 11–12). In a poem like Maurice Sendak's "Pierre" there is a parody of parodies. The lion does eat Pierre, expected punishment for a child who resolutely doesn't care, but he is extracted and, finally reformed of his indifference, shown eating with the lion rather than being eaten by it.

Parodies of cautionary tales usually keep the dark ending of the original. Both Jane Taylor's "Playing with Fire" in her *Select Rhymes for the Nursery* (20) and Heinrich Hoffmann's "The Dreadful Story of Harriet and the Matches" (*Struwwelpeter*, 10–11) end in sorrow for the protagonists. In the earlier serious verse, a mother explains in detail the sufferings of a little girl "That had got such a dreadful scar" from catching on fire while playing with matches. Its realism does indeed create the intended revulsion, and undoubtedly bred some nightmares in timid children. Hoffmann has his foolish Harriet absolutely consumed after she plays with matches in spite of the warning of two pussy-cats who chorus, "me-ow, me-o, / You'll burn to death, if you do so." We know that Hoffmann, a physician, wrote these poems to amuse young patients who came to his office, but some find his humor as frightening, if not more so, than the originials he parodies. "The Story of Little Suck-a-Thumb" in which "The great, long, red-legged scissor man" (20) cuts off the child's thumbs, while funny to many adults, is considered a bit strong for young children.

Edward Lear, in "The History of the Seven Families of the Lake Pipple-Popple," distances the violent deaths of the seven children of each of the seven families by making his characters birds, guinea pigs, cats, and fish and by employing nonsense sequences like "huffled, / and ruffled, / and shuffled, / and puffled" (*Complete Nonsense*, 111) to describe the deadly scuffle of the young parrots. Even so, as Leo Schneiderman points out in the section on the psychological benefits of nonsense, the universal destruction in this story might disturb some children. But some children love humorous violence. Else Holmelund Minarik's story "No Fighting, No Biting," in which two small alligators who don't abide by this stricture are eaten by a large male alligator while involved in one of their petty battles, was a favorite in this writer's household and the title became a byword.

Nonsense writers also turn pious tales with conventional happy endings into mock tragedies. Edward Gorey has some wickedly funny inversions of this sort. In "The Hapless Child" the standard Victorian plot of a pretty and virtuous little heroine being finally rescued by a parent, rich aunt or uncle, or a potential husband after her trials and tribulations as an orphan is knocked flat, along with the heroine, when the story ends after the searching father runs over little Charlotte Sophia and "She was so changed, he did not recognize her" (*Amphigorey*, n.p.). In "The Gashly-crumb Tinies" Gorey takes the usually cheery genre of the alphabet rhyme and, as mentioned in the discussion of alphabet books, uses it to chronicle a series of grisly child deaths. Children enjoy such parodies of genres they have encountered all too often in bland forms. As Linda Geller notes, children view parodies as one way to "deliver a fatal blow to 'babyhood'" (*Wordplay*, 87).

Gorey's masterpiece satire on children's verse is "The Wuggly Ump." This dinosaur-like monster who seems harmlessly ridiculous in its eating habits ("gunny sacks, / Brass doorknobs, mud, and carpet tacks") turns out to eat children also. But the poem and the children are persistently cheerful while the Wuggly Ump is on the way:

> We pass our happy childhood hours
> In weaving endless chains of flowers.
> . . . .
> When play is over, we are fed
> On wholesome bowls of milk and bread.
>
> (n.p.)

Their refrains progress from "tirraloo . . . tirralay," "Jigglepin . . . jogglepen," "hushaboo . . . hushaby," "twiddle-ear . . . twaddle-or" to the final "Sing glogalimp, sing glugalump / From deep inside the Wuggly Ump." In one sense this verse is simply a parody of the type of idyllic poetry for juveniles that Robert Louis Stevenson, A. A. Milne, and countless other, lesser versifiers have written. But in a broader sense, Gorey is taking on that whole area of children's literature that lives by the creed that children should be protected from harsh reality. The Wuggly Ump, although only a nonsense creature, devours that notion along with eveything else he eats.

Gorey's humor is related to that in anonymous poems like those about Little Willie:

> Willie, with a thirst for gore,
> Nailed his sister to the door.
> Mother said, with humor quaint:
> "Now, Willie dear, don't scratch the paint."
> (In Cole, Beastly Boys and Ghastly Girls, 95)

He shares their absurdly understated reaction to serious disasters. It is a type of humor that has proved very popular in the twentieth century. Generated at times by the fact that some things are so horrific they can be dealt with only with laughter, nonsense attacks didacticism and simplistic piety in a manner similar to that used in the theater of the absurd.

Hilaire Belloc is the undisputed master of parody of cautionary tales, but besides him and the others mentioned, countless other writers have turned their hand to nonsense parodies of moralistic verse for children. Ogden Nash, John Ciardi, Shel Silverstein, Ted Hughes, and Spike Milligan are among the more famous. The entire group constitutes a healthy antidote to priggishness and pomposity. Children who read and enjoy such literature have a strong advantage in understanding and dealing with the complexity of our not always sensible and rational world. Others who have, like Theodor Seuss Geisel, used the humor of nonsense to make a serious point have also challenged children to think about how many sides there are to most issues. The relationship between the nonsense tradition and the didactic tradition has been a healthy one.

Adoff, Arnold. *The Cabbages Are Chasing The Rabbits*. San Diego and New York: Harcourt, 1985.

————. "Politics, Poetry, and Teaching Children: A Personal Journey." *Lion and Unicorn* 10 (1986): 9–14; rpt. in *ALAN Review* 14.3 (Spring 1987): 11–12.

Belloc, Hilaire. *Hilaire Belloc's Cautionary Verses*. New York: Knopf, 1951.

Carroll, Lewis. *The Annotated Alice*. Ed. Martin Gardner. New York: World, 1963; rpt. 1972.

Cole, William, ed. *Beastly Boys and Ghastly Girls*. Illus. Tomi Ungerer. Cleveland and New York: World, 1964.

Darton, William. *The Third Chapter of Accidents and Remarkable Events: containing caution and instruction for children*. London, 1807; in *Flowers of Delight*. Ed. Leonard De Vries. New York: Pantheon, 1965. 211.

Dr. Seuss [Theodor Seuss Geisel]. *And to Think I Saw It on Mulberry Street*. New York: Random, 1936.

————. *Green Eggs and Ham*. New York: Beginner/Random, 1960.

————. *I Can Read with My Eyes Shut*. New York: Beginner/ Random, 1978.

————. *If I Ran the Circus*. New York: Random, 1956.

————. *If I Ran the Zoo*. New York: Random, 1950.

————. *Oh the Thinks You Can Think*. New York: Beginner/ Random, 1975.

————. *On Beyond Zebra*. New York: Random, 1955.

————. *One fish two fish red fish blue fish*. New York: Beginner/Random, 1960.

Espeland, Pamela and Marilyn Waniek. *The Cat Walked Through the Casserole*. Minneapolis: Carolrhoda Books, 1984.

Geller, Linda Gibson. *Wordplay and Language Learning for Children*. Urbana, IL: NCTE, 1985.

Gorey, Edward. *Amphigorey*. New York: Putnam, 1972.

Hoffmann, Heinrich. *Struwwelpeter*. 1847. London: Pan Books, 1972; rpt. from Blackie and Son, 1903.

Joslin, Sesyle. *What Do You Do, Dear*. Illus. Maurice Sendak. New York: Harper, n.d.; rpt. from Addison-Wesley, 1961.

————. *What Do You Say, Dear?*. Illus. Maurice Sendak. New York: Harper, n.d.; rpt. from Addison-Wesley, 1958.

Leaf, Munro. *Gordon the Goat*. New York and Philadelphia: Lippincott, 1944. Rpt. Hamden, CT: Library Professional Publications, 1988.

————. *Grammar Can Be Fun*. New York: Stokes, 1934.

————. *Manners Can Be Fun*. New York: Stokes, 1936. Rev. ed. New York and Philadelphia: Lippincott, 1958.

————. *Robert Francis Weatherby*. New York: Stokes, 1935; rpt. Hamden, CT: Library Professional Publications, 1988.

————. *The Story of Ferdinand*. Illus. Robert Lawson. New York: Viking, 1936; rpt. 1969.

————. *The Watchbirds: A Picture Book of Behavior*. New York: Stokes, 1939.

Lear, Edward. *The Complete Nonsense of Edward Lear*. Ed. Holbrook Jackson. New York: Dover, 1951.

Minarik, Else Holmelund. *No Fighting, No Biting!* Illus. Maurice Sendak. New York: Harper, 1958.

Oxenbury, Helen and Fay Maschler. *A Child's Book of Manners*. New York: Viking/ Penguin, 1984; rpt. 1986.

Taylor, Jane. "Playing with Fire." *Select Rhymes for the Nursery*. London, 1808. In *Flowers of Delight*. Ed. Leonard De Vries. New York: Pantheon, 1965. 20.

Part IV THE NONSENSE VISION

12

Perhaps the most fundamental form of picture play is that which violates our visual common sense.

Peggy Whalen-Levitt, "Picture Play in Children's Books: A Celebration of Visual Awareness" in Barron and Burley, 169

Nonsense Illustrations

An Overview

Nonsense illustrations have a long history, and they seem to be increasingly popular in the twentieth century. Maurice Sendak, Arnold Lobel, Dr. Seuss, Shel Silverstein, James Marshall, and Edward Gorey are among the famous author-illustrators who include the absurdities and grotesqueries associated with nonsense in the pictures for their own and others' books. Steve Kellogg, Ellen Raskin, Paul Zelinsky, Graham Oakley, and James Stevenson are also major contributors to the field. Many of the books by these artists remain in print year after year, because children show their appreciation of this form of humor by their purchases and their selections at libraries, where nonsense remains a favorite. The number of contemporary illustrators creating nonsense indicates that the field is alive and well and should continue to be so.

These contemporary nonsense illustrators are part of a long tradition established by such laureates of nonsense as Edward Lear, John Tenniel, and Heinrich Hoffman. All three used exaggeration, humorous allusions, and impossible combinations of objects and characteristics, to support or to enhance the nonsense elements of the accompanying texts. And their followers have continued to use similar methods. Pictorial nonsense shares with verbal nonsense the tendency to cross the boundaries set by everyday systems of classification, to place incongruous elements together, and to create a visual play that is a counterpart of wordplay. However, nonsense illustration is not limited to a simple translation of humor from a verbal medium to a graphic medium, and, in the next chapter we will examine the techniques by which artists convey a nonsense vision.

There are a number of perspectives from which to view nonsense illustrations, a number of ways to categorize the field:

The Relationship between Artist and Author

1. Author-artists may have a double perspective which includes both the visual and verbal, and illustrate their own writing.
2. These same illustrators may sometimes interpret the writing of others.
3. Artists may work strictly with the words of others.

The Relationship between Artist and Intended Audience

1. Pictorial nonsense may be aimed at the adult.
2. It may be aimed at the child.
3. It may be aimed at both.

The Relationship between Illustration and Text

1. Illustrations can adhere to the text and merely support it by picturing the nonsense described.
2. Illustrations can enhance or heighten the nonsense in the text.
7. Illustrations can contradict the text and subvert it, thereby creating another kind of nonsense.

THE AUTHOR-ARTIST CONNECTION

A simple division to consider is between those who illustrate their own writing and those who illustrate the work of others. Because the majority of illustrators have done both, these two categories overlap and are perhaps more useful in theory than in practice, but the relationship can influence the nature of the nonsense. When, for example, both text and pictures are by the same person, the two may be more interdependent than when two creators are involved.

AUTHOR-ILLUSTRATORS

Many author-illustrators have such strong visions of their creations that their illustrations become an inseparable part of their verbal nonsense. When readers recall Heinrich Hoffmann's *Struwwelpeter*, for instance, the picture of the title character, Shock-headed Peter, is likely to come to mind more vividly than the poem describing him. And most readers will remember Hoffmann's picture of "The great, long, red-legged scissor-man" (20) rushing across the room to cut off the thumbs of poor Conrad (Little Suck-a-Thumb). Other favorite characters come to mind exactly as Hoffmann created them. Developing their own nonsense visions and individual styles, many modern illustrators have carried on the traditions of Hoffman and other nineteenth-century nonsense author-illustrators. In our own century, who would attempt to redraw a Thurber dog, a Charles Addams character, Edward Gorey's Gashlycrumb Tinies, or Maurice Sendak's Wild Things.

Another instance of closely interrelated text and picture occurs in a genre that Lear developed—his nonsense botanies. In these, the nonsense is mainly visual although the title under each drawing is also humorous. Lear placed nonsensical Latinate labels under sketched absurdities such as the "Phattfacia Stupenda" (*Complete Nonsense*, 128), which shows a round face on a stem. Lear also classified and drew specimens of the "Smalltoothcombia Domestica" (127), a plant with combs growing off its stems, and of the "Piggiawiggia Pyramidalis" (129) a plant with pigs for flowers. These nonsense botanies inspire imitation or parody rather than reinterpretation. The June 1, 1987, cover of the *The New Yorker* by R. Chast features nine nonsense seed packets, among them "Morning Magic French Toast" (toast forms the flower's center), "Bowlscraper Oatmeal" (the bowls are the flowers), and "Mom's Best Fried Chicken Drumsticks" (eight drumsticks sprout on a weed-like plant). The packets also promise a harvest of "Patsy's Pride Swiss Cheese" and "Summer De-Lite Chocolate-covered Cherries." Chast's dig at the silly names on seed packets is extremely clever although her drawings are not as madly imaginative as Lear's. But then who can contend with a "Tigerlillia Terribilis" (155) or a "Crabbia Horrida" (162). Lear's botanical creations are difficult to improve upon.

Cover-drawing by R. Chast; © 1987, The New Yorker Magazine, Inc.

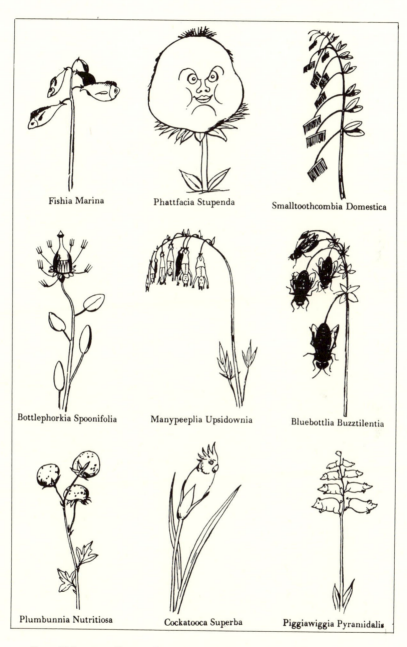

Fishia Marina

Phattfacia Stupenda

Smalltoothcombia Domestica

Bottlephorkia Spoonifolia

Manypeeplia Upsidownia

Bluebottlia Buzztilentia

Plumbunnia Nutritiosa

Cockatooca Superba

Piggiawiggia Pyramidalis

From "Nonsense Botany," written and illustrated by Edward Lear.

New Illustrations for Old

Lear's limericks and longer nonsense poems, on the other hand, have inspired artists to try their own visions of his words. In *The Penguin Book of Limericks*, compiled by E.O. Parrott, the illustrator Robin Jacques gives us elaborate renditions of the "Old Man with a beard" (cover and frontpiece) and the "Young Lady of Portugal" (253) as she stands in her tree "just to look at the sea" (252). Many pictorial versions of "The Owl and the Pussycat" exist. Kevin Madison drew elaborate illustrations for a book containing "The Yonghy-Bonghy-Bo" and "The New Vestments." Nancy Elkholm Burkert's ethereal rendition of the kingdom of "The Scroobious Pip" raises nonsense to an almost mystical level. And these are only a few examples of the many pictorial renditions of Lear's nonsense.

The Dolomphious Duck,
who caught Spotted Frogs for her dinner
with a Runcible Spoon.

Picturing Another Author's Words

While innumerable works of nonsense are written and illustrated by the same person, some artists prefer to create their own nonsensical renditions of the work of others. A glance through the nonsense works listed in our bibliography will show that about a third of them are illustrated by someone other than the author. There are countless collaborations between modern authors and illustrators to produce works of whimsical nonsense. Even those well known as author-illustrators have frequently drawn for other writers. Maurice Sendak, for example, gave us a joyful visual accompaniment for Ruth Krauss's *A Hole Is to Dig*. James Marshall provided some suitably silly pictures for Jane Yolen's *How*

Beastly! A Menagerie of Nonsense Poems. And Steven Kellogg created what can best be called explosive illustrations to complement Trinka Hakes Noble's accounts of the adventures of Jimmy's boa constrictor (*The Day Jimmy's Boa Ate the Wash* and *Jimmy's Boa Bounces Back*). Edward Gorey illustrated several of John Ciardi's books for children (*The Man Who Sang the Sillies*, *You Read to Me, I'll Read to You*, and *The Monster Den*), and his pictures bring out the latent nonsense in even the more sedate of Ciardi's poems. Ellen Raskin turned her artistic talents to illustrating Renee Karol Weiss's collection of modern American animal poems, *A Paper Zoo*. The few examples given here make it evident that although a single author-illustrator may be held up as the ideal for a book of nonsense, excellent creations can result from collaborations as well.

Sometimes the combination works so well that the author and illustrator are paired for any number of books. Quentin Blake is one example of this. He has illustrated many books, a number of them written by Roald Dahl (*Charlie and the Chocolate Factory*, *Charlie and the Glass Elevator*, *The BFG*, *The Witches*, and *The Giraffe and the Pelly and Me*). Blake's humorous line drawings are a perfect accompaniment for Dahl's nonsense. Any illustrator would be challenged by Dahl's sense of humor and his constant playing with words, as when the Giant explains to Sophie in *The BFG* that "every human bean is diddly and different. Some is scrumdiddlyumptious and some is uckyslush" (20). Later, when the giant is catching dreams, he shouts, "'It's a trogglehumper! . . . Oh, save our solo!' he cried. 'Deliver us from weasels! The devil is dancing on my dibbler!'" (84). Blake, working in black and white line drawings, is able to capture the Giant blowing the trogglehumper nightmare into the sleeping Fleshlumpeater's face and then to depict the writhing reaction. On some pages (113–15, for example) the illustrations occupy far more space than the text—and have far more silliness: a young boy squeezing toothpaste into a car's gas tank claims, in the illustration, "I IS INVENTING A CAR THAT RUNS ON TOOTHPASTE" (113).

When the BFG (Big Friendly Giant) leaves Giant Country, he is like Gulliver among the Lilliputians, his size creating all kinds of problems. He and Sophie go to visit the Queen of England, and even her ballroom is a tight squeeze for him. His chair consists of a chest of drawers put on top of a grand piano. His table (they have been invited for breakfast) is created by putting a pingpong table on top of four grandfather clocks which are twelve feet high, and the silverware is a garden fork, a spade, and "the great sword hanging on the wall" (174). Blake captures the scene admirably, showing the butler with perfect aplomb serving the Giant by walking up a ladder, serving tray balanced in one hand, the coffeepot in the other.

The Big Friendly Giant from *The B.F.G.* by Roald Dahl,
illustrated by Quentin Blake.

The following year the Dahl-Blake duo produced the *The Witches*, another romp with the ridiculous. The hero, an orphan being raised by his cigar-smoking grandmother, is fascinated by the tales of witches his grandmother tells him, how they make children disappear or turn them into something else—a chicken, or a stone statue. The grandmother also tells him what to look for in a witch: "Witches' . . . feet have square ends with no toes at all . . . it does give them a problem with their shoes. . . . A witch . . . has the most awful job squeezing her feet into those neat little pointed shoes" (26–27). Again working in black and white, Blake captures Dahl's rogue's gallery of characters. He also successfully renders "the claw of a crrrabcrrruncher, the beak of a blabbersnitch, the snout of a grrrobblesquirt, and the tongue of a catsprrringer" (90–91), and he has a comical series picturing the transformation of Bruno Jenkins from a boy to a mouse. In *Witches*, Dahl has transformed the traditional tales about giants and witches. Such metamorphosis is common in nonsense stories. Writing of this genre, Bettina Hurlimann has stated,

> The time-honoured rules which govern [fairy tales] are frequently broken, for there are no rules in nonsense, which exists in a no-man's land between the fairy-tale world and the real one. . . . There is a clear distinction in the nature of the characters taking part, those in the nonsense books being individual conceptions and not stock types as in the fairy story." ("Fantasy and Reality" in *Three Centuries of Children's Books*, 76).

Roald Dahl's creations are certainly individualistic, and Quentin Blake captures this individuality in his illustrations.

ILLUSTRATING FABLES

Besides working with contemporary nonsense writers, illustrators have tackled fables, nursery rhymes, and tall tales with hilarious results. Randolph Caldecott and Edward Gorey have given us two very good examples of the power of illustration to enliven well-known classics. In *Some of Aesop's Fables with Modern Instances Shewn in Designs* (1883), Caldecott presented both conventional and highly inventive illustrations for twenty of Aesop's fables. For each fable there are one or more illustrations depicting the animals and situations found in the original fable and an accompanying illustration which relates the fable to some nineteenth-century human situation. For example, for "The Dog and the Wolf" (the story in which the wolf initially envies the dog's sleekness but comes to pity it for having to wear a collar), Caldecott draws a contented bachelor, lounging on a bench before his pint, blissfully smoking a pipe whose wreath of smoke encircles a picture of a young man dancing dutifully at a formal ball, while a seated middle-aged husband nods in sad-faced sleep beside his stout-figured chaperone wife (*The Caldecott Aesop*, 26–27). For "The Fox and the Stork" (in which the stork repays the fox's stingy trick of offering the long-billed bird liquid in a shallow dish by offering the fox a long narrow jug to eat from), Caldecott parallels this by having a maiden lady send to a hunting gentleman *Harvey's Meditations Among the Tombs* in vengeful exchange for the hunter's gift to her of a sporting magazine (42–43). Seven of Caldecott's illustrated fables were included in a late Victorian edition of Charles H. Bennett's Aesop. Bennett's pictures also "Translated into Human Nature" the meaning of the fables, but by the clothing of the characters (who keep their animal forms) and by the settings and the props used. For example, Bennett illustrates "The Hare and the Tortoise" by showing a portly and prosperously dressed tortoise stepping out of a guildhall entrance and over the reclining form of a disgruntled hare, whose trousers and coat are patched and whose crumpled top hat is filled with rolls of paper marked "PLAN" and "INVENTION" (50–51). More recently, Edward Gorey's spritely illustrations of *Lions and Lobsters and Foxes and Frogs*, Ennis Rees's retelling of some Aesop fables, reawaken the sly humor that underlies these tales with a moral.

Illustrating Nursery Rhymes

Nursery rhymes have been a perennial source of nonsense illustrations. The Baring-Goulds' *Annotated Mother Goose* has selections of these that include anonymous woodcuts, and pictures by Kate Greenaway, Walter Crane, Randolph Caldecott, Arthur Rackham, and Maxfield Parrish. Not all of these stress the nonsense elements, and neither do some current renditions of Mother Goose in pictures. Many popular editions contain illustrations that are simply brightly colored and innocuous. Nursery rhymes do, however, inspire visual nonsense. Nicola Bayley's and Wallace Tripp's illustrations for such verse are two recent examples of the numerous available editions that contribute to the nonsense tradition of nursery rhymes. At first glance, the illustrations in *Nicola Bayley's Book of Nursery Rhymes* seem merely brightly colored and based on early nineteen-century picture book scenes. A closer look shows elements of exaggeration—Doctor Foster's "puddle" floods all of Gloucester (n.p.)—and parody—the double-page spread for "As I was going to St. Ives" derives from William Dyce's nineteenth-century painting of the sea and cliffs, "Pegwell Bay,

Kent, A Recollection of October 5th, 1858," the scene in Bayley's version swarming with cats and kittens. Bayley also uses accumulated detail to create a contrast between action and scene. In the picture for "Three Blind Mice" the cosy warm tones of the old-fashioned, elaborately equipped kitchen serve to set off the cold gleam of the knife as the farmer's wife, one hand still on the tail of a fish on her cutting board, reaches her other knife-wielding hand below the table where the helpless blind mice flounder on the table's leg brace. There is a determined, murderous gleam in the wife's eye. Stare at this illustration long enough and the seemingly simple little rhyme that inspired it will divide and subdivide into multiple and contradictory meanings.

Wallace Tripp's book of nursery rhymes *Granfa' Grig Had a Pig* includes nonsense elements in the illustrations beyond those found in the verses. He has transformed even human characters in the rhymes into animals, and, using the cartoon device of speech in a balloon, provided an additional layer of humor with the characters' comments. For example, his Dr. Foster is an elephant and the double-page spread shows the elephant doctor in a waist-deep puddle with other animals working with ropes, pulley, and lever to dislodge him. It is still raining hard (water pours from his hat) as an animal nurse tells him, "Sir Richard is feeling much better, so you can run along home now" (14–15). The elephant's expression accurately reveals his feelings about this turn of events. In "Hickory, Dickory Dock" the mouse runs down a ladder from the clock tower holding his ears and saying, "Wooeee! Talk about loud!" while a pigeon responds, "Just be glad you weren't up there at noon" (24).

Nicola Bayley and Wallace Tripp are only two of many modern illustrators who have tried to capture the spirited nonsense of nursery rhymes. Each generation reinterprets these verses, sometimes by actually rewriting them, but more frequently by seeing them anew through the eyes of illustrators. In this century Mother Goose has had no difficulty moving out into space, as Frederick Winsor's *Space Child's Mother Goose* proves. After all, long before the astronaut set foot there, her man in the moon had made the reverse trip to earth, and her "old woman toss'd in a blanket / Seventeen times as high as the moon" went, broom under arm, "To sweep the cobwebs from the sky" (Baring-Goulds, 50).

ILLUSTRATING TALL TALES

Like the nursery rhymes, tall tales have been a source of inspiration for writers and illustrators, the former with their retellings and the latter with their transformations of words into imaginative, singular images.

The exaggerations of tall tales especially lend themselves to absurd illustrations. Steven Kellogg, for instance, has taken the tall tales of Paul Bunyan and Pecos Bill and given them special treatment, his visual exaggerations matching the far-fetched texts. Kellogg already had many devoted fans of his earlier books with their often nonsensical situations; American tall tales was a natural area for him to explore.

In his *Paul Bunyan* the fun starts immediately with a sign on the endpapers announcing Paul's birth: "weight: 156 pounds." Then Paul is shown as a super-baby, uprooting trees and causing various calamities, many of which Kellogg has added to his pictures although they are not delineated in the text. There is an especially fine double-page spread depicting the damage caused when Paul rocks in his cradle in the harbor. The townspeople are reacting by carrying signs that read, "Imprison the Giant Brat" and "Send the Beast to England," etc. (n.p.). Kellogg improves upon the already absurd exaggerations that are recounted in the tales. For example, in one tale, Paul's enormous flapjack griddle is greased by having kitchen helpers skate around with slabs of bacon lashed to their feet. Kellogg's double-page illustration shows the helpers playing hockey on their bacon-skates, with a big cheering section behind them and other workers in the background mixing the milk and the flapjack flour. In *Pecos Bill*, Kellogg continues in the same vein, using elaborate and exuberant double-page spreads that match his tongue-in-cheek retelling of this popular tall tale. Pecos Bill is a Texan-born cowboy who is raised by coyotes and capable of such feats as killing a giant rattlesnake and "a critter that was part grizzly, part puma, part gorilla, and part tarantula" (n.p.).

Paul Bunyan and Pecos Bill are mythical figures who have existed only in the stories told of them. However, some American tall-tale heroes like Davy Crockett, Johnny Appleseed, and John Henry actually existed and were a source for the legends that grew up around them about their endurance and strength. We tend to claim the tall tale for this side of the Atlantic, but the genre goes far back in European and Middle Eastern tradition. Homer's Odysseus is something of a tall-tale hero. Sinbad the Sailor, whose adventures are recounted in the *Arabian Nights*, definitely is. In 1785 a small collection of the extraordinary adventures of Baron Munchausen, written by the German author Rudolph Erich Raspe, appeared. Two hundred years later the baron's exploits are still bringing laughter to readers. They are currently available in English in retellings by Adrian Mitchell that are deftly illustrated by Patrick Benson.

There was a real Baron Munchausen, said to have been displeased by the boasting fictional namesake that Raspe created. The fictional baron, however, is not like some of the triumphant folk heroes of the American

From *The Baron Rides Out* by Adrian Mitchell, illustrated by Patrick Benson.

tall tale. He relies more on bravado than brawn, his adventures have much more literary underpinning, and boast he does—so outrageously that his statements go beyond what Mark Twain called "stretchers" and must be classed as self-contradictory, bold-faced lies. But on the title page of *The Baron Rides Out* the adventures are purported to be the truth, as sworn by Captain Sinbad, Lemuel Gulliver, Aladdin, and Pinocchio.

Baron Munchausen's proclivity for making outlandish claims seems to be catching because the title page also reads, "With pictures drawn on horseback by Patrick Benson" and in two subsequent books, *The Baron on the Island of Cheese* and *The Baron All at Sea*, the claim for the illustrations is that they have been "drawn in the belly of a whale" or "drawn under water." The title pages again contain statements that undercut the claim for veracity: "I would like to state that every word of these adventures is true, or I'm a Dutchman. . . . [signed] Hans Brinker, Amsterdam" (*Island of Cheese*) and "Do you, reader, doubt my word? You do? Well, name your weapon. I will meet you for a duel at the south gate of the Garden of Eden next February 31st" (*At Sea*).

The absurd exaggerations continue in the text and are marvelously captured in Benson's ink and watercolor illustrations. In *The Baron Rides Out*, for example, when, during a battle in which the baron, leading the armies of Tsar Peter the Great, routs the Turks, his horse, Never You Mind, is cut in two, Benson's illustration shows water pouring out of the severed horse while it drinks. The baron simply sews him together again. Except for an inordinate thirst the horse is as good as new. In fact, a preposterous but beneficial side effect to this miracle operation makes Never You Mind better than new. The stitching was done with laurel shoots which eventually grow into a tree that provides the baron with shade as he rides. Benson has drawn birds flying from the tree (one is on the baron's hat) and a camel eating the laurel leaves. The baron sits astride Never You Mind, nonchalantly holding a many-scooped ice-cream cone.

In *The Baron on the Island of Cheese*, one illustration depicts the island's odd inhabitants. Slightly larger than Lilliputians, they have no bodies but merely heads, long legs and short arms. Other peculiarities on the island are a bird's nest with 504 eggs, "each of them as large as eight beer barrels," and a stag with a cherry tree growing from its head (it had been shot with a cherry stone). The first is reminiscent of Sinbad's encounter with the Roc. The second, with its blending of the animal and vegetable kingdoms, seems to be one of Raspe's favored forms of nonsense. Benson captures the spirit of these and other absurdities in this and in the latest book *The Baron All at Sea*. Here, his depiction of "a forty-leven-storey hotel upon wheels, which comfortably housed the Choir of One Thousand, together with Queen Mab's servants" and whose weight "was somewhat relieved by a pair of large balloons," is a wonderful flight of fancy in itself, taking up most of two pages. Benson the illustrator and Mitchell the translator prove to be a perfect team for bringing the baron's exploits to a twentieth-century, English-speaking audience.

Other writers and illustrators have found tall tales to be fertile ground for imaginative growth. Among them are Alvin Schwartz (already discussed), Adrien Stoutenburg, James Cloyd Bowman, and Glen Rounds. One author-illustrator, James Stevenson, has modernized the tall tale both in content and graphic format. In his Grandpa books (*Grandpa's Great City Tour: An Alphabet*, *The Great Big Especially Beautiful Easter Egg*, *What's Under My Bed?*, *Worse Than Willy*, *No Friends*, *There's Nothing to Do*, *Will You Please Feed Our Cat?*, and *Could Be Worse!*), Stevenson's lively watercolor illustrations in comic-book style with speech balloons and plenty of sound words in oversized, often brightly colored letters (CRASH!, WHEEEEE!, KLUNK!, etc) accompany the wild exuberance and exaggeration of the text. When, for instance, Grandpa recounts how two bullies used his brother Wainey for a football, turning him literally into a bouncing baby boy, the comic-book style is the perfect form for giving a visual rendition of the verbal joke. One running joke in the illustrations is that as Grandpa tells Mary Ann and Louie all these whoppers about his childhood and youth, he and Wainey are always, even as infants and children, shown with their moustaches. The story of the enormous Easter egg, a variation on a traditional tall-tale motif, gives Stevenson as artist the additional advantage of bright colors to work with. Stevenson is a good example of that total nonsense vision that delights in both verbal and visual exaggeration. His dual talents have produced a vivacious series of modern tall tales. However, in both writing and illustrating his tall tales, he is an exception in this particular subgenre.

It is evident that literary works of nonsense have attracted a wide range of illustrators who are able to catch the spirit of this genre whether the writing is contemporary or traditional. The fact that so many illustrators have been successful in envisioning and portraying nonsense written by others suggests that this humorous perspective is readily shared by people with a certain bent of mind and that it can be expressed with facility through both words and pictures.

THE ARTIST-AUDIENCE CONNECTION

Another possible division when discussing nonsense illustration is by audience: adult, child, or both. The nonsense art of the surreal paintings of Salvador Dali, some political cartoons, and some of Charles Addams's and Edward Gorey's work is mainly adult. On the other hand, much of the artwork of Ellen Raskin, Steve Kellogg, Shel Silverstein (to name only a few prime examples) seems to be primarily for children. A third type of nonsense illustration is that which appeals to both audiences, having both widely accessible visual humor and a sophistication of concept or a richness of reference that presupposes a knowledgeable person as viewer. This last category has produced an abundant selection of nonsense illustration.

Although the picture book is almost universally regarded as a genre for young children, more and more artists are revealing that such a belief may be misguided since pictures, like words, can tell many tales to a variety of audiences. As Roger Duvoisin stated in "Children's Book Illustration: The Pleasures and Problems," "The modern picture book, with its large pages, its wealtlh of color made possible by modern processes of reproduction, is a tempting invitation to the artist to play with his brush and pen" (178). Because of this, some very sophisticated artwork can be found in picture books. Furthermore, while young children can see a literal tale unfold before their eyes, older children and adults may discover symbolism, puns, satire, and other nuances in the same illustrations and stories. Many illustrators have thus reached out to a dual audience in their picture books, especially in those containing nonsense, which, by its very nature, requires a double vision. Nonsense authors also employ irony, satire, and parody, all of which require a rather large store of knowledge for their appreciation. Pictures as well as text can have many referential layers and promote the understanding of complex allusions, an understanding that gives pleasure to both adults and children.

VISUAL FEASTS FOR THE WHOLE FAMILY

Pictures and text produced mainly for children but with appeal for adults are not new. In the Alice books Lewis Carroll and his illustrator John Tenniel both included material beyond the ken of a young child. Tenniel, for example, inserted some caricatures of the prime ministers Disraeli and Gladstone in the guise of Looking-Glass characters. Both Caldecott and Bennett have political and social references in their illustrations for Aesop's fables. In fact an artist can get away with more referential material in a work for children than the writer can. This is because a picture is more immediately accessible than a written text. A child can, for instance, laugh at the silly objects, characters, or antics in a drawing even while missing the added dimension of historical or literary allusions, whereas a similar allusion in writing would of necessity include words outside the child's vocabulary and could cause more puzzlement than amusement.

The practice of slipping allusions into illustrations continues today. Such allusions may or may not have a close connection with the text. Mitsumasa Anno's journey books, which rely almost totally on the pictures (some have no words at all), contain references to adult works and famous landmarks as well as references to classic children's books. An author-illustrator like Maurice Sendak has a different ratio of text and illustration. Only occasionally, as in the center pages of *Where the Wild Things Are*, does he let the picture take over entirely. However, he too makes many of his allusions pictorially rather than verbally. How many children would recognize that it is Mozart who is sitting, playing a musical instrument in the cottage that Ida passes while carrying her rescued sister home (*Outside Over There*, n.p.)? A child can recognize the visual references to kitchen implements and packaged goods that make up the city skyline for *In the Night Kitchen*, but how many children will realize that the bakers are portraits of Oliver Hardy of the Laurel and Hardy comedy team who made movies two generations ago?

Two Illustrators who seem to be quite deliberate in aiming elements in their pictures at both adults and children are Wallace Tripp and Graham Oakley. In Wallace Tripp's anthology *Marguerite, Go Wash Your Feet*, recognizable, famous characters and speech balloons filled with puns and jokes (many of them old chestnuts) add a zany quality to the already humorous collection. The illustration for the limerick "There was a young bugler named Breen" features General Grant commenting, "I know only two tunes. One of them is 'Yankee Doodle,' and the other isn't" (11). In the background stand Laurel and Hardy with food on their bayonets. Most of Tripp's illustrations feature amusing animal characters dressed as people, but where actual people are depicted, many are recognizable. The limerick about the "wonderful family called Stein" (16) depicts Einstein, Epstein (the sculptor), and Gertrude Stein. The Gertrude in the illustration is writing, "'Rose is arose and tows of her toes is pigeons alas so the point of the joint is in from the shin and woofer and tweeter have outsung St. Peter.' Is that clear, Jake?" (16). This is an extremely clever and complex parody of Stein's work. Jake is modelling a head out of clay while Einstein plays his violin, a slate with his workings on MC² on the floor at his feet. Only a well educated person—child or adult—will recognize all the allusions in this illustration.

Some of Tripp's pictorial allusions are, however, intended for a juvenile audience. Emily Dickinson's poem "I'm nobody! Who are you?" is accompanied by a lavish, double-page spread full of "somebodies": Pinocchio, Robinson Crusoe, Charlie Chaplin, Struwwelpeter, the Gingerbread Boy, Alice, Humpty Dumpty, Goldilocks and the littlest bear, the four friends from *The Wind in the Willows*, Dorothy and her three companions from *The Wizard of Oz*, and others (28–29). A child who loves to read would recognize the majority of these.

Drawing for the Child's Visual World of Reference

James Marshall has some visual jokes that allude specifically to a popular type of children's picture book. In the Stupids series, which he illustrated for author Harry Allard, Marshall places mislabeled pictures on the walls. In *The Stupids Step Out*, the mislabelings include "Flower" under the picture of an evergreen (5), followed in the next illustration by "TREE" as designation for a blue, rose-like flower. Separate pictures of a bird and a fish are labelled "DOG" (9, 21). In *The Stupids Die*, this last is reversed and a picture of a dog has "FISH" written under it (27). This same book also has pictures of a bird labelled "BUS" (11), beach balls called "THE PYRAMIDS" (31), a bucket of water named "LAKE STUPID" (9), and two appearances of an oval-framed picture of a butterfly, labelled "COW" (19). *The Stupids Have a Ball* has equally ridiculous misnomers and one specific literary reference: a picture of a single red and white ball is labelled "THE BUTTERFLIES' BALL" (27). The book also includes a large landscape of a flat plot of grass inscribed "MOUNT STUPID" (7), an apple labelled "TOAD" (15) and a tulip labelled "FROG" (23). This humor may be a bit simple for adults, but what a delight it must be for children just old enough to be bored by the many, many picture books that have been prosaically insisting that an apple is an apple, that the small brown animal that wags its tail and barks is a dog, and the one with green eyes and whiskers that says "meow" is a cat. Illustrators of nonsense literature for children have not hesitated to try the traditions of satire and topical allusion, and the pictures they have produced are all the richer for it.

The Picture-Text Connection

Considering the various possible relationships between text and picture in nonsense books also produces insights. As with all illustrations, nonsense ones can follow the text closely and add to the pleasure gained from story or poem rather than to its meaning. John Tenniel's drawings for the Alice books fall into this category, as do some of Lear's illustrations for his limericks and David McPhail's detailed black and white, fine-line illustrations for Nancy Willard's *Sailing to Cythera*. In other cases, the illustrations can create additional areas of humor and absurdity. Many nursery rhyme illustrations and other complex pictures like those by Graham Oakley are good examples of how verbal nonsense can be enhanced by nonsense pictures. Sometimes the picture is absolutely essential in creating the nonsense. For instance, Crockett Johnson's Harold books, in which the boy draws the scenes of which he is a part, would be incomprehensible as text alone.

One final way in which text and illustration can interact in a nonsense work is by disjunction. A sensible, even a somber picture can be made ridiculous by its attendant commentary (portraits of famous people or reproductions of famous artworks accompanied by highly inappropriate descriptions or identifications are examples, as are James Marshall's similar mislabelings of wall pictures). L. Leslie Brooke, in his illustration for "This Little Pig Went to Market," includes a framed picture of a pigsty with sow and piglets and the words "There's no place like home" (*Ring o' Roses*, n.p.), showing that while both text and picture may be quite ordinary by themselves, bringing them together can create an incongruity that disrupts sense.

A very interesting combination of text and illustration occurs in *Rain Makes Applesauce*. This Caldecott Honor Book, written by Julian Scheer and illustrated by Marvin Bileck, was also selected as one of the ten best illustrated books of 1964 by the *New York Times*. Taken alone, the text would appear to be completely nonsensical. The book's title, along with "Oh you're just talking silly talk" is used as a refrain. For example: "The stars are made of lemon juice and rain makes applesauce / I wear my shoes inside out and rain makes applesauce" (n.p.) or "Candy tastes like soap soap soap and rain makes applesauce Oh you're just talking silly talk." Although the extraordinary illustrations are full of all sorts of details and oddities, which at first glance appear to be nonsensical as well, a closer scrutiny reveals sense among the nonsense. The entire process of making applesauce is depicted. We see two children buy seeds, dig a hole, watch the tree grow to a fully laden tree, gather the apples and cart them home, pare and core the fruit, mix it with spices and sugar, and cook it until it is ready. This perfectly sane sequence moves sedately on page by page, afloat on the droll refrain, and arrives at the "Sea of Applesauce," a busy, final picture that is a visual feast.

Scheer and Bileck's collaboration reveals that one of the ways to create incongruities is by having text and illustration deliberately contradict each other; in this instance a nonsense text has illustrations that depict a sensible series of events. Similarly, a sensible narrative may be undermined by absurd or surreal pictures. Anthony Browne's illustrations for

Annalena McAfee's *The Visitors Who Came to Stay* and his own *Piggybook* (which will both be discussed in the next chapter) are examples of contradictions between sober statements and surreal pictures.

Connections between illustration and text are related closely to artists' use of detail. Therefore, let us turn to an examination of the techniques that illustrators employ to convey a nonsense vision in a graphic medium.

Aesop. *The Caldecott Aesop*. Illus. Randolph Caldecott. New York: Doubleday, 1978; facsimile rpt. from 1883.

———. *Aesop's Fables*. Illus. Charles H. Bennett. London: Bracken Books, 1986; rpt. from original edition.

———. *Lions and Lobsters and Foxes and Frogs* (retold by Ennis Rees). Illus. Edward Gorey. Reading, MA: Addison- Wesley, 1971.

Baring-Gould, William S. and Ceil Baring-Gould. *The Annotated Mother Goose*. New York: Times Publishing, 1972.

Bayley, Nicola. *Nicola Bayley's Book of Nursery Rhymes*. London: Jonathan Cape, 1975; rpt. 1977.

Chast, R. Cover illustration. *The New Yorker*, June 1, 1987.

Ciardi, John. *The Man Who Sang the Sillies*. Illus. Edward Gorey. New York and Philadelphia: Lippincott, 1961.

———. *The Monster Den: Or Look What Happened at My House— and to It*. Illus. Edward Gorey. New York and Philadelphia: Lippincott, 1963.

———. *You Read to Me, I'll Read to You*. Illus. Edward Gorey. New York and Philadelphia: Lippincott, 1962.

Carroll, Lewis. *The Annotated Alice: Alice's Adventures in Wonderland & Through the Looking Glass*. Ed. John Gardner. Illus. John Tenniel. New York: World, 1963; rpt. 1972.

Dahl, Roald. *The BFG*. Illus. Quentin Blake. New York: Farrar, 1982.

———. *Charlie and the Chocolate Factory*. Illus. Joseph Schindelman. New York: Knopf, 1964.

———. *The Giraffe and the Pelly and Me*. New York: Farrar, 1985.

———. *The Witches*. Illus. Quentin Blake. New York: Farrar, 1983.

Duvoisin, Roger. "Children's Book Illustration: The Pleasures and Problems." In *Only Connect: Readings on Children's Literature*. Eds. Egoff, Stubbs, and Ashley. New York: Oxford UP, 1980. 357–74.

Gorey, Edward. *Amphigorey: Fifteen Books by Edward Gorey*. New York: Putnam, 1972; Perigee/Putnam, 1981.

Hoffmann, Heinrich. *Struwwelpeter*. 1847. First English edition, London: Blackie and Son, 1903. London: Pan Books, 1972.

Hurlimann, Bettina. "Fantasy and Reality: Nonsense from *Peter Pan* to *Pippi Longstocking*." In *Three Centuries of Children's Books in Europe*. Trans. and ed. Brian W. Alderson. London: Oxford UP, 1967.

Kellogg, Steven, auth. and illus. *Paul Bunyan*. New York: Morrow, 1984.

———. *Pecos Bill*. New York: Morrow, 1986.

Krauss, Ruth. *A Hole Is to Dig: A First Book of First Definitions*. Illus. Maurice Sendak. New York: Harper, 1952. Rpt. Bodley, 1976.

Lear, Edward. *The Complete Nonsense of Edward Lear*. Ed. Holbrook Jackson. New York: Dover, 1951.

———. *The Courtship of the Yonghy-Bonghy-Bo & The New Vestments*. Illus. Kevin Maddison. New York: Viking, 1980.

———. *The Scroobious Pip* (completed by Ogden Nash). Illus. Nancy Ekholm Burkert. New York: Harper, 1968; rpt. 1987.

Marshall, James. *The Stupids Die*. Author Harry Allard. Boston: Houghton, 1981.

———. *The Stupids Have a Ball*. Boston: Houghton, 1978.

———. *The Stupids Step Out*. Boston: Houghton, 1974.

Noble, Trinka Hakes. *The Day Jimmy's Boa Ate the Wash*. Illus. Steven Kellogg. New York: Dial, 1980.

———. *Jimmy's Boa Bounces Back*. Illus. Steven Kellogg. New York: Dial, 1984.

Parrott, E.O., ed. *The Penguin Book of Limericks*. Illus. Robin Jacques. New York: Viking/Penguin, 1986.

Raspe, Rudolph Erich. *The Baron All at Sea*. Retold by Adrian Mitchell. Illus. Patrick Benson. New York: Philomel, 1987.

———. *The Baron on the Island of Cheese*. Retold by Adrian Mitchell. Illus. Patrick Benson. New York: Philomel, 1986.

———. *The Baron Rides Out*. Retold by Adrian Mitchell. Illus. Patrick Benson. New York: Philomel, 1985.

Scheer, Julian. *Rain Makes Applesauce*. Illus. Marvin Bileck. New York: Holiday House, 1964.

Sendak, Maurice. *In the Night Kitchen*. New York: Harper, 1970.

———. *Outside Over There*. New York: Harper, 1981.

———. *Where the Wild Things Are*. New York: Harper, 1963; rpt. Scholastic, 1969.

Stevenson, James, auth. and Illus. *Could Be Worse!* New York: Morrow/Mulberry, 1987.

———. *Grandpa's Great City Tour: An Alphabet Book*. New York: Greenwillow, 1983.

———. *The Great Big Especially Beautiful Easter Egg* New York: Greenwillow, 1983.

———. *No Friends*. New York: Greenwillow, 1986.

———. *There's Nothing to Do!* New York: Greenwillow, 1986.

———. *What's Under My Bed!* New York: Greenwillow, 1983.

———. *Will You Please Feed Our Cat?* New York: Greenwillow, 1987.

———. *Worse Than Willy!* New York: Greenwillow, 1984.

Tripp, Wallace, ed. and illus. *Granfa' Grig Had a Pig and Other Rhymes Without Reason from Mother Goose*. Boston: Little, Brown, 1976.

———. *Marguerite, Go Wash Your Feet*. Boston: Houghton, 1985.

Weiss, Renee Karol. *A Paper Zoo: A Collection Animal Poems by Modern American Poets*. Illus. Ellen Raskin. New York: Macmillan, 1968; rpt. 1987.

Whalen-Levitt, Peggy. "Picture Play in Children's Books: A Celebration of Visual Awareness." *Jump Over the Moon: Selected Professional Readings.*" Eds. Pamela P. Barron and Jennifer Q. Burley. New York: Holt, 1984. 167–74.

Yolen, Jane. *How Beastly! A Menagerie of Nonsense Poems*. Illus. James Marshall. New York and Cleveland: William Collins, 1980.

13

In one wordless picture book for small children a mouse eats around a piece of paper, creating a window through which we can see a farm, and then folds the paper into a plane on which it sails down to the wheatfields. The appeal of this silent narrative lies undoubtedly in the leap from one symbolic system to another.

Margaret Higonnet, "Narrative Fractures and Fragments" in Children's Literature *15: 41*

Techniques of Nonsense Illustration

Visual nonsense shares many elements and techniques with verbal nonsense. Both use exaggeration and peculiar mixtures to create a surrealistic effect. In some cases the immediacy of a graphic representation heightens the humor and makes the nonsense more obvious. We often laugh more heartily at a silly sight than at a silly sentence. Also, nonsense strongly depends on internal contradictions, and when these contradictions can be seen at one glance of the eye rather than gathered sequentially from a text, the disparity hits the reader/viewer with more force. Pictures can be more effective than words in conveying other aspects of nonsense. The possibility of infinite regression, so central to nonsense and so difficult to explain verbally, can be shown rather simply by drawing a picture within a picture within a picture ad infinitum. Tricks of perspective can create an effect similar to that achieved by folding a triptych mirror into such an angle that your reflection repeats itself to a vanishing point.

Nonsense illustration is, of course, simply a subcategory that comes under much the same rubric as any other type of illustration. The range of graphic media and styles is not limited by the nonsense vision. By and large, the relationship between text and illustration is similar whether the pictures are realistic or nonsensical. There are some ways, however, by which nonsense illustration distinguishes itself from other types. One important exception occurs when picture and words deliberately undercut each other, as happens in Scheer's *Rain Makes Applesauce*. Another element found mainly within the province of humor and nonsense illustration is the use of words in the pictures, a crossing of visual/verbal boundaries.

EXAGGERATION

Exaggeration and distortion are key techniques that nonsense illustrations share with nonsense texts. Clothing, actions, expressions, and movement are pictured in hyperbolic forms; people and animals are caricatured; perspective or proportions are skewed. Numerous examples of exaggeration in nonsense illustrations have already been given, especially in conjunction with those drawn for tall tales. The depiction of nonsense beasts also calls for exaggerations and distortions of normal animal traits. Numerous other examples could be cited of the pictorial extremes which result from an artist's nonsense vision, but a few will suffice to make the point.

Shel Silverstein, for instance, draws "Twistable Turnable Squeezeable Pullable / Stretchable Foldable Man" (*A Light in the Attic*, 138), more pretzeled in on himself than any human contortionist could ever be. And when Jack Prelutsky writes of the fate of Herbert Glerbert who dissolves into "a puddle thing, a gooey pile" (*Queen of Eene*, 20), illustrator Victoria Chess draws a fat, gluttonous, checker-shirted young man who melts like candlewax onto the floor (21). Even the chaise-lounge on which Herbert is napping loses its contours somewhat. Such pictorial exaggeration makes the expression "glob of fat" seem quite literal. In fact illustrations can often reveal word-for-word misinterpretations much more easily than a verbal explanation can. Take, for one more example, Kellogg's rendering of "Mrs. Rosebud's wig flew off'" (*Jimmy's Boa Bounces Back*, n.p.). Meggie is relating the story to Jimmy, and a "thought balloon" (signalled by that ingenious short-cut symbol of bubbles from the forehead) pictures Jimmy imagining a blonde wig with white angel wings flapping off the head of an unaware Mrs. Rosebud. Obviously, graphic representations of the extremes that result from nonsensical conjectures can be very effective.

From Japan comes a very different kind of exaggeration and illustration. Mitsumasa Anno, already mentioned for his *Topsy-Turvies* and journey books, also wrote *The King's Flower* in which "there once was a king who had to have everything bigger and better than anyone else" (4). The illustrations show outsized furniture, dining utensils, toothbrush and the like, dwarfing the people and creating absurd situations. However, when the king tries to grow the biggest flower and gets only a small red tulip, its beauty makes him realize that "perhaps biggest is not best after all" (29). In his afterword Anno reveals the inspiration for the book:

> One day, when I was looking at a gas storage tank, I wondered what it would be like if there was a coffee cup as large as one of those big containers. I imagined myself climbing up a tall ladder and creeping along the edge on my hands and knees, lapping up the coffee, and I felt almost dizzy. (30)

As a result, Anno begins to imagine all sorts of huge things, but with his imaginings comes the recognition "that each flower, each worm, is natural and indispensable" (30). He ends his story by having the king observe that "not even I could make the biggest flower in the world. And perhaps that is just as well" (29). This rejection of hyperbole and exaggeration may seem to be anti-nonsense, but actually Anno is showing how such distortions can lead us back to a more sane interpretation of the world around us. Nonsense proceeds to sense by indirection.

The grotesque landscapes and creatures in the world of Dr. Seuss result from a more direct form of exaggeration. Not even Hieronymous Bosch drew as many strange habitats and peculiar inhabitants as Seuss has. We have commented on the lessons in language Seuss conveys as author, and Leo Schneidermann, in his essay on the psychological benefits of nonsense, noted that Dr. Seuss's plots challenge the child to take risks and move out into life. Seuss's drawings suggest a similar message. As illustrator, he pictures a teetering universe, which is nevertheless strangely safe for the young protagonists who wander through it. Seuss's soaring flights of visual fancy result in precarious, free-standing stairways, bridges with high, narrow arches, and other fragile-appearing labyrinthine constructions. His creatures and artifacts are often the most unlikely conglomeration of characteristics. There are no ears too weird, no necks too long, no contraptions too complex for the pages of Seuss's books. Elizabeth Segel and Joan Friedberg, in their essay "From Mulberry Street to Stethoscope Row: Fifty Years of Dr. Seuss," hold that Seuss's "vigorous, innovative style of illustration draws his audience into his world, delighting them with wild wackiness" (14). His pictures are among the more

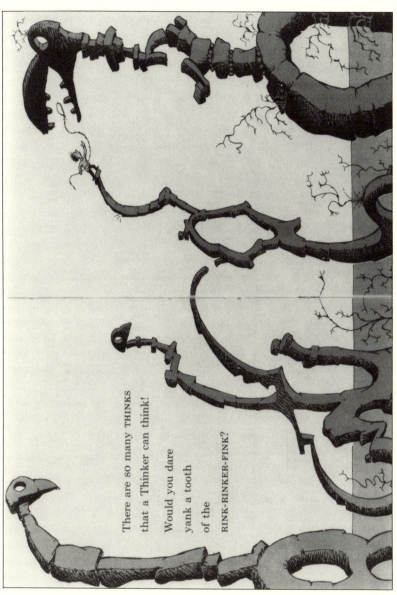

There are so many THINKS
that a Thinker can think!

Would you dare
yank a tooth
of the
RINK-RINKER-FINK?

From *Oh, the Thinks You Can Think!*, written and illustrated by Dr. Seuss.

idiosyncratic and effective illustrations for children's books, and they give us a visual subuniverse where obedience to everyday laws of anatomy, architecture, and gravity have been set aside in favor of the rule of nonsense.

Odd Assortments

In addition to exaggeration, nonsense illustrations share with verbal nonsense the technique of juxtaposing incongruous objects. James Marshall straps a chicken to Aunt Dottie's head (*The Stupids Have a Ball*, n.p.); Steven Kellogg draws a beribboned poodle floating paws up in a punch bowl (Noble, *Jimmy's Boa Bounces Back*, n.p.); Edward Lear creates a jutting black beard, large enough and bushy enough to house the "Two Owls and a Hen, four Larks and a Wren" that his limerick enumerates (*Complete Nonsense*, 3). An attempt to catalog the numerous instances of crazy combinations in nonsense illustrations could reach encyclopedic length. We challenge the reader to look through a book with nonsense illustrations and not find an instance of ridiculous juxtaposition, such as the strange conglomeration of packages, kitchen utensils, and tools that make up the skyline of Sendak's *In the Night Kitchen*. Then there are the humorous collections that result from such categories as "Things That Can Tickle You," "Things You See on the Ground," and "Things That Make So Much Noise You Can't Hear Yourself Think" (Stiles and Wilcox n.p.), all of which Grover the Muppet encounters in *Grover and the Everything in the Whole Wide World Museum*. Creating absurdities simply by grouping disparate objects or features together is a major element in nonsense illustration.

Nonsense in the General Context of Illustration

Graphic renditions of exaggerations and incongruous groupings are usually within the the province of humor and nonsense. Illustrations for nonsense literature also share many traits with illustrations of other kinds. In a recent article in *The Five Owls*, Uri Shulevitz enumerates three ways in which illustrations can function: (1) as an unessential enhancement of the text, (2) an extension of the text that can "stretch the action of the story," and (3) as a necessary clarification of the text ("What Is a Picture Book?," 51). He holds that we have a true picture book only when the illustrations are necessary to our understanding of the action. He goes on to say, "But there are degrees of understanding, and it is this factor that will determine whether the book is a straight storybook or a combined picture book/storybook" (51).

A great many illustrations for nonsense literature, delightful as their artwork may be, are indeed mainly a decoration and do little or nothing to change the reader's interpretation. Take, for example, Kate Greenaway's charming drawings for nursery rhymes, which convey a vision of childhood rather than of humor and nonsense. Other nonsense illustrations do interpret the text in ways that influence the reader's appreciation of it. Some of Edward Gorey's illustrations for his own and others' work are good instances of this. Sometimes the illustrations carry all or most of the nonsense. Mitsumasa Anno's wordless book *Topsy-Turvies: Pictures to Stretch the Imagination*, in which the laws of physics and space are twisted and turned inside out or upside down is an example. Another is Ellen Raskin's *Twenty-two, Twenty-Three*, in which the piled up antics of the various nonsensically clothed animals, "the dove with gloves on his feet" (7), "gibbons in ribbons" (8), are only minimally conveyed by a text that has been pushed to the edge of the pages by the robust illustrations.

Three works by Gorey (all reprinted in *Amphigorey*) provide a good spectrum of the ways in which nonsense pictures can merely influence the text or consume it entirely. In *The Doubtful Guest* the verse gives much information about the peculiar creature who arrives unexpectedly and during its seventeen-year stay does such things as stand "with its nose to the wall," eat "part of a plate," and hide in the soup tureen. The guest is not described, however, and, without the illustrations, we could hardly guess that it looks like a cross between a seal, a penguin, and a morose crow. In Gorey's *The Sinking Spell* the illustrations are more essential for whatever meaning can be derived. In this story, the "guest," though stared at by the puzzled members of the household, is never visible, and it is the reaction of the other characters, who are simply referred to as "we" and not mentioned specifically in the text, that sets the tone. The reader only learns of the various locations of the whatever-it-is as it sinks. After "It's gone beneath the cellar floor," the last line, "We shall not see it any more," is especially nonsensical as the reader has never seen it at all. Finally, in Gorey's nonsense ghost story *The West Wing*, a somewhat absurd eeriness is conveyed wordlessly by floating objects (a candle, a shadow, sheets), an earthquake-like crack in a carpeted floor, a water-filled room, and various strange inhabitants. No one of these possible connections between text and picture is intrinsically better than the others, but, for purposes of trying to discover what constitutes a nonsense illustration, the approaches that involve strong interaction with the text may yield the most interesting answers.

NONSENSE AND GRAPHIC TECHNIQUES

Certainly no particular medium or graphic technique seems to be best for creating nonsense illustrations. They range from very simple line drawings to elaborate, full-color paintings. Comparing the work of Crockett Johnson and Henrik Drescher reveals how two very different artistic styles can use the same nonsense device. In both books, the craziness of the plots comes directly from the illustrations, the characters being led through a series of developments as a result of what appears in the pictures as the story progresses. Both are clear examples of what Shulevitz means by a true picture book.

Johnson's Harold books move the boy from crisis to crisis as a result of what he draws with his purple crayon (a dragon, an ocean, mountain, lion, etc. in *Harold and the Purple Crayon* and *Harold's Circus*). The books are small in format, the pages bare of illustration except for Harold and what he draws. This simplicity and the fact that Harold is drawn with the same serious, deadpan expression on almost every page tends to make the reader giggle. (Some adults will recognize his similarity to old-time film comic, Buster Keaton.) In *A Picture for Harold's Room*, Johnson uses the purple crayon to reveal the relation between nonsense and common sense. Harold draws himself into a village, where, by a trick of perspective (the broad path narrowing to nothing at the horizon) he is a giant in relation to his surroundings. This heady experience then diminishes as Harold draws an ever-widening railroad track back the other way and, he grows proportionately smaller until he realizes that his drawing of an enormous bird and flower "is only a picture" and "he took his crayon and he crossed it out" (54–55). Safely back in his room, Harold draws another picture, this one framed and thus contained, carefully delimited, and distinguished as art, not reality. But in these self-creating illustrations, Johnson has meshed the two worlds.

Henrik Drescher's *Simon's Book* uses a similar device—a story that draws itself—but his illustrations are more elaborate than Johnson's. Drescher's book begins with a young boy working at a drawing board. When the boy falls asleep, the pens and ink come alive to help the drawn character, Simon, escape from the scary monster he has been left with on the page. What follows is a rollicking adventure as the snake-like pens and the ink bottle do their best to help, but to no avail: the monster catches Simon, and then, to everyone's surprise, gives him a big kiss. "When they arrived at the last page, the pens drew a soft, warm bed and cover, using the last drop of ink" (n.p.). Simon and his new friend go to bed, the pens retreat to their jars to sleep, and the next morning the real boy awakens to find his book completely finished, "And that is the same book you've just finished reading."

Drescher's illustrations are far more complex than Johnson's, whose simplicity is used to delineate the nonce worlds Harold creates. The only color in the Johnson books is the purple in the line drawings Harold makes. Johnson's pages are clear and uncluttered, and Harold has a charming, childlike simplicity, creating, for instance, a picnic supper of nine different pies, sampling each, then drawing animals to finish the feast. Drescher's illustrations, in contrast, are in full color with many extraneous scribbles, some even outside of the margins. His colors are bright, but there is also a darkness underneath, which gives the child reader a feeling of trepidation and excitement. Some of the scratchings are of creatures and people, shapes, an occasional word. Drescher's margins seem to be created for creatures to walk on, lean through from the outside, or break out of from inside. All of these factors combine in zany, exuberant illustrations for the child to delight in and puzzle and shiver over. In contrast, Harold holds his purple crayon firmly, in control of the strange settings he creates; Drescher's protagonist is more subject to outside forces, existing in a world where neither boundaries nor expectations hold firm. The two sets of illustrations reinforce these differences. They share, however, a means of creating a picture world where the child can explore relationships and problems and then come safely back to a home reality. Johnson's and Drescher's shared technique of having a character or implement already within the illustration produce further pictures is an ingenious method of crossing boundaries between reality and art and of creating a visual paradox, a chicken and egg puzzle about what precedes what.

CROSSING VISUAL-VERBAL BOUNDARIES

A similar technique that nonsense illustrators employ is that of crossing the boundary between writing and drawing. They sometimes insert pictures into the text. The rebus is a formalized example of this. They also use words in the pictures to create humor and nonsense. James Marshall's mislabellings and speech balloons are examples that we have already mentioned. Some illustrators go further and concoct a mad mixture of visual and verbal puns and other jokes. Wallace Tripp and Graham Oakley are masters at this latter technique (which overlaps with their practice of inserting references to famous persons, paintings, or pieces of literature or music). Tripp, for example, in his illustration for Beasley's poem about Noah and the ark, has drawn a tiny ark with a

A hedge between,
Keeps friendship green.

From *Granfa' Grig Had a Pig*, compiled and illustrated by Wallace Tripp.

speech balloon coming from it that reads: "Now I herd everything" (*Marguerite, Go Wash Your Feet*, 9). Although this and some of the puns in Tripp's *Granfa' Grigg Had a Pig*, such as the king's comment about the splattered Humpty Dumpty, "Is this someone's idea of a yolk?" (30) or the Yankee Doodle cat saying "spaghetti" instead of "macaroni'" (74), are accessible to younger children, many are for older children and adults. Accompanying "An Apple a Day," for example, is a drawing of a rabbit throwing an apple at Dr. Duck and saying, "Scram, you quack! You hippocratic oaf!" (23). There are some referential puns: the room of Old King Cole contains busts and paintings of famous animal musicians such as J.S. Bark, Giacomo Pooch, and Clawed Depussey. For two boating rhymes, one illustration has a direct classical reference—"Argonaut" for the bowl of the "Three Wise Men of Gotham" (91)—but the tub in "Rub-a-dub dub" is called "Quiet Desperation" (92), a joke that requires both a knowledge of Thoreau and of the many problems involved in handling small craft in order to be appreciated. These jokes and puns in the illustrations add another level of combined visual-verbal nonsense to the original verses.

Graham Oakley is an author-illustrator whose text and pictures are both heavily laden with puns and satire. He seems unable to resist using these forms of humor in either medium. Oakley has definite ideas about picture books: "What I want to do is to use as few descriptive passages as possible, to show almost everything in the pictures. . . . I think it is the artist's duty to cram in as much as possible" (quoted in Duvoisin 165). Anyone familiar with Oakley's work knows that it is in the extraordinarily rich and complicated illustrations that children and adults alike can find tidbits to chuckle over. A recent book of his, *Henry's Quest*, employs puns, mixes incongruous elements together, and casually crosses time boundaries. The book's opening illustrations show a curious mixture of the Arthurian age and contemporary artifacts, which are used for other than their original purpose. Twentieth-century cars have become hen houses and resting places for pigs. A television set now serves as a rabbit cage. Oakley is also partial to puns and satiric historical references in his illustrations. When Henry enters the evil city, he sees advertising for some of Shakespeare's plays, including "King Leer." A nightclub is named "Caligula's," and included in the large portraits on the walls of the emperor's palace are Al Capone, Attila, and Hitler.

In this futuristic fantasy the only surviving books are a collection of fairy tales and *King Arthur and the Knights of the Round Table*, which so fascinates the newly crowned king that he changes his name to King Arthur II, and his subjects become caught up in the mania for chivalry and knightly derring-do, albeit somewhat strangely mounted and accoutred. The illustrations for a joust feature one opponent on a bicycle and chased by dogs. Another knight is about to be thrown by his cowmount. The wielded shields carry an array of crests, including baked goods, a high-topped shoe with tools crossed behind it, and a mortar and pestle (in other words, these knights errant are tradesmen of various sorts). Buckets and football helmets, among other types, serve as headgear for the fighters. The royal coat-of-arms has a car on the shield. The clothing too reflects a variety of styles and periods. Hats range from the tall, pointed cones ladies wore in King Arthur's day to straw hats and derbies. The queen's crown-topped snood sits on the shoulders of her housedress as she clutches a pocketbook. This strange, nonsensical juxtaposition of old and new in the illustrations sets the tone of the book.

Earlier Oakley wrote a series of "Church Mice" books, beginning with *The Church Mouse*, which explains how the mice and Sampson the cat get to stay in the church. In this book, as in the others that follow, Oakley places signboards in his illustrations for an added dimension, especially for his adult audience. Although children might enjoy such jokes as the "Cuddles" nametag on the collar of a ferocious-looking dog, they might regard as gibberish the scientific terminology that lists all the ingredients of a can of tomato puree as chemicals.

The church setting offers Oakley the chance to use wall memorials for his humor, and he makes the most of the opportunity. One of them reads, "In Memory of / Admiral Sir Horatio Flounder / . . . / Drowned in the Municipal / Boating Pond on / Trafalgar Day 1892 / R.I.P." (n.p.). The memorial also contains a series of letter abbreviations after the Admiral's name, among them, Q.E.D. and R.S.V.P., perpaps Oakley's way of commenting on modern mania for abbreviations and acronyms as well as on the British love for titles.

The second book in the series is *The Church Cat Abroad*, and again signs are abundant. The ocean liner on which Sampson and two mice travel to the South Seas is the *Plummet*, a name which, like Tripp's *Quiet Desperation*, is not likely to inspire confidence. The following book, *The Church Mice and the Moon*, pokes fun at scientists, especially those involved in space explorations. Here, Oakley enjoys himself thoroughly with signs, labels, book titles, and the like. For example, one sign reads: "WOMUMP Astronaut Training Department / Special One Day Course" (n.p.). In the laboratory a complicated-looking piece of equipment is labeled "The Whizzo Encephalograph / Mark II Economy Model / 1934 / Chung Ho Novelties Ltd. / Hong Kong." Among the books the two mice are supposed to read before supper are "Calculus in 2073 Easy Stages," "The Story of Relativity Without Tears," and "Spacecraft Piloting for Beginners." Food labels become another source of satiric and punning silliness.

From *The Church Mice and the Moon*, written and illustrated by Graham Oakley.

The two scientists toast themselves with cooking sherry "Bottled by Hartburn Insecticides Limited." They eat cornflakes, "The Breakfast with the Farmyard Smell." The cornflakes box boasts of a "Great Offer / Send Only / 1500 Packets / Tops Plus / 50p for / FREE / Plastic / Shoe Horn."

Oakley's *The Church Mice at Christmas* contains new, humorous signs and labels. One shopping bag reads "W.M. Binge & Son Ltd. / Wine & Spirits"; it is located on High Street. More grimly, inside a toy shop, one wall advertises "Mayhem Toys Ltd. / Real Replicas." Displayed are rocket launchers, tanks, all kinds of guns, and three games: one features an atomic warhead; the second is "Mega Deth / A New Game for the Whole Family," and the third, "Axeman," is an assassination game. Oakley's humor connects with that of schoolchildren who delight in parodying brand names (as Geller noted) and with the dark comedy of the theater of the absurd. He is also working the same territory that Dr. Seuss covers in *The Butter Battle Book*.

SURREALISM IN NONSENSE ILLUSTRATION

Surrealistic elements are perhaps more common in nonsense illustrations than they are in nonsense texts. For instance, in an Arnold Lobel limerick and its illustration we have both an echo of Carroll's mad tea party and a parody of Dali's painting of drooping timepieces:

> There was an old pig with a clock
> Who experienced anguish and shock,
> For he greased it with butter,
> Which cause it to sputter
> And drowned both its tick and its tock.
>
> (*Pigericks*, 25)

The illustration is in two frames. The first frame shows a perfectly normal-looking grandfather clock (rather stunted, but erect); in the second, the clock is bent over, its hand and clapper laden with butter, and it is in obvious distress.

Jack Prelutsky's Aunt Samantha, complacent about the "middle-sized rhinocerous" (*Queen of Eene*, 24) that has appeared on her head, would not, as pictured by Victoria Chess, seem out of place if she wandered through the set of a Beckett play. And in Sendak's *Outside Over There*, the sunflowers that grow and burgeon through one window while the scene seen through another changes from picture to picture add surrealistic details not found in the text.

The Disjunction of Picture and Text in Nonsense Illustration

As many of the examples given prove, nonsense illustration is often not confined to the text it accompanies. In fact, one strange use of illustration may well fall entirely within the range of what can be defined as nonsense. This is the practice of creating pictures that contradict or undercut the text. One early, classic example of this is Dr. Seuss's *And to Think That I Saw It on Mulberry Street*, in which the increasingly extravagant scenarios of the illustrations belie the prosaic account the son gives his father of the trek home from school. Ellen Raskin also lets the illustrations carry the nonsense and excitement in her tongue-in-cheek *Nothing Ever Happens on My Block* in which Chester Filbert sits on a curb and gives a first-person account of how dreary and uninteresting life is on his block, while behind him an astonishing array of activities occurs. In her *Franklin Stein*, Raskin uses a similar construction. The text is almost deadpan serious while the illustrations show a monstrosity being built as the family begins to miss a variety of objects (potato masher, tie, mop, plumber's helper, etc.) The resulting creation is dubbed Fred and ultimately wins a contest for "most unusual pet." When Franklin meets a friend, he decides that Fred needs one too, so he and his new friend go to the butcher's for "1 heart 2 lungs 2 kidneys." This is typical Raskin humor and both an interesting parody of Mary Shelley's novel *Frankenstein* and a good example of the kind of nonsense that contemporary children find amusing. The illustrations are essential for conveying that nonsense.

One of the most extreme cases of this yoking together of contradictory pictures and story occurs in the individual and collaborative works of British author/illustrator Anthony Browne. In *Piggybook*, which he both wrote and illustrated, he has combined a straightforward, realistic text with initially sane and sensible illustrations that evolve into humorously nonsensical ones. Although his vocabulary is carefully selected to contribute to the effect of the changing illustrations, it is the latter that carry the main weight of mood and meaning. The Piggott family is introduced as a fairly typical twentieth-century human family: a father, two sons, and a beleagured mother who does all of the work in the house in addition to working outside of the home. One day she leaves. Her note tells her family, "YOU ARE PIGS" (n.p.). As days pass and she does not return, the house comes to resembles a pigsty, and the pictures reveal that father and sons are actually turning into pigs.

The paintings begin realistically enough with a normal-looking, smiling father and sons shown before a typical house with a typical car in the garage. But pictorial hints of the departure from reality come quickly. On the second page (a double spread) both boys have their mouths wide open

From *Piggybook*, written and illustrated by Anthony Browne.

as they call to their mother to hurry with their breakfast, while in the newspaper their father is reading there is a picture of a gorilla with an identical, open-mouthed expression. (Browne is also the author of *Gorilla*, and at least one such animal can be found in the illustrations of most of his books.) More significantly for *Piggybook*, the cereal boxes on the table feature pictures of pigs. When Mr. Piggott and the boys return at the dinner hour, their mouths (including Mr. Piggott's) are again shown wide open, and the surrealism has increased. Mr. Piggott's shadow on the wall is a pig's head. The illustrations in the newspaper are now entirely of pigs, and the boutonniere he is wearing has a pig's face.

On the following page an over-sized close-up of Mr. Piggott at the table (from the end of his nose to half of his full plate) discloses that his vest has buttons with pigs' faces on them. The next few pages' illustrations also reveal the sharp contrast between the male Piggotts's lifestyle and that of the mother.

Four drably colored squares that depict her at various chores contrast sharply with the facing, brightly colored picture of the father at the dinner table. The contrast is reemphasized when another bright, double-page spread shows the males lazily watching television.

After Mrs. Piggott leaves, the visual references to pigs increase markedly. The doorknobs, outlets, wallpaper design, pictures, vases, erasers, fireplace decorations, clock, salt and pepper shakers, and other household objects acquire the faces of pigs. Even the moon now has a porcine visage, and the dog's nose has become a snout. Most surrealistic of all, the males' hands have become pigs' feet and their heads become pig heads and remain that way until Mrs. Piggott returns. Browne's increasingly piggish word choices ("grunted," "snuffled," "root around") accentuate the visual transformations, which culminate in a picture showing the three on their pigsfoot "hands" and knees, directly facing the reader.

Mrs. Piggott returns, and they beg her to stay. When she does, it is to a reformed family that now helps with the household tasks. All the pigs disappear from the illustrations, and the three males regain their human forms. The reader finally gets to see Mrs. Piggott with bright clothing and a smiling face. This typical modern tale showing the influence of the feminist movement seems, in its text, perfectly realistic. That illusion is quickly dispelled, however, by the illustrations, which have carried the implications in the phrase "male chauvinist pig" to a vivid conclusion.

In *The Visitors Who Came to Stay*, written by Annalena McAfee and illustrated by Browne, sense in the text is again juxtaposed with nonsense illustrations. There is, in fact, an even greater disparity between the two than that found in *Piggybook*, where multiple pictures of pigs create a running joke on a single theme. In *The Visitors* Browne uses a wide range of humorous surrealistic images to reveal the anger and psychological upset of the young girl in this sedately narrated story. The plot is perfectly logical, one that could be listed under a "Modern Problem" heading. A young girl, Katy, lives happily with her father (her parents are divorced) until Mary and her son Sean come to visit. Katy does not like Sean at all because of the tricks he plays on her. The visits increase, and eventually Sean and Mary move in. Katy becomes upset, finally voicing her feelings to her father, and the next day the visitors are gone. Gradually Katy realizes how much Mary and Sean have enriched their lives, and she suggests that they visit Sean and Mary. On the story level, the book seems a simple, realistic one about a girl who comes to realize that the visitors she thought were a nuisance were good company after all, a reaction reminiscent of Robert's in John Steptoe's *Stevie*.

The illustrations are another matter entirely. Hints of the unusual appear on the front cover, the most obvious one the giraffe's head appearing above the horizon at sea. A closer look reveals that the top of one of the railing posts is a teapot, that a woman is wearing a plate of food on her head, and that, although she is in a sleeveless dress, one of the figures on the beach is bundled into a heavy coat, boots, and winter scarf. The effect of the cover is tantalizing: what will the book have to offer?

The title page with Katy holding her teddy bear seems ordinary except for the teddy bear's eyes and mouth which look human and have a surprised expression. The picture book begins quite realistically with Katy and her dad shown in a snapshot and then watching television together, and then in a normal breakfast scene. The scene at a train station portrays the first decisive break with reality. As Katy and her father wait for the train, the view on their side of an overpass is of trees barren of leaves and a wintry gray sky. The sky through the overpass archway, however, is a bright, sunny blue, and the trees are fully in leaf. On the following page Mary and Sean appear for their first visit, and the departure from pictorial realism is even more apparent. In a wall picture of a train engine, the smoke comes out past the frame. The chair in the room is suspended above the floor, and the bookcase-cabinet is filled with such oddities as flying loaves of French bread, a tiny person asleep on one of the shelves, window and sky scenes instead of wood panels, flying seagulls, and a wine bottle that tapers into a carrot. The teddy bear held by Katy again has human eyes and mouth, now with an expression of fear.

Surrealism, and the escape from the literal that it implies, becomes full-blown in a double-page merry-go-round scene. Two flags flying above are supposedly British and American, but the colors are rearranged; a third flag is black with a white skull and crossbones; the fourth is a polka-dotted pair of men's undershorts. More nonsense appears in the portrayals of the carousel riders, an unlikely lot: the Lone Ranger, carrying bananas for guns; a businessman reading a newspaper while sitting on a toilet seat, his derby hat topped with a seagull; a very fat woman in green high heels, carrying an alligator instead of a purse and riding a horse that also sports green high heels. Other objects being ridden are also unusual. There is a rooster and a creature with a rhino's head in front, an elephant's trunk behind, and the body and legs of a horse. The colors and designs of all the animal bodies are lavish and ornate.

After Mary and Sean have moved in with Katy and her dad, Sean's tricks turn up in the illustrations. In one the father has apparently put Sean's trick sugar in his coffee, for it is foaming. Katy's shoelace is tied to something. More grotesquely, a monster's hand with warts and a real nail in place of a fingernail and a variety of other prank gimmicks (false eyeballs, fake snake, spider, mouse, fried egg, etc.) are scattered about the second breakfast scene, which presents a startling contrast to the earlier uncluttered and realistic one. In addition to Sean's silly objects, the seagull has reappeared, now wearing dark glasses, and the cereal boxes bear the satiric names "Corny Flakes" and "Dry Old Bones."

The narrative continues realistically, but a beach scene, earlier depicted as deserted except for Katy and her dad, is now transformed into an extravagant surrealistic painting. What were white cliffs have become a finger; the ship from the earlier illustration is now a bus; one seagull has a pig's body; a shark's fin slices through the sand; doffed sunglasses have eyes, a child's sand sculpture is the Empire State Building; a dog urinates, creating a moat around another sand structure; a woman's bare feet have high heels, matching the shoes near them; another pair of shoes ends in toes; Sean holds the top to a woman's bikini, her breasts now covered with two fried eggs; and a boy's snorkel mask has a goldfish swimming around in it. Across from this crowded, surrealistic beach, a pear, an apple, and an orange serenely grace the opposite page.

When the visitors leave, the full-page illustration is appropriately bare, although not yet free of surrealistic elements. The kitchen window frames a seagull with the body of a teddy bear. The curtains move even though the window appears to be closed. Other stark illustrations follow as Katy ponders what now seems to be missing from her life. When she and her father go to visit Sean and Mary, the illustration is again filled with a wealth of nonsense: a man's pipe sticks out of the house's chimney; a penguin is on the roof; one seagull has the body of a fish; a fried egg floats cloud-like; one window contains an upside down vase of flowers; others have slot-machine fruit in them. There are also visual puns, most of them in the yard: a small tree bears apples that form crab bodies (a crabapple

Illustration by Anthony Browne from *The Visitors Who Came to Stay*,
written by Annalena McAfee.

tree); another tree has shoes instead of fruit (a shoe tree); the rubber plant has boots, a tire, and a rubber glove hanging from it; the birdbath is a literal bathtub with one seagull sitting atop the water and the other, wearing a shower cap, stretched out in it; the flower bed is literal too, the tulips growing out of a brass bed. New delightfully daffy details can be found with every fresh look at this and others of the illustrations. To complete the book, the endpaper contains a picture of the teddy bear, now with appropriate button eyes and stitched mouth, but wearing eyeglasses with false nose, bushy eyebrows and moustache attached, one of Sean's speciality items depicted earlier.

Here, then, is a picture book with a remarkable blending of sense and nonsense, of real and surreal. Anyone listening to the story without seeing the illustrations would think it a simple, straightforward, realistic narrative. When Browne's pictures are added, however, so is an entirely new dimension of meaning and a visual banquet of the unusual, the intriguing, the nonsensical. The paintings lift the book from ordinary, modern problem story to being a *pièce de résistance*. Browne and McAfee's collaboration is a fitting finale to this study of nonsense literature and illustration.

Anno, Mitsumasa, auth. and illus. *The King's Flower*. New York: William Collins, 1979.

———. *Topsy Turvies: Pictures to Stretch the Imagination*. New York: Walker-Weatherhill, 1970.

Browne, Anthony, auth. and illus. *Gorilla*. New York: Knopf, 1985.

———. *Piggybook*. New York: Knopf, 1986.

Dr. Seuss. *And to Think That I Saw It on Mulberry Street*. New York: Vanguard, 1936.

———. *The Butter Battle Book*. New York: Random House, 1984.

Drescher, Henrik, auth. and illus. *Simon's Book*. New York: Lothrop, 1983.

Gorey, Edward, auth. and illus. *Amphigorey: Fifteen Books by Edward Gorey*. New York: Putnam, 1972; Perigee/Putnam, 1981.

Higonnet, Margaret R. "Narrative Fractures and Fragments." *Children's Literature* 15 (1987): 37–54.

Johnson, Crockett, auth. and illus. *Harold and the Purple Crayon*. New York: Harper, 1945; rpt. Scholastic, 1973.

———. *A Picture for Harold's Room*. 1960. New York: Scholastic, 1968.

Lear, Edward. *The Complete Nonsense of Edward Lear*. Ed. Holbrook Jackson. New York: Dover, 1951.

Lobel, Arnold. *The Book of Pigericks*. New York: Harper, 1983.

Marshall, James (pseudonym as author: Harry Allard), auth. and illus. *The Stupids Have a Ball*. Boston: Houghton, 1978.

McAfee, Annalena. *The Visitors Who Came to Stay*. Illus. Anthony Browne. New York: Viking/Kestrel, 1984.

Noble, Trina Hakes. *Jimmy's Boa Bounces Back*. Illus. Steven Kellogg. New York: Dial, 1984.

Oakley, Graham. *The Church Cat Abroad*. New York: Atheneum, 1973.

————. *The Church Mice and the Moon*. New York: Atheneum, 1974.

————. *The Church Mice at Christmas*. New York: Atheneum, 1980.

————. *The Church Mouse*. New York: Atheneum, 1972.

————. *Henry's Quest*. New York: Atheneum, 1986.

Prelutsky, Jack. *The Queen of Eene*. Illus. Victoria Chess. New York: Greenwillow, 1987.

Raskin, Ellen, auth. and illus. *Franklin Stein*. New York: Atheneum, 1972.

————. *Nothing Ever Happens on My Block*. New York: Atheneum, 1969.

————. *Twenty-two, Twenty-three*. New York: Atheneum, 1976.

Scheer, Julian. *Rain Makes Applesauce* Illus. Marvin Bileck. New York: Holiday House, 1964.

Segel, Elizabeth and Joan Friedberg. "From Mulberry Street to Stethoscope Row: Fifty Years of Dr. Seuss." *Carnegie Magazine*. 58:6 (Nov.-Dec. 1986): 8–15.

Sendak, Maurice. *In the Night Kitchen*. New York: Harper, 1970.

Shulevitz, Uri. "What Is a Picture Book?" *The Five Owls*. 2:4 (Mar./Apr. 1988): 49–51.

Silverstein, Shel. *A Light in the Attic*. New York: Harper, 1981.

Steptoe, John. *Stevie*. New York: Harper, 1969.

Stiles, Norman and Daniel Wilcox. *Grover and the Everything in the Whole Wide World Museum*. New York: Random/Children's Television Workshop, 1974.

Tripp, Wallace, ed. and illus. *Granfa' Grig Had a Pig and Other Rhymes Without Reason from Mother Goose*. Boston: Little, 1976.

————. *Marguerite, Go Wash Your Feet*. Boston: Houghton, 1985.

Afterword

We have surveyed much of the terrain of nonsense land. In these concluding pages Nancy Willard presents her vision of that land as a garden where a perpetual game of renewal is played. Willard, as most readers interested in children's literature know, is a winner of the Newbery Medal for her book of poems, *A Visit to William Blake's Inn* (Harcourt Brace Jovanovich, 1981). She has also written, among her other books for children, a fantasy trilogy: *Sailing to Cythera: And Other Anatole Stories*, *The Island of the Grass King: The Further Adventures of Anatole*, and *Uncle Terrible*. All four of these books are flavored with nonsense, and so Willard, who also teaches at Vassar College, writes on the subject both as author and literary scholar. Her essay, which is excerpted from a longer version, sums up eloquently many of the points we have stressed throughout this book.

A Lively Last Word on Nonsense

by Nancy Willard

I once had an aunt whom everyone admired as a fountain of good sense, except in matters of travel. She bought tickets to well-known places—Paris, Bermuda, Berlin—but she seemed never to arrive in them, for on her postcards she always wrote of places that could never be found on any map. Portapooka. Pannyfanny Islands. And what she did in these places was a perfect mystery:

> Arrived in Portapooka last night and had a delicious feel of mesh bears. Have taught a new crock to take me up in the morning.

Excerpted from "The Game and the Garden: The Lively Art of Nonsense" from *Angel in the Parlor*, copyright 1983 by Nancy Willard. Reprinted by permission of Harcourt Brace Jovanovich, Inc., pages 258-282.

My mother explained to me that my aunt's secret life in these places was the result of her bad handwriting, and when we'd translated this nonsense we would find out what she'd really been up to.

> Arrived in Puerto Rico last night and had a delicious meal of fresh pears. Have bought a new clock to wake me up in the morning.

I found her nonsense much more entertaining than her sense. How delightful to feel a mesh bear and to travel by crock every morning! Even after the misunderstanding was explained to me, her encounters with crocks and bears seemed quite as real as her purchase of clocks and pears, perhaps because I had already picked up the habit of hiding common sense with nonsense.

. . . .

I especially treasured one postcard from my aunt that no one could ever reduce to sense. The picture showed a formal garden: an elegant maze of shaped hedges, arbors, beds of herbs and flowers. On the reverse side she had scrawled her message:

> You'd love this place. The roaring shillilies san sea whet all and the pappasnippigoo are zooming.

It's right and fitting that a sensible garden and a nonsensical message should be two sides of a single card. Nonsense is both logical and absurd, like the games we play as children. Some years ago I was out walking and found myself treading on a game of hopscotch, chalked out on twelve squares. The last square, which we called "Home" when I played the game, was marked "Heaven" in this one. I am told by those who play this version of hopscotch that it's harder to get into heaven than to go home. You must throw your stone into heaven, jump to the eleventh square, pick up the stone, jump to the spot where it landed, and recite at top speed the alphabet forward and backward, your name, address, and telephone number, your age, and the name of your boyfriend or girlfriend. If I were to tell a clergyman that I got into heaven by throwing a stone into it, he would say, "Nonsense!" In life, yes, but in the game, no. In the game it makes perfect sense. Nonsense too is a game, and a great part of learning to write it is learning to play it.

When I was little and the prospect of reaching heaven seemed closer than it does now, I heard the story of the Minotaur, half man, half bull, whom King Minos kept in a maze and to whom every year the most beautiful young Athenians were sacrificed. I didn't know that when Theseus killed the Minotaur, the Athenians celebrated by drawing the maze on the ground and dancing through it. I didn't know that hopscotch may have come down to us from that custom (Healy, 55, 75). Where else but in children's games and nursery rhymes do the ancient and the modern so amiably link hands?

. . . .

Some fine books [like Susan Stewart's *Nonsense, Aspects of Intertextuality in Folklore and Literature* and Elizabeth Sewell's *The Field of Nonsense*] have been written on the connections between nonsense and play, and I recommend them to you. My task here is much humbler: to look at two of my favorite nonsense writers for children, Lewis Carroll and Edward Lear, and to consider a few of the ways they can teach writers how to start on the downward path to wisdom. It's not the wisdom of Solomon we're after here, but Blake's wise foolishness: "If the fool would persist in his folly he would become wise" (*The Poetry and Prose of William Blake*, Erdman, editor, 36). Perhaps if I ever translate the babble on my aunt's postcard, I'll find her saying that she's having a wonderful time in the Garden of Eden, and the roses are lovely but not as fragrant as the ones in her garden in Detroit. I wish this revelation about the roses would turn out to be true. I wish paradise was all around us and finding it was as easy as recognizing it. I hope Blake is right when he says, "If the doors of perception were cleaned every thing would appear to man as it is, infinite" (39). The proper name of that celestial cleaning person is Faith, but perhaps the nickname for Faith is Nonsense.

. . . .

If you want to play the game of nonsense, the best way to start is by playing with words. Imagine that nonsense is like hopscotch and to reach the first square you must invent twenty-five words, all recognizable as parts of speech. That is, the reader or listener must be able to recognize a verb, and adjective, and so on. To Lear, the gift for playing with language came so easily that it overflows from his poems into his letters. Of the weather he writes, "The day is highly beastly & squondangerlous" and "The views over the harbour are of the most clipfombious and ompsiquillious nature" (*Letters of Edward Lear*, Constance Strachey, editor, 58–59). From his "Nonsense Cookery" you may learn how to make crumbobblious cutlets and an amblongus pie—easy, if you can find an amblongus. And what is an amblongus? Lear never tells. It is not customary for a writer of recipes to stop and define his ingredients; he merely tells you what to do with them. It you invent imaginary things, you must also invent names for them. Lear's long poem "The Quangle Wangle's Hat" introduces a congerie of imaginary creatures so matter-of-factly that you feel in some far corner of the known world they must have always existed.

. . . .

The Pobble, the Attery [venomous] Squash, the Bisky Bat—fantastic creatures all—could I have met them in dreams? Not likely. There's nothing dreamlike about their appearance here. Strict meter and form keep each thing in its place, much as the squares in hopscotch order the moves of the players. None of these images are allowed to run together, the way images do in dreams; they are introduced, one by one, in a stanza that is both a litany and a catalog. Lear writes in conventional forms about unconventional things.

. . . .

If you play by the rules—that is, if you follow the rules of syntax and grammar and if you write in a regular meter and stanza form—you can walk the thin line between chaos and nonsense without a qualm. When Lewis Carroll included "Jabberwocky" in *Through the Looking Glass*, he could scarcely have imagined what James Joyce would borrow and transform in *Finnegan's Wake*. For every unfamiliar word in "Jabberwocky," Carroll has not only a definition but an explanation.

. . . .

Some of Carroll's neologisms are, like Lear's Quangle Wangle, names for things that never were. Having never seen a tove, I take Carroll's word for it that it is something like a badger, a lizard, and a corkscrew, which nests under sundials and lives on cheese. But "slithy" is an invention of a different kind. It means lithe and slimy. It is, we are told, like a portmanteau; there are two meanings packed up into one word. Nonsense was never so clearly taught, I think, as in this passage from Carroll's introduction to *The Hunting of the Snark*:

> . . . take the two words "fuming" and "furious." Make up your mind that you will say both words, but leave it unsettled which you will say first. Now open your mouth and speak. If your thoughts incline ever so little towards "fuming," you will say

"fuming-furious"; if they turn, by even a hair's breadth, towards "furious," you will say "furious-fuming"; but if you have that rarest of gifts, a perfectly balanced mind, you will say "frumious." (*The Complete Illustrated Works of Lewis Carroll* Edward Guiliano, ed., 181)

Playing with words leads to playing on words and a whole range of puns, malapropisms, and intentional misunderstandings. One of the commonest misunderstandings among children—and one that Carroll makes use of—is taking a figure of speech literally. When my son was about five or six, we were finishing our dinner at a restaurant and the waiter glided over to our table and magnanimously announced, "Dessert is on the house." A look of panic came over my son's face. Was that dish of chocolate ice cream worth the danger of scaling Howard Johnson's orange roof? Such logical misunderstandings run through both the Alice books.

. . . .

The inappropriate word as a literary device comes into its own with Edward Lear. We have all heard people misuse words, often choosing not the right word but a word similar to it in sound. A passage from Lear's "The Story of the Four Little Children Who Went Round the World" shows this device in its glory, with a few of Lear's invented words thrown in for good measure:

The Moon was shining slobaciously from the star- bespangled sky, while her light irrigated the smooth and shiny side and wings and backs of the Blue-Bottle- Flies with a peculiar and trivial splendor, while all Nature cheerfully responded to the cerulean and conspicuous circumstances. (*Nonsense Books*, 107–08)

The more high-flown the rhetoric, the greater the incongruity between what the writer seems to say and what he actually says.

When Lewis Carroll uses the wrong but similar-sounding word, he depends on our knowing the right word so that we can enjoy the incongruity, just as we enjoy the parody of a poem more when we know the original. [Examples are the Mock Turtle's lessons in "reeling and writhing" and "branches of arithmetic—Ambition, Distraction, Uglification, and Derision" (*Complete Illustrated Works*, 61)]

. . . .

The secret heart of nonsense is the amiable incongruity. One of the ways I first discovered this was through a game, "Peter Coddle's Trip." The game involves a printed story and a pack of cards on which are named a miscellaneous assortment of things: a yellow nightcap, an insane bedbug, an intoxicated clam, an old hairbrush, a red wig, an elderly porcupine, and so on. The leader reads the story aloud until he comes to a blank. One of the players draws a card and what is written on that card fills the blank and becomes part of the story. The story describes Peter Coddle's trip to New York, and if the player were to draw the cards I have just mentioned, Peter's description of the Statue of Liberty would read as follows:

> Squire Mildew wanted to go down to the Statue of Liberty, which loomed up down the bay like an elderly porcupine. . . . As we came near the statue the hand holding the torch seemed about the size of an old hairbrush. We landed and went up into the head. On the way up we met some people coming down the narrow winding stairs: one of them said it was as close as an intoxicated clam. I thought the lights were no better than a red wig. From the head we had a splendid view. We saw a steamer passing out of the harbor; . . . she was going like an insane bedbug. (*Peter Coddle's Trip*, 5)

[A similar game is called "Mad Libs," currently available in a series of notebooks by Roger Price and Leonard Stern. It requires the player to list a series of words in various parts of speech and then fill in the blanks of the story with the listed words.]

Literary nonsense differs from [such] game[s] . . . in this way: the nonsense writer needs a reason other than chance for linking incongruous things together. He needs an arbitrary convention that will free the words from the categories of everyday use and from our sense of what belongs with what. One of the most useful of these conventions is alliteration. In *Through the Looking Glass*, Alice plays a game that both Carroll and Lear use in their poetry: "I love my love with an H" (*Complete Illustrated Works*, 143).

· ·

Lear builds many of his nonsense alphabets around alliteration, which leads him to some very odd combinations:

The Melodious Meritorious Mouse,

. . . .

The Visibly Vicious Vulture,
who wrote some Verses to a Veal-cutlet in a
Volume bound in Vellum. (*Nonsense Books*, 313, 321)

Students in search of subjects for nonsense can turn to the yellow pages of the telephone directory and read the categories at the top of adjacent pages. In our directory I discovered a Burglar Bus, a Calculating Canvas, Chimney Churches, Cleaning Clergy, Dancing Dentists, Karate Kindergartens, and Musical Nurserymen. Sometimes when I bring nonsense poetry into a class of very sensible people, I say, "For the next hour I am going to ask you to make some changes in your vocabulary. Instead of the word *door*, I want you to use the word *rainbow*. Instead of the verb *to open*, please use the verb *to skin*. For the word *light*, please substitute the word *cat*. And for the verb *to turn on*, use the verb *to hassle*. Remember: the door is the rainbow, to open is to skin, the light is the cat, to turn on is to hassle. Now, in this new language please tell me to open the door and turn on the light." A deep silence follows. And then very slowly, somebody says, "Skin the rainbow and hassle the cat. Please." "Thank you. What else can you say about the door and the light?" "The cat is by the rainbow." "The rainbow is already skinned," adds another student. Though we would sound like lunatics to a visitor, we understand each other. Following the rules of nonsense, we speak a common language.

. . . .

The writer who uses double talk has taken a road that followed far enough, leads to surrealism. It should come as no surprise that when André Breton wrote his pamphlet, *What is Surrealism?* in 1936, he named Lewis Carroll among its patron saints (See Jeffrey Stern in *Lewis Carroll: A Celebration*, 133).

. . . .

Breton recommended automatic writing as a way of bringing to the conscious act of writing the unconscious freedom of dreaming. "Forget about your genius, your talents, and the talents of everyone else. . . . Write quickly, without any preconceived subject, fast enough so that you will not remember what you're writing and be tempted to reread what you have written" (*Manisfestoes of Surrealism*, 29–30). In automatic writing, the freedom of association found in dreams becomes the ability to make connections between remote parts of one's experience. Robert Bly calls this "leaping," and what he says about "leaps" in poetry would have interested Lear and Carroll. "In a great ancient or modern poem, the considerable distance between the associations, the distance the spark has to leap, gives the lines their bottomless feeling, their space . . ." (Bly, *Leaping Poetry: An Idea With Poems and Translations*, 4). Nonsense poetry can set up absolute polarities between associations, creating impossiblities.

. . . .

The White Queen . . . maintained she could believe as many as six impossible things before breakfast. . . . [But] believing the impossible isn't easy. While sitting in the waiting room of a doctor's office recently, I overheard a mother trying to entertain her young daughter with a game in a children's magazine. The game was, How many things can you find wrong in this picture? I could not see the picture, but the conversation had me riveted.

> *Mother*: What do you mean there's nothing wrong with the pic-
> ture? Look at the tree. It's full of carrots.
>
> *Child*: Maybe it's a carrot tree.
>
> *Mother*: You know carrots don't grow on trees. Now, what's wrong
> with the train?
>
> *Child*: Nothing.
>
> *Mother*: You don't see it? The train has wings. Choo-choo trains
> don't have wings.

I felt sure the child knew the right answer, but who among us would not like to see a carrot tree or ride a train with wings? And I thought of the child Stephen in *A Portrait of the Artist as a Young Man*, who muses on red roses and white roses, cream and pink and lavender roses. "But you could not have a green rose," he tells himself, adding wistfully, "But perhaps somewhere in the world you could" (James Joyce, 13).

Perhaps among the roaring shillilies and the pappasnippigoo on my aunt's postcard, a green rose is growing. I've never been to the Garden of Nonsense to see for myself. But one night I dreamed myself in a very different garden, and persisting in my folly, like the fool in Blake's proverb, I woke a little wiser. Since the dream took the shape of a story, let me tell you the story.

Once upon a time at the edge of town grew a garden about which I knew nothing except that some called it the Garden of Reason and I was forbidden to go there. Eve conversing with the serpent was not more curious than I, and I headed straight for the garden the first chance I got. The gatekeeper was a magician, and the gatehouse was his cottage. He let me into the house and told me I must wait to be admitted but I might sit at his table and drink a cup of tea while I waited. This I declined to do, as the table was cluttered with papers and dirty dishes, and I could not find a clean cup. Suddenly a young woman rushed in, clutching a book and pounding the title with her fist: THE LIFE AND DEATH OF SHEILA HOROWITZ.

"Don't tell me this is the way it's got to be!" she shouted. "Tell me there's more to my life than this book!"

The magician folded his hands over his chest, unmoved. If to be admitted I had to accept the magician's version of my life, then I would go back the way I came. But now I saw that the front door had vanished and the only door open to me led into the garden itself. The magician turned his back on me for an instant, and I jumped up and fled through the door.

The garden was as formal as that in my aunt's picture: a maze of hedges, beds of herbs, long walks under wisteria arbors. But hers was empty and this one was full of people. I knew from their clothes that some had come here a long time ago. Those old men in Greek togas— how many hundreds of years had they wandered these paths? That handsome woman in flowered brocade skirts and a farthingale—what was she looking for? Weren't we all looking for the same thing, the way out? Far behind me I could hear the magician beating down bowers and running through rosebeds, shouting, "You have not been admitted! You have not been admitted!" Suddenly I spied two familiar figures ahead of me, Martin and Alice Provensen, who in our waking lives had just finished the illustrations for our book *A Visit to William Blake's Inn*. "If we don't hurry, the magician will catch us," I said. "If we don't look back," said Alice, "the magician won't catch us." A high, smooth wall let us know we had reached the back boundary of the garden; reason has its limits. Against the wall leaned an old ladder, which was not even suitable for apple picking; the rungs were broken. "Let's put our feet where the rungs were," suggested Martin. My common sense said, What nonsense! But my uncommon sense whispered, If a fool persists————.

One by one, under our feet, the rungs healed themselves and grew whole enough to hold us. Now we stood on top of the wall. Facing us was an angel so tall that we brushed the hem of its gown like grasshoppers.

"You are free," said the angel. It pointed over trees and fields, to the far-off world-town we'd started from, sparkling on the horizon. Sunlight slanted from its sleeve, touched down in the world-town. On that broad road of sunlight we slid like children playing, all the way back to the beginning.

Blake, William. *The Poetry and Prose of William Blake*. Ed. David Erdman. Garden City, NY: Doubleday, 1970.

Carroll, Lewis. *The Complete Illustrated Works of Lewis Carroll*. Ed. Edward Guiliano. New York: Avenel, 1926.

Evans, Patricia Healy. *Rimbles: A Book of Children's Classic Games, Rhymes, Songs and Sayings* Garden City, NY: Doubleday, 1961.

Joyce, James. *A Portrait of the Artist as a Young Man*. New York: Viking, 1957.

Lear, Edward. *Letters to Edward Lear*. Ed. Constance Strachey. New York: Duffield, 1907.

———. Nonsense Books. *Boston: Little, 1888*.

"*Peter Coddle's Narrative*." Peter Coddle's Trip. Springfield, MA: Bradley, 1970.

Sewell, Elizabeth. *The Field of Nonsense*. London: Chatto and Windus, 1952.

Stern, Jeffrey. "Lewis Carroll the Surrealist." In *Lewis Carroll: A Celebration*. Ed. Edward Guiliano. New York: Potter, 1982.

Stewart, Susan. *Nonsense, Aspects of Intertextuality in Folklore and Literature*. Baltimore: Johns Hopkins UP, 1979.

Willard, Nancy. *The Island of the Grass King: Further Adventures of Anatole*. New York: Harcourt, 1979.

———. *Sailing to Cythera, and Other Anatole Stories*. New York: Harcourt, 1974.

———. *Uncle Terrible: More Adventures of Anatole*. San Diego: Harcourt, 1982.

———. *A Visit to William Blake's Inn: Poems for Innocent and Experienced Travelers*. San Diego: Harcourt, 1981.

Bibliographies

Cockatooca Superba

Primary Sources

Note: Includes all works cited and a selected list of additional works that contain nonsense for children. When possible, we note current editions. Most of these books are, however, available in the children's section of libraries, even if out of print.

When the title is not self-explanatory, the code given below indicates the type of book. When a series of books by the same author are similar, only the first entry listed is annotated. Those noted (X) are discussed in this book; see the Index under the author's name.

Code:
123 = Counting Book
ABC = Alphabet Book
C = Comic Strip/Cartoon
F = Fiction
G = Games
J = Jokes
R = Riddles
TT = Tall Tale
V = Verse
WP = Wordplay
X = See index.

Adams, Pam. *There was an Old Lady Who Swallowed a Fly*. New York: Grosset, 1975. (V)

————. *This Old Man*. New York: Grosset, 1975.

Addams, Charles. *Addams and Evil*. New York: Simon, 1974. (C/X)

————. *The Charles Addams Mother Goose*. New York: Windmill Books, 1967.

————. *Black Maria*. New York: Simon, 1960. (X)

————. *Homebodies*. New York: Simon and Schuster, 1954. (X)

Adler, David A. *The Dinosaur Princess and Other Prehistoric Riddles*. Illus. Loreen Leedy. New York: Holiday House, 1988.

Adoff, Arnold. *The Cabbages Are Chasing The Rabbits*. Illus. Janet Stevens. San Diego and New York: Harcourt, 1985. (X)

————. *Outside-Inside Poems*. Illus. John Steptoe. Wooster, OH: Lathrop, 1981.

Aesop. *Aesop's Fables*. Illus. Charles H. Bennett. With additional fables illus. by Randolph Caldecott. London: Bracken, 1986; facs. of 19th century edition. (X)

————. *Aesop's Fables*. Retold by Blanch Winter. New York: Airmont, 1965. (X)

————. *The Caldecott Aesop*. Intro. Michael Patrick Hearn. Illus. Randolph Caldecott. Garden City, NY: Doubleday, 1978; 1st edition, London: Macmillan, 1883. (X)

————. *Lions & Lobsters & Foxes & Frogs: Fables from Aesop*. Retold by Ennis Rees. Illus. Edward Gorey. Reading, MA: Young Scott Books/ Addison-Wesley, 1971. (X)

Aiken, Conrad Potter. *A Little Who's Zoo of Mild Animals*. Illus. John Vernon Lord. New York: Atheneum, 1977.

Albee, Edward. *Tiny Alice: A Play*. New York: Atheneum, 1965. (X)

————. *Who's Afraid of Virginia Woolf*. New York: Atheneum, 1963. (X)

Alderson, Brian, ed. *The Helen Oxenbury Nursery Rhyme Book*. Illus. Helen Oxenbury. New York: Morrow, 1987. (X)

Allen, Jonathan, ed. *A Bad Case of Animal Nonsense: Featuring the Animal Alphabet, Poems, I Know an Old Lady, Rhyming Animals*. Boston: Godine, 1981.

Amerey, Heather. *The Alphabet Book*. Illus. Colin King. London: Usborne, 1979. (X)

Andersen, Hans Christian. *The Complete Fairy Tales and Stories*. Trans. Erik C. Haugaard. Garden City, NY: Anchor/ Doubleday, 1983. (X)

Anno, Mitsumasa. *Anno's Alphabet: An Adventure in Imagination*. New York: Crowell, 1975. (X)

————. *The King's Flower*. New York: William Collins Pubs., 1979. (X)

————. *Topsy Turvies: Pictures to Stretch the Imagination*. New York: Walker-Weatherhill, 1970. (X)

Anno, Mitsumasa and Masaichiro Anno. *Anno's Magical ABC: An Anamorphic Alphabet*. New York: Philomel/Putnam, 1981.

Anthony, Edward. *Oddity Land*. Illus. Erik Blegvad. New York: Doubleday, 1957.

Aristophanes. *The Wasps, The Poet and the Women, The Frogs*. Trans. David Barrett. Baltimore: Penguin, 1970. (X)

Asch, Frank. *Gia and the One Hundred Dollars Worth of Bubblegum*. New York: McGraw, 1974. (F)

————. *MacGoose's Grocery*. Illus. James Marshall. New York: Dial, 1978.

————. *Yellow, Yellow*. Illus. Mark Alan Stumaty. New York: McGraw-Hill, 1971. (F)

Baring-Gould, Sabine. *A Book of Nursery Songs and Rhymes*. London: Methuen, 1895.

Baring-Gould, William S. and Ceil Baring-Gould. *The Annotated Mother Goose*. New York: World, 1972. (X)

Barrett, Judi. *Cloudy With a Chance of Meatballs*. Illus. Ron Barrett. New York: Scholastic, 1978. (X)

Barry, Katharina, auth. and illus. *A Is for Anything: An ABC Book of Pictures and Rhymes*. New York: Harcourt, 1961.

Barton, Bryon, auth. and illus. *Applebet Story* New York: Viking, 1973. (ABC)

Baum, L. Frank. *The Emerald City of Oz*. Chicago: Rand, 1972; rpt. from Chicago: Reilly & Britton, 1910.

————. *Dorothy and The Wizard of Oz*. Chicago: Reilly and Lee, 1908. (X)

————. *The Marvellous Land of Oz*. Illus. John R. Neill. Intro. by Martin Gardner. New York: Dover, 1969. Rpt. from Chicago: Reilly & Britton, 1904. (X)

————. *Ozma of Oz*. Illus. John R. Neill. New York: Dover, 1985; rpt. from Chicago: Reilly & Burton, 1907. (X)

————. *The Road to Oz*. Chicago: Rand, 1971; rpt. from Reilly & Burton, 1909. (X)

————. *The Wizard of Oz*. Illus. W. W. Denslow. Chicago: Rand, 1956; rpt. from G. M. Hill, 1900. (X)

Bayer, Jane. *A My Name is Alice*. Illus. Steven Kellogg. New York: Dial, 1984. (ABC)

Bayley, Nicola. *As I Was Going Up and Down*. New York: Macmillan, 1986. (V)

————. *Nicola Bayley's Book of Nursery Rhymes*. London: Jonathan Cape, 1975; rpt. 1977. (X)

Beckett, Samuel. *Endgame*. New York: Grove, 1958. (X)

————. *Poems in English*. New York: Grove, 1961. (X)

————. *Waiting for Godot*. New York: Grove 1954. (X)

Beisner, Monika. *Monika Beisner's Book of Riddles*. New York: Farrar, 1983.

————. *Secret Spells & Curious Charms*. New York: Farrar, 1985.

Belloc, Hilaire. *The Bad Child's Book of Beasts*. London: Alden, 1896. New York: Knopf, 1965. (V/X)

————. *Cautionary Tales for Children*. London: Everleigh Nash, 1908. (V)

————. *Cautionary Verses: Collected Humorous Poems*. Illus. B.T.B. [Basil T. Blackwell] and Nicolas Bentley. London: Duckworth, 1940. New York: Knopf, 1951. (X)

————. *Matilda Who Told Lies and Was Burned to Death*. Illus. Steven Kellogg. New York: Dial, 1970. (V)

————. *New Cautionary Tales*. London: Duckworth, 1930.

————. *A Moral Alphabet: In Words of from One to Seven Syllables*. Illus. Basil T. Blackwood. London: E. Arnold, 1899. London: Duckworth, 1973. Chelmsford, England: Tindal Press, 1974.

————. *More Beasts for Worse Children*. London: E. Arnold, 1897. New York: Knopf, 1966. (V/X)

————. *The Yak, the Python, the Frog*. Illus. Steve Kellogg. New York: Parents Magazine Press, 1975.

Benjamin, Alan. *1000 Inventions*. Illus. Sal Murdocca. New York: Four Winds, 1980.

————. *1000 Space Monsters (Have Landed)*. Illus. Sal Murdocca. New York: Four Winds, 1980.

————. *Ribtickle Town*. Illus. Ann Schweninger. New York: Four Winds, 1983.

Bennet, Jill, ed. *A Packet of Poems*. Illus. Paddy Mounter. New York: Oxford UP, 1987.

Berenstain, Stanley and Janice Berenstain. *The Big Honey Hunt*. New York: Beginner/Random, 1962.

Bernstein, Joanne and Paul Cohen. *Creepy, Crawly Critter Riddles*. Illus. Rosekrans Hoffman. Niles, IL: Robert Whitman, 1986.

————. *Un-Frog-Gettable Riddles*. Illus. Alexandra Wallner. Niles, IL: Robert Whitman, 1986.

Berson, Harold. *Barrels to the Moon* New York: Putnam/Coward, 1982.

Bishop, Ann. *A Riddle-iculous Rid-alphabet Book*. Illus. Jerry Warshaw. Chicago: Whitmore, 1979.

Blair, Walter. *Tall Tale America: A Legendary History of Our Humorous Heroes*. Illus. Glen Rounds. New York: Coward, 1944.

Blake, William. *The Poetry and Prose of William Blake*. Ed. David Erdman. Garden City, NY: Doubleday, 1970.

Bodeker, N.M., author and illus. *Hurry, Hurry, Mary Dear! and Other Nonsense Poems*. New York: Atheneum, 1976.

———. *It's Raining Said John John Twaining: Danish Nursery Rhymes*. New York: Atheneum, 1973. (X)

———. *Let's Marry Said the Cherry And Other Nonsense Poems*. New York: Atheneum, 1974. (X)

Bonini, Marinella. *I Can Be the Alphabet*. New York: Viking, 1987.

Bowman, James Cloyd. *Mike Fink*. Illus. Leonard Everett Fisher. Boston: Little, 1957. (TT)

———. *Pecos Bill*. Illus. Laura Bannon. Niles, IL: Whitman, 1937. (TT, X)

Brandreth, Gyles. *The Puzzle Mountain*. Harmondworth, Middlesex, England: Penguin, 1981. London: Treasure Press, 1986. (WP)

———. *Word Games*. New York: Harper, 1986. (X)

Brown, Margaret Wise. *The Fish with the Deep Sea Smile: Stories and Poems for Reading to Young Children*. Illus. Roberta Rauch. Hamden, CT: Linnet Books, 1988; rpt. from Dutton, 1938, 1966.

———. *Goodnight Moon*. Illus. Clement Hurd. New York: Harper 1947; rpt. 1975. (X)

———. *Wonderful Storybook: 25 Stories and Poems*. Illus. J.P. Miller. New York and Racine, WI: Golden/Western, 1948; rpt. 1984.

Browne, Anthony, auth. and illus. *Gorilla*. New York: Knopf, 1985. (X)

———. *Piggybook*. New York: Knopf, 1986. (X)

Burningham, John. *John Patrick Norman McHennessy—the boy who was always late*. New York: Crown, 1988. (F)

Cameron, Polly, auth. and illus. *"I can't," said the ant: A Second Book of Nonsense*. New York: Coward, 1961. (V)

Camus, Albert. *The Rebel*. Trans. Anthony Bower. Harmondsworth Middlesex, England: Penguin, 1971. (X)

Carroll, Lewis. *The Annotated Alice: Alice's Adventures in Wonderland & Through the Looking Glass*. Annotator, Martin Gardner. New York: World, 1972. (X)

———. *The Complete Illustrated Works of Lewis Carroll*. Ed. Edward Guiliano. New York: Avenel, 1926. (X)

———. *The Complete Works of Lewis Carroll*. New York: Random, 1976. (X)

———. *The Hunting of the Snark*. Illus. Kelly Oechsli. New York: Pantheon, 1966.

———. *The Selected Letters of Lewis Carroll*. Ed. Morton N. Cohen. New York: Pantheon, 1982. (X)

Casterline, H. E., ed. *Jabberwocky and Other Nonsense Verses*. Illus. Jean Chandler. New York and Racine, WI: Golden/Western, 1986.

Causley, Charles. *As I Went Down Zig Zag*. Illus. John Astrop. London and New York: Warne, 1974. (V)

Cerf, Bennett. *Bennett Cerf's Book of Animal Riddles*. Illus. Roy McKie. New York: Random, 1964.

———. *Bennet Cerf's Book of Laughs*. Illus. Carl Rose. New York: Random, 1959.

———. *Bennett Cerf's Book of Riddles*. Illus. Roy McKie. New York: Random, 1960.

———. *More Riddles* Illus. Roy McKie. New York: Random, 1961.

Chast, Roz. Cover illustration. *The New Yorker*, June 1, 1987. (X)

Chaucer, Geoffrey. *The Parliament of Fowls*. In *The Poetical Works of Chaucer*. Ed. F.N. Robinson. Boston: Houghton, 1933. (X)

Children's Television Workshop. *The Sesame Street Book of Letters*. Illus. Boston: Little, 1969. (ABC)

Ciardi, John. *An Alphabestiary*. Illus. Milton Hebald. New York and Phildelphia: Lippincott, 1966. (ABC/WP)

———. *Doodle Soup*. Illus. Merle Nacht. Boston: Houghton Mifflin, 1985. (V)

———. *I Met a Man*. Illus. R. Osburn. Boston: Houghton, 1961.

———. *The Man Who Sang the Sillies*. Illus. Edward Gorey. New York: Lippincott, 1961. (X)

———. *The Monster Den: Or Look What Happened at My House— and to It*. Illus. Edward Gorey. New York and Philadelphia: Lippincott, 1963. (X)

———. *The Reason for the Pelican*. Illus. Madeleine Gekiere. New York and Philadelphia: Lippincott, 1959. (X)

———. *You Read to Me, I'll Read to You*. Illus. Edward Gorey. New York and Philadelphia: Lippincott, 1962. (X)

Cleary, Beverly. *Ramona the Pest*. Illus. Louis Darling. New York: Scholastic, 1975; rpt. from Morrow, 1968. (X)

Cleave, Elizabeth, auth. and illus. *ABC*. New York: Atheneum, 1985.

Cole, Joanna and Stephanie Calmenson, eds. *The Laugh Book: A New Treasure of Humor for Children*. New York: Doubleday, 1986. (X)

Cole, William, ed. *An Arkful of Animals: Poems for the Very Young*. Illus. Lun Munsinger. Boston: Houghton, 1978.

———, ed. *Beastly Boys and Ghastly Girls*. Illus. Tomi Ungerer. Cleveland and New York: World, 1964. (X)

———. *A Boy Named Mary Jane and Other Silly Verse*. Illus. George Maclain. New York: Watts, 1977.

———, ed. *Oh, Such Foolishness!* Illus. Tomie de Paola. New York and Philadelphia: Lippincott, 1978. (X)

————, comp. *Oh, That's Ridiculous*. Illus. Tomi Ungerer. New York: Viking, 1972. (X)

————. *Oh, What Nonsense!*. Illus. Tomi Ungerer. New York: Viking, 1966. (X)

————. *Poem Stew*. Illus. Karen Weinhaus. New York: Harper, 1983.

————. *The Square Bear and Other Riddle Rhymes*. New York: Scholastic, 1987.

Cole, William and Mike Thaler. *Monster Knocks Knocks*. Archway, 1982.

Cooney, Barbara, auth. and illus. Letters by Suzanne R. Morse. *A Garland of Games and Other Diversions: An Alphabet Book*. New York: Holt, 1969.

Cooper, Helen, ed. *Great Grandmother Goose*. Illus. Krystyna Tursha. New York: Greenwillow, 1978. (X)

Cooper, M. *Tommy Thumb's Pretty Song Book*. London, 1744. (X)

Corbet, Sybil. *Animal Land Where there are no People*. London, 1897. (X)

Corbett, Scott. *The Mysterious Zetabet*. Illus. Jon McIntosh. Boston: Atlantic/Little, 1979. (ABC/X)

Cox, James A. *Put Your Foot in Your Mouth and Other Silly Sayings*. Illus. Sam Q. Weissman. New York: Random, 1980.

Craft, Ruth. *Carrie Hepple's Garden*. Illus. Irene Haas. New York: Macmillan, 1979.

Craig, Bobbie, auth and illus. *A Comic and Curious Collection of Animals, Birds and Other Creatures*. New York: Modern Promotions, 1981.

Crane, Walter, auth. and illus. *An Alphabet of Old Friends and the Absurd ABC* New York: Metropolitan Museum of Art, 1981.

Cullen, Countee and Christopher Cat. *The Lost Zoo*. Illus. Joseph Low. Toronto: Ryerson, 1940; rpt. 1968. (X)

Cummings, E.E. *Hist Whist and other poems for children*. New York: Liveright, 1983. (X)

————. *Fairy Tales*. Illus. John Eaton. New York: Harcourt, 1965. (X)

————. *in Just-/spring*. Illus. Heidi Goennel. Boston: Little, 1988. (V/X)

Dahl, Roald. *The BFG*. Illus. Quentin Blake. New York: Farrar, 1982. (X)

————. *Charlie and the Chocolate Factory*. Illus Joseph Schindelman. New York: Knopf, 1964; Bantam, 1984. (F/X)

————. *Dirty Beasts*. Illus. Rosemary Fawcett. New York: Farrar, 1983. (V/X)

————. *The Giraffe, the Pelly, and Me*. New York: Farrar, 1985. (V/X)

————. *James and the Giant Peach*. New York: Knopf, 1961. (F/X)

————. *Roald Dahl's Revolting Rhymes*. New York: Bantam, 1986. (X)

————. *The Witches*. Illus. Quentin Blake. New York: Farrar, 1983. (X)

de Gasztold, Carmen Bernos. *Prayers from the Ark*. Trans. Rumer Godden. Illus. Jean Primrose. New York: Viking, 1969. (X)

De Regniers, Beatrice S. *May I Bring a Friend*. Illus. Beni Montresor. New York: Macmillan, 1974.

De Vries, Leonard, ed. *Flowers of Delight: An agreeable Garland of Prose and Poetry for the Instruction and Amusement of little Masters and Misses and their distinguished Parents*. New York: Pantheon, 1965. (X)

Demers, Patricia and Gordon Moyles, eds. *From Instruction to Delight: An Anthology of Children's Literature to 1850*. Toronto: Oxford UP, 1982.

Donn, Jack and Gardner Dozois, eds. *Bestiary!* New York: Ace, 1985.

Dr. Seuss [Theodor Seuss Giesel], auth. and illus. *And to Think That I Saw It on Mulberry Street*. New York: Vanguard, 1936. (X)

———. *The Butter Battle Book*. New York: Random, 1984. (X)

———. *The Cat in the Hat*. New York: Beginner Books/Random, 1957. (X)

———. *The Cat in the Hat Comes Back*. New York: Beginner/ Random, 1958; 1986.

———. *Did I Ever Tell You How Lucky You Are?* New York: Random, 1973.

———. *Dr. Seuss's ABC*. New York: Beginner/Random, 1960. (X)

———. *Dr. Seuss's Sleep Book*. New York: Random, 1962. (X)

———. *Fox in Socks*. New York: Beginner/Random, 1965.

———. *Green Eggs and Ham*. New York: Beginner/Random, 1960. (X)

———. *Hop on Pop*. New York: Beginner/Random, 1963.

———. *Horton Hatches the Egg* New York: Random, 1940.

———. *Horton Hears a Who*. New York: Random, 1954.

———. *How the Grinch Stole Christmas*. New York: Random, 1957.

———. *I Can Lick Thirty Tigers Today and Other Stories*. New York: Random, 1969. (X)

———. *I Can Read with My Eyes Shut*. New York: Beginner/ Random, 1969. (X)

———. *I Had Trouble in Getting to Solla Sollew*. New York: Random, 1965.

———. *If I Ran the Circus*. New York: Random, 1956. (X)

———. *If I Ran the Zoo*. New York: Random, 1950. (X)

———. *Lorax*. New York: Random, 1971.

———. *McElligot's Pool*. New York: Random, 1947.

———. *Oh, Say Can You Say?* New York: Beginner/Random, 1979. (X)

———. *Oh, the Thinks You Can Think!* New York: Beginner/ Random, 1975. (X)

———. *On Beyond Zebra*. New York: Random, 1955. (X)

———. *One fish two fish red fish blue fish*. New York: Beginner/Random, 1960. (X)

———. *Scrambled Eggs Super*. New York: Random, 1953.

———. *Sneetches and Other Stories*. New York: Random, 1961.

———. *There's a Wocket in My Pocket!* New York: Random, 1974.

———. *The Tough Coughs As He Ploughs the Dough: Early Writings and*

Cartoons by Dr. Seuss. Ed. Richard Marschall. New York: Morrow, 1987. (X)

Drescher, Henrik. *Look Alikes.* New York: Lothrop, 1985.

———. *Looking for Santa Claus.* New York: Lothrop, 1984.

———. *Simon's Book.* New York: Lothrop, 1983. (X)

Dulac, Edmund. *Lyrics Pathetic and Humorous from A to Z.* New York: Warne, 1908. (ABC)

Dugan, Michael, comp. *Stuff and Nonsense.* Illus. Deborah Miland. Cleveland, OH: Collins, 1974; rpt. 1977. (V)

Edens, Cooper. *A Phenomenal Alphabet Book* Illus. Joyce Eide. La Jolla, CA: Green Tiger Press, 1981. (WP)

Eichenberg, Fritz, auth. and illus. *Ape in a Cape: An Alphabet of Odd Animals.* New York: Harcourt, 1952. (X)

Einsel, Walter. *Did You Ever See?* New York: Scholastic, 1962.

Emrich, Duncan, ed. *The Nonsense Book of Riddles, Rhymes, Tongue Twisters, Puzzles and Jokes* from *American Folklore.* Illus. Ib Orlsson. New York: Four Winds, 1970.

Espeland, Pamela and Marilyn Waniek. *The Cat walked through the Casserole and other poems for Children.* Minneapolis: Carolrhoda Books, 1984. (X)

Espy, Willard R. *A Children's Almanac of Words at Play* Illus. Bruce Cayard. New York: Potter, 1982.

Ets, Marie Hall. *Beasts and Nonsense.* New York: Viking, 1952.

Evans, Patricia Healy. *Rimbles: A Book of Children's Classic Games, Rhymes, Songs and Sayings.* Garden City, NY: Doubleday, 1961. (X)

Fadiman, Clifton. *Wally the Wordworm.* Illus. Lisa Atherton. Owings Mills, MD: Stemmer House, 1983. (X)

Feiffer, Jules. *Passionella and Other Stories.* New York: McGraw, 1959. (X)

Fisher, Robert, ed. *Amazing Monsters: Verses to Thrill and Chill.* Illus. Rowena Allen. London and Boston: Faber, 1982. (X)

Fitzhugh, Louise. *Harriet the Spy.* 1964. New York: Dell, 1983. (X)

Flanders, Michael. *The Sloth and the Gnu.* Illus. Peter Swan. London and New York: Warne, 1974.

Folsom, Marcia and Michael. *Easy as Pie: A Guessing Game of Sayings.* Illus. Jack Kent. New York: Clarion/Houghton, 1985.

———. *Q is For Duck: An Alphabet Guessing Game.* Illus. Jack Kent. New York: Clarion-Houghton, 1987

Frisch, Max. *Biedermann and the Firebugs* New York: Methuen, 1962. (X)

Gackenback, Dick. *Arabella and Mr. Crack.* New York: Macmillan, 1982.

———. *Timid Timothy's Tongue Twisters* New York: Holiday House, 1986.

Gantz, David. *The Genie Bear with the Light Brown Hair Word Book.* Garden City, NY: Doubleday, 1982. (ABC)

Gardner, Beau, auth. and illus. *Have You Ever Seen . . . ? An ABC Book*. New York: Dodd, 1986.

Gardner, John. *A Child's Bestiary*, with added poems by Lucy Gardner and Eugene Rudzewicz. Illus. Lucy, Joel, Joan, and John Gardner. New York: Knopf, 1977. (X)

———. *Dragon, Dragon and Other Tales*. Illus. Charles Shields. New York: Knopf, 1975. (F/X)

Gomme, Alice Bertha. *Children's Singing Games, with the tunes to which they are sung*. New York: Dover, 1967.

Gorey, Edward, auth. and illus. *Amphigorey: Fifteen Books by Edward Gorey*. New York: Putnam, 1972, Perigee/Putnam, 1981. (X)

———. *Amphigorey Too*. New York: Putnam, 1975.

———. *The Vinegar Works* (including *The Gashlycrumb Tinies*, *The Insect God*, and *The West Wing*). New York: Simon, 1963. (X)

———. *The Glorious Nosebleed: Fifth Alphabet*. New York: Dodd, 1974.

———. [Pseudonym Mrs. Regera Dowdy]. *The Pious Infant*. New York: Fantod, 1966.

———. *The Utter Zoo*. New York: Meredith, 1967.

———. *The Wuggly Ump*. New York and Philadelphia: Lippincott, 1963.

Grahame, Kenneth. *The Reluctant Dragon* Illus. E. H. Shepard. New York: Holiday House, 1938. First published in *Dream Days*. London: John Lane, 1898. (X)

Green, Roger Lancelyn, ed. *The Book of Nonsense by Many Authors*. Illus. Charles Folkard. New York: Dutton, 1956. (X)

———, ed. *A Century of Humorous Verse: 1850–1950*. New York: Dutton, 1961.

Hale, Lucretia. *The Peterkin Papers*. New York: Random House, n.d. (F)

Hall, Rich. *Angry Young Sniglets*. Illus. Arnie Ten. New York: Collier/Macmillan, 1987. (WP/X)

———. *More Sniglets*. New York: Collier/Macmillan, 1985.

———. *Sniglets*. New York: Collier/Macmillan, 1984.

———. *Unexplained Sniglets of the Universe*. New York: Collier/Macmillan, 1986.

Halliwell, J. O. *Popular Rhymes and Nursery Tales*. 1842. London: Bodley Head, 1970. (X)

Hamilton, Mary. *A New World Bestiary*. Illus. Kim La Fave. Vancouver and Toronto: Douglas and McIntyre, 1985. (X)

Hamoy, Carol, auth. and illus. *What's Wrong? What's Wrong?* New York: Astor-Honor, 1965.

Heide, Florence Parry. *Alphabet Zoop*. Illus. Sally Matthews. New York: McCall, 1970.

Hendra, Judith, ed. *The Illustrated Treasury of Humor for Children*. New York: Grosset, 1980.

Heilbroner, Joan. *This Is the House Where Jack Lives*. Illus. Aliki. New York: Harper, 1987.

Hoff, Syd. *Syd Hoff's Nutty Noodles*. New York: Scholastic, 1987.

Hoffmann, Heinrich. *Struwwelpeter [Shockheaded Peter]*. Frankfort, 1847. London: Blackie and Son, 1903. London: Pan Books, 1972. (X)

Holland, Marion. *Big Ball of String*. New York: Beginner/ Random, 1958.

Holme, Bryan, ed. *A Present of Laughter*. New York: Viking, 1982. (V)

Hotchpotch, Horatio. *Nursery Rhymes for Modern Times*. New York: Sutter House, 1976.

Hughes, Dean. *Nutty and the Case of the Mastermind Thief*. New York: Atheneum, 1985. (F)

———. *Nutty and the Case of the Ski-Slope Spy*. New York: Atheneum, 1985.

———. *Nutty Can't Miss*. New York: Atheneum, 1987.

———. *Nutty for President*. New York: Atheneum, 1981.

Hughes, Ted. *Moon-Whales and Other Moon Poems*: New York: Viking, 1976.

Hunt, Bernice Kohn. *Your Ant is a Which: Fun with Homophones*. Illus. Jan Pyk. New York: Harcourt, 1976.

Hunter, Julius. *Absurd Alphabedtime Stories*. Illus. Ronald Gomez. St. Louis: CBP, 1976.

Hutchins, Pat. *The Very Worst Monster*. New York: Greenwillow, 1985. (F)

———. *1 Hunter*. New York: Greenwillow, 1982. (123)

Ionesco, Eugene. *Four Plays by Eugene Ionesco*. Trans. Donald M. Allen. New York: Grove, 1958. (X)

Jacobs, Leland B. ed. *Funny Bone Ticklers in Verse and Rhyme*. Illus. Edward Malsberg. Chicago: Garrard, 1973.

———. *Poetry for Chuckles and Grins*. Illus. Tomie De Paola. Chicago: Garrard, 1968.

Johnson, Crockett. *Harold and the Purple Crayon*. New York: Harper, 1955. New York: Scholastic, 1973. (X)

———. *Harold at the North Pole: A Christmas Journey with the Purple Crayon*. New York: Harper, 1958.

———. *Harold's ABC*. New York: Harper, 1963.

———. *Harold's Circus: An Astounding, Colossal Purple Crayon Event*. New York: Harper, 1959. (X)

———. *Harold's Fairy Tale: Further Adventures with the Purple Crayon*. New York: Harper, 1956.

———. *Harold's Trip to the Sky*. New York: Harper, 1957.

———. *A Picture for Harold's Room: A Purple Crayon Adventure*. 1960. New York: Scholastic, 1968. (X)

Johnson, Jane, comp. and illus. *A Book of Nursery Riddles*. Boston: Houghton, 1985.

Jones, Kathryn Amanda, auth. and illus. *Can You Guess What I Am?* New York: Carlton, 1984. (ABC)

Joslin, Sesyle. *What Do You Do, Dear*. Illus. Maurice Sendak. Reading, MA: Addison-Wesley, 1961. New York: Harper, 1987. (X)

———. *What Do You Say, Dear*. Illus. Maurice Sendak. Reading, MA: Addison-Wesley, 1958. New York: Harper, 1986. (X)

Joyce, James. *Finnegans Wake*. New York: Viking, 1959. (X)

———. *A Portrait of the Artist as a Young Man*. New York: Viking, 1957. (X)

Juster, Norton. *The Phantom Tollbooth*. 1961. New York: Random, 1964. (X)

Justus, May. *Peddler's Pack*. Illus. Jean Tanburine. New York: Holt, 1957.

Kahn, Peggy. *The Wuzzles' Alphabet Book*. Illus. Bobbi Barto. New York: Random, 1986. (X)

Kellogg, Steven. *Aster Aardvark's Alphabet Adventures*. New York: Morrow, 1987.

———. Reteller and illus. *Chicken Little*. New York: Morrow, 1985.

———. *Paul Bunyan*. New York: Morrow, 1984. (X)

———. *Pecos Bill*. New York: Morrow, 1986. (X)

———. *There Was an Old Woman*. New York: Four Winds, 1980.

Kelly, Walt. *Pogo*. New York: Simon, 1951.

———. *Songs of Pogo*. New York: Simon, 1956. (X)

Kennedy, X. J. *Brats* Illus. James Watts. New York: Atheneum, 1986. (V)

———. *Did Adam Name the Vinegaroon?* Boston: Godine, 1982. (V/ABC)

———. *The Forgetful Wishing Well: Poems for Young People*. Illus. Monica Incisa. New York: McElderry/Atheneum, 1985.

———. *One Winter Night in August and Other Nonsense Jingles*. Illus. David McPhail. New York: Atheneum, 1975.

———. *The Phantom Ice Cream Man: More Nonsense Verse*. Illus. David McPhail. New York: Atheneum, 1979.

Kipling, Rudyard. 1902. *Just So Stories*. New York: Airmont, 1966. (FX)

Klein, Robin. *Snakes and Ladders*. New York: Oxford UP, 1986. (V)

Knight, Hilary. *Hilary Knight's ABC*. Illus. New York: Golden Press, 1961.

———. *Hilary Knight's The Owl and the Pussy-Cat*. New York: Four Winds, 1981.

Kohl, Marguerite and Frederica Young. 1963. *Jokes for Children*. New York: Hill and Wang, 1985. (X)

———. *More Jokes for Children*. 1966. New York: Hill and Wang, 1986. (X)

Kohn, Michael. *There Was an Old Woman Who Swallowed a Fly*. Illus. Bari Weissman. Lancaster, NH: Dandelion Press, 1987.

Kroll, Steven. *Gobbledygook*. Illus. Kelly Oechsli. New York: Avon, 1985.

———. *Sleepy Ida and Other Nonsense Poems*. Illus. Seymour Chwast. New York: Pantheon, 1977.

Larrick, Nancy, ed. *Green Is Like a Meadow of Grass*. Illus. Kelly Oeschli. Champaign, IL: Garrard, 1968. (X)

Latta, Richard. *This Little Pig had a Riddle*. Illus. Lynn Munsinger. Niles, IL: Whitman, 1986.

Lawson, Robert. *Ben and Me*. Boston: Little, 1951. (X)

———. *Mr. Revere and I*. Boston: Little, 1953. (X)

Le Seig, Theo [Pseudonym for Dr. Seuss]. *Hooper Humperdink . . . Not Him!* Illus. Charles E. Martin. New York: Random House, 1976. (ABC)

———. *I Wish I Had Duck Feet*. Illus. Barney Tobey. New York: Beginner/ Random, 1965.

———. *Maybe You Should Fly a Jet! Maybe You Should Be a Vet*. Illus. Michael J. Smollin. New York: Random, 1980.

———. *Would You Rather Be a Bullfrog?* Illus. Roy McKie. New York: Random, 1975.

Le Tord, Bijou. *Arf, Boo, Click*. New York: Four Winds, 1981. (X)

Leaf, Munro *The Story of Ferdinand*. Illus. Robert Lawson. New York: Viking, 1936; rpt. 1969. (X)

———, auth. and illus. *Flock of Watchbirds*. New York and Philadelphia: Lippincott, 1946,

———. *Fly Away Watch Bird! A Picture Book of Behavior* New York and Philadelphia: Stokes (Lippincott), 1941.

———. *Gordon the Goat*. New York and Philadelphia: Lippincott, 1944; rpt. Hamden, CT Library Professional Publications, 1988.

———. *Grammar Can Be Fun*. New York: Stokes, 1934. (X)

———. *Manners Can Be Fun*. Stokes, 1936. Rev. ed. New York and Philadelphia: Lippincott, 1958.

———. *More Watchbirds: A Picture Book of Behavior*. New York and Philadelphia: Stokes (Lippincott), 1940.

———. *Robert Francis Weatherbee*. New York: Stokes (Lippincott), 1935; rpt. Hamden CT: Library Professional Publications, 1988.

———. *Three and Thirty Watchbirds: A Picture Book of Behavior*. New York and Philadelphia: Lippincott, 1944.

———. *The Watchbirds: A Picture Book of Behavior*. New York and Philadelphia: Stokes (Lippincott), 1939. (X)

———, reteller. *Aesop's Fables*. Illus. Robert Lawson. New York: Heritage Press, 1941.

Leander, Ed. *Q Is for Crazy*. Illus. Josef Sumichrast. New York: Harlin Quest, 1977.

Lear, Edward. *The Complete Nonsense of Edward Lear*, ed. Holbrook Jackson. New York: Dover, 1951. (X)

———. *The Courtship of the Yonghy-Bonghy-Bo & The New Vestments*. Illus. Kevin Maddison. New York: Viking, 1980.

———. *An Edward Lear Alphabet*. Illus. Carol Newsom. New York: Lothrop, 1983.

———. *Nonsense Books*. Boston: Little, 1888. (X)

———. *The Scroobious Pip* (completed by Ogden Nash). Illus. Nancy Ekholm Burkert. New York: Harper, 1968; rpt. 1987. (X)

Lee, Dennis. *Alligator Pie*. Illus. Frank Newfield. Toronto: Macmillan of Canada, 1974. (X)

———. *Garbage Delight*. Illus. Frank Newfield. Boston: Houghton, 1987. (X)

———. *Jelly Belly*. Illus. Juan Wijngaard. New York: Bedrick Blackie, 1985.

———. *Nicolas Knock and other People*. Illus. Frank Newfield. Boston: Houghton, 1974.

———. *Wiggle to the Laundromat*. Toronto and Chicago: New Press, 1970. (X)

Leedy, Loreen. *The Dragon ABC Hunt*. New York: Holiday House, 1986.

Levine, Caroline. *Silly School Riddles and Other Classroom Crack-ups*. Illus. Lynn Munsinger. Niles, IL: Robert Whitman, 1986.

Libbey, Rutt Everding. *Silly Billy's Alphabet*. Illus. Gene Holton. San Carlos, CA: Golden Gate, 1964.

Lindgren, Astrid. *Pippi Goes on Board*. New York: Viking, 1957. (X)

———. *Pippi in the South Seas*. New York: Viking, 1957.

———. *Pippi Longstocking*. Trans. Florence Lamborn. Illus. Louis S. Glanzman. New York: Viking, 1950, rpt. 1963. (X)

Lindsay, Vachel. *Johnny Appleseed and Other Poems*. Illus. George Richards. New York: Macmillan, 1928; 1961; rpt. Cutchogue, NY: Buccaneer, 1981.

———. *Springfield Town Is Butterfly Town and Other Poems for Children*. Kent, OH: Kent State UP, 1969. (X)

Lionni, Leo, auth. and illus. *The Alphabet Tree*. New York: Pantheon, 1968.

Lippman, Peter, auth. and illus. *One and Only Wacky Wordbook*. Racine, WI: Western, 1979.

Lobel, Arnold, auth. and illus. *The Book of Pigericks*. New York: Harper, 1983. (X)

———. *Days with Frog and Toad*. New York: Harper, 1978; rpt. 1985. (F)

———, illus. *Fables*. New York: Harper, 1980; rpt. 1983.

———. *Frog and Toad All Year*. New York: Harper, 1976; rpt. 984, 1985. (F)

———. *Frog and Toad Are Friends*. New York: Harper, 1970. (F)

———. *Frog and Toad Together*. New York: Harper, 1979. (F)

———. *Giant John*. New York: Harper, 1964.

———. *Grasshopper on the Road*. New York: Harper, 1978; rpt. 1986.

———. *Great Blueness and Other Predicaments*. New York: Harper, 1968.

———. *Gregory Griggs and Other Nursery Rhyme People*. New York: Greenwillow, 1978.

———. *Holiday for Mister Muster*. New York: Harper, 1978.

———. *How the Rooster Saved the Day*. Illus Anita Lobel. New York: Greenwillow, 1977.

———. *The Ice-Cream Cone Coot and Other Rare Birds*. New York: Four Winds, 1980.

———. *Martha the Movie Mouse*. New York: Harper, 1977.

———. *Mouse Soup*. New York: Harper, 1977; rpt. 1983, 1986.

———. *Mouse Tales*. New York: Harper, 1972; rpt. 1978, 1985.

———. *On Market Street*. Illus. Anita Lobel. New York: Greenwillow, 1981; Scholastic, 1985. (ABC)

———. *Owl at Home*. New York: Harper, 1975, 1982, 1987.

———. *Prince Bertram the Bad*. New York: Harper, 1965.

———, illus . *The Random House Book of Mother Goose*. New York: Random, 1986.

———. *The Rose in My Garden*. Illus. Anita Lobel. New York: Greenwillow, 1984.

———. *Small Pig*. New York: Harper, 1969.

———. *Treeful of Pigs* New York: Greenwillow, 1979.

———. *Uncle Elephant*. New York: Harper, 1981.

———. *Whiskers and Rhymes*. New York: Greenwillow, 1985. (X)

———. *Zoo for Mister Muster*. New York: Harper, n.d.

Lopshire, Robert. *Put Me in the Zoo*. New York: Beginner/ Random, 1960.

Lord, John V. and Burroway, Janet. *The Giant Jam Sandwich*. Illus. John V. Lord. Boston: Houghton, 1973.

Low, Alice. *If Dinosaurs Were Cats and Dogs*. New York: Four Winds, 1981.

Low, Joseph, ed. and illus. *Adam's Book of Odd Creatures*. New York: Atheneum, 1962. (ABC)

———. *Beastly Riddles: Fishy, Flighty and Buggy, Too*. New York: Macmillan, 1983.

———. *Five Men under the Umbrella and Other Ready-to-Read Riddles*. New York: Macmillan, 1975.

———. *There Was a Wise Crow*. Chicago: Follett, 1969. (X)

MacDonald, George. *The Complete Fairy Tales of George MacDonald*. Intrd. Roger Lancelyn Green. Illus. Arthur Hughes. New York: Schocken, 1978. (F)

————. *The Light Princess*. New York: Farrar, 1969. (X)

MacDonald, Suse. *Alphabatics*. New York: Oxford, 1987.

Maestro, Giulio. *Razzle-Dazzle Riddles*. New York: Clarion/ Houghton, 1985.

————. *A Raft of Riddles*. New York: Clarion/Houghton, 1982.

————. *Riddle Romp*. New York: Clarion/Houghton, 1983.

————. *What's a Frank Frank? Tasty Homograph Riddles*. New York: Clarion-Houghton, 1984.

————. *What's Mite Might? Homophone Riddles to Boost Your Word Power!*. New York: Houghton, 1986. (X)

Marshall, James. *George and Martha*. Boston: Houghton Mifflin, 1972.

————. *George and Martha Encore*. New York: Houghton, 1973.

————. *George and Martha One Fine Day*. New York: Houghton, 1987.

————. *George and Martha Tons of Fun*. New York: Houghton, 1980.

————. *George and Martha Back in Town*. New York: Houghton, 1984.

————, selector. *James Marshall's Mother Goose*. New York: Farrar, 1979.

————. *Red Riding Hood*. New York: Dial, 1987.

————. *Yummers*. Boston: Houghton Mifflin, 1973.

————. *Yummers Too: The Second Course*. Boston: Houghton Mifflin, 1986.

————. *The Stupids Die*. Author Harry Allard. Boston: Houghton Mifflin, 1981. (X)

————. *The Stupids Have a Ball*. Author Harry Allard. Boston: Houghton Mifflin, 1978. (X)

————. *The Stupids Step Out*. Author Harry Allard. Boston: Houghton Mifflin, 1974. (X)

Mayer, Mercer. *A Silly Story*. New York: Four Winds, 1980.

McAfee, Annalene. *The Visitors Who Came to Stay*. Illus. Anthony Browne. New York: Viking Kestrel, 1984. (X)

McCord, David. *All Day Long*. Illus. Henry B. Kane. Boston: Little, 1966.

————. *All Small*. Illus. Madelaine G. Linden. Boston: Little, 1986.

————. *Every Time I Climb a Tree*. Illus. Marc Simont. Boston: Little, 1967.

————. *Far and Few*. New York: Dell, 1972.

————. *For Me to Say*. Illus. Henry B. Kane. Boston: Little, 1970.

————. *One at a Time*. Illus. Henry B. Kane. Boston: Little, 1977.

————. *Speak Up: More Rhymes of the Never Was and Always Is*. Illus. Marc Simont. Boston: Little, 1980.

————. *The Star in the Pail*. Illus. Marc Simont. Boston: Little, 1975.

————. *Take Sky*. Illus. Henry B. Kane. Boston: Little, 1962.

McGinn, Maureen. *I Used to Be an Artichoke*. lllus. Anita Norman. St. Louis: Concordia, 1973. (ABC/X)

McGinley, Phyllis. *All Around Town*. New York and Philadelphia: Lippincott, 1948.

McGovern, Ann. *Mr. Skinner's Skinny House*. Illus. Mort Gerberg. New York: Four Winds, 1981. (X)

McNaughton, Colin, auth. and illus. *Colin McNaughton's ABC and 123* Garden City, NY: Doubleday, 1976.

Merriam, Eve. *The Birthday Cow*. Illus. Guy Michel. New York: Knopf, 1978.

Milne, A. A. *The World of Christopher Robin:* The Complete *When We Were Very Young* and *Now We are Six*. New York: Dutton, 1958. (X)

————. *The World of Pooh:* The Complete *Winnie-the-Pooh* and *The House at Pooh Corner*. Illus. E.H. Shepard. New York: Dutton, 1957. (X)

Mills, Carol. *A-Z and Back Again: An ABC Book*. Illus. Susanne Ferrer. London: Tiger Books, 1986. (Originally published as *The A-Z of Absolute Zaniness*. Australia: RPLA, 1984.)

Minarik, Else Holmelund. *No Fighting, No Biting*. Illus. Maurice Sendak. New York: Harper, 1958. (X)

Mitchell, Adrian, reteller. *See* Raspe, Rudolph Erich.

Moncure, Jane Bell. *Magic Monsters Act the Alphabet*. Illus. Helen Endres. Elgin, IL: Child's World, 1980.

Morrison, Bill. *Squeeze a Sneeze*. Boston: Houghton, 1977.

Moscovitch, Rosalie. *What's in a Word? A Dictionary of Daffy Definitions* Illus. Andy Myer. Boston: Houghton, 1985.

Mosel, Arlene, reteller. *Tikki Tikki Tembo*. Illus. Blair Lent. New York: Holt, 1968.

Moss, Jeffrey. *Oscar-the-Grouch's Alphabet of Trash*. Illus. Sal Murdocca. Racine, WI: Western, 1977.

Moss, Jeffrey, et al. *The Sesame Street Storybook*. New York: Children's Television Workshop, 1971. (X)

Mullen, Michael. *Magus the Lollipop Man*. 1981. Edinburgh: Canongate, 1983. (F)

Murdocca, Sal, auth. and illus. *Grover's Own Alphabet*. New York Racine, WI: Western/Children's Television Workshop, 1978.

Murphy, Jim. *Guess Again: More Weird and Wacky Inventions*. New York: Bradbury, 1986.

Myers, Bernice. *The Extraordinary Invention*. New York: Macmillan, 1984. (F)

Nash, Ogden. *The Adventures of Isabel*. Boston: Little, 1963. (V/X)

————. *The Animal Garden*. Illus. Hillary Knight. M. New York: Evans, 1965.

————. *The Bad Parents Garden of Verse*. New York: Simon, 1936.

————. *Custard and Company*. Illus. and comp. Quentin Blake. London: Kestrel/Penguin, 1979.

————. *Custard the Dragon and the Wendigo*. Illus. J. Astrop. London and New York: Warne, 1978.

————. *Custard the Dragon and the Wicked Knight*. Illus. Linell Nash. Boston: Little, 1961.

————. *Ogden Nash's Musical Zoo*. Music by Vladimire Dukelsky. Boston: Little, 1947.

————. *Parents Keep Out: Elderly Poems for Youngerly Readers*. Illus. Barbara Corrigan. Boston: Little, 1951.

————. *Verses from 1929 On*. Boston: Little, 1959. (X)

Nerlove, Miriam. *I Made a Mistake* New York: Atheneum , 1985. (V)

Nesbit, E. *Five Children and It*. New York: Viking/Penguin, 1985. (F/X)

————. *The Phoenix and the Carpet*. New York: Viking/ Penguin, 1984. (X)

————. *The Story of the Amulet*. New York: Viking/Penguin, 1985. (X)

Neumeier, Marty and Byron Glaser. *Action Alphabet*. New York: Greenwillow, 1985.

Newbery, John. *A Little Pretty Pocket-Book: Intended for the Instruction and Amusement of Little Master Tommy and Pretty Miss Polly*. London, 1744. (X)

Niland, Deborah, auth. and illus. *ABC of Monsters*. New York: McGraw, 1978.

Noble, Trinka Hakes. *The Day Jimmy's Boa Ate the Wash*. Illus. Steven Kellogg. New York: Dial, 1980. (F)

————. *Jimmy's Boa Bounces Back*. Illus. Steven Kellogg. New York: Dial, 1984. (X)

Nolan, Dennis, auth. and illus. *Alphabrutes*. Englewood Cliffs, NJ: Prentice, 1977. (X)

Oakley, Graham. *The Church Cat Abroad*. New York: Atheneum, 1973. (F/X)

————. *The Church Mice Adrift*. New York: Atheneum, 1976.

————. *The Church Mice and the Moon* New York: Atheneum, 1974. (X)

————. *The Church Mice at Bay*. New York: Atheneum, 1978.

————. *The Church Mice at Christmas*. New York: Atheneum, 1980.

————. *The Church Mice in Action*. New York: Atheneum, 1982.

————. *The Church Mouse*. New York: Atheneum, 1972. (X)

————. *Henry's Quest*. New York: Atheneum, 1986. (X)

Obligado, Lilian, auth. and illus. *Faint Frogs Feeling Feverish and Other*

Terrifyingly Tantalizing Tongue Twisters. New York: Viking, 1983. (ABC)

Oechsli, Kelly. *The Monkey's ABC Book.* New York and Racine, WI: Golden/Western, 1982.

O'Neill, Mary. *Hailstones and Halibut Bones* Illus. Leonard Weisgard. Garden City, NY: Doubleday, 1961. (V)

Orgel, Doris. *Merry, Merry Fibruary.* Illus. Arnold Lobel. New York: Parents Magazine Press, 1977.

Oxenbury, Helen and Fay Maschler. *A Child's Book of Manners.* New York: Viking/Penguin, 1984; rpt. 1986. (X)

Pape, D. L. *King Robert the Resting Ruler.* Fayetteville, GA: Oddo, 1968. (WP)

———. *Liz Dearly's Silly Glasses.* Fayetteville, GA: Oddo, 1965.

———. *Professor Fred and the Fid-Fuddlephone.* Fayetteville, GA: Oddo, 1965.

———. *The Three Thinkers of Thay-lee.* Fayetteville, GA: Oddo, 1965.

———. *Scientist Sam.* Fayetteville, GA: Oddo, 1968.

Parish, Peggy. *Amelia Bedelia.* Illus. Fritz Siebel. New York: Scholastic, 1963; rpt. 1969. (X)

———. *Amelia Bedelia and the Baby.* Illus. Lynn Sweat. New York: Avon, 1981. (X)

———. *Amelia Bedelia and the Surprise Shower.* Illus. Fritz Siebel. New York: Scholastic, 1966. (X)

———. *Amelia Bedelia Goes Camping.* Illus. Lynn Sweat. New York: Greenwillow, 1985. (X)

———. *A Beastly Circus.* Illus. Peter Parnall. New York: Simon, 1969. (ABC)

———. *Come Back, Amelia Bedelia.* Illus. Wallace Tripp. New York: Scholastic, 1971. (X)

———. *Play Ball, Amelia Bedelia.* Illus. Wallace Tripp. New York: Scholastic, 1972. (X)

———. *Teach Us, Amelia Bedelia.* Illus. Lynn Sweat. New York: Scholastic, 1977. (X)

Parrott, E. O. *Limericks.* New York: Viking Penguin, 1983. (X)

Patience, John, auth. and illus. *An Amazing Alphabet.* New York: Derrydale Books, 1984.

Patz, Nancy. *Moses Supposes His Toeses Are Roses: And Seven Other Silly Old Rhymes.* New York: Harcourt, 1983.

Peet, Bill. *The Kweeks of Kookatumdee* Boston: Houghton, 1985.

———. *No Such Things.* Boston: Houghton, 1985. (V)

"Peter Coddle's Narrative." *Peter Coddle's Trip.* Springfield, MA: Bradley, 1970. (WP/X)

Peter Piper's Practical Principles of Plain and Perfect Pronunciation with Manifold Manifestations. 1813. Illus. Marcia Brown. New York: Scribner's, 1959. Also in de Vries. *Flowers of Delight*, 80–85. (ABC/WP/X)

Phillips, Louis. *Going Ape: Jokes from the Jungle*. Illus. Bob Shein. New York: Viking/Kestrel, 1988.

Pinkwater [Daniel] Manus. *Around Fred's Bed*. Illus. Robert Mertens. Englewood Cliffs, NJ: Prentice, 1976.

———, auth. and illus. *Blue Moose*. New York: Dodd, 1975.

———, auth. and illus. *The Blue Thing*. Englewood Cliffs, NJ: Prentice-Hall, 1977.

———, auth. and illus. *Return of the Blue Moose*. New York: Dodd, 1979.

———. *The Wuggie Norple Story*. Illus. Tomie de Paolo. New York: Four Winds, 1980. (F)

Portugal, Jan, auth. and illus. *ABC Sillies*. Palo Alto, CA: Wild Horse, 1983.

Potter, Beatrix. *The Tale of Squirrel Nutkin*. London: Warne, 1903; rpt. 1931. (R/X)

Potter, Charles Francis. *More Tongue Tanglers and a Rigamarole*. Illus. William Wresner. New York: World, 1964.

———. *Tongue Tanglers*. Illus. William Wresner. New York: World, 1962.

Prelutsky, Jack. *A Gopher in the Garden*. Illus. Robert Leydenfrost. New York: Macmillan, 1967. (V)

———. *The New Kid on the Block* Illus. James Stevenson. New York: Greenwillow, 1984. (V/X)

———. *No End of Nonsense: Humorous Verses*. Illus. Wilfrid Blecher. New York: Macmillan, 1968.

———. *The Pack Rat's Day* Illus Margaret Bly Graham. New York: Macmillan, 1974.

———. *The Queen of Eene*. Illus. Victoria Chess. New York: Greenwillow, 1978. (X)

———, comp. *The Random House Book of Poetry*. Illus. Arnold Lobel. New York: Greenwillow, 1984.

———. *Ride a Purple Pelican*. Illus. Garth Williams. New York: Greenwillow, 1986. (X)

———. *The Sheriff of Rottenshot*. Illus. Victoria Chess. New York: Greenwillow, 1982.

———. *The Snopp on the Sidewalk and Other Poems*. Illus. Byron Barton. New York: Greenwillow, 1977.

———. *Toucans Two*. Illus. Jose Aruego. New York: Macmillan, 1970. Printed in England as *Zoo Doings and Other Poems*. London: Hamilton, 1971. (X)

————. *Zoo Doings: Animal Poems*. Illus. Paul O. Zelinsky. New York: Greenwillow, 1973.

Price, Roger and Leonard Stern. *Off-the-Wall: Mad Libs # 6*. Los Angeles: Price/Stern/Sloan, 1970; 1982; 1987. (X)

Provensen, Alice and Martin. *Play on Words*. New York: Random, 1972.

Ra, Carol F. *Trot, Trot to Boston: Play Rhymes for Baby*. Illus. Catherine Stock. New York: Lothrop, 1987.

Raffel, Burton, trans. *Poems from the Old English*, 2nd ed. Lincoln: U of Nebraska P, 1964. (X)

Raposo, Joe and Jon Stone. *The Songs of Sesame Street*. New York: Columbia Records, 1970. (X)

Raskin, Ellen, auth. and illus. *A & THE: or, William T. C. Baumgarten Comes to Town*. New York: Atheneum, 1970.

————. *And It Rained*. New York: Atheneum, 1969.

————. *Franklin Stein*. New York: Atheneum, 1972. (X)

————. *Nothing Ever Happens on My Block*. New York: Atheneum, 1966. (X)

————. *Silly Songs and Sad*. New York: Crowell, 1967.

————. *Spectacles*. New York: Atheneum, 1968.

————. *Twenty-Two, Twenty-Three*. New York: Macmillan, 1976. (X)

————. *Who, Said Sue, Said Whoo?* New York: Atheneum, 1973.

————. *The World's Greatest Freak Show*. New York: Atheneum, 1971.

Raspe, Rudolph Erich. *The Baron All at Sea*. Retold by Adrian Mitchell. Illus. Patrick Benson. New York: Philomel, 1987. (X)

————. *The Baron on the Island of Cheese*. Retold by Adrian Mitchell. Illus. Patrick Benson. New York: Philomel, 1986. (X)

————. *The Baron Rides Out*. Retold by Adrian Mitchell. Illus. Patrick Benson. New York: Philomel, 1985. (X)

Reed, Langford. *A Book of Nonsense Verse*. New York: Putnam, 1926.

Rees, Ennis, reteller. Illus. Edward Gorey. *Lions and Lobsters and Foxes and Frogs: Fables from Aesop*. Reading, MA: Addison-Wesley, 1971. (X)

Reid, Alastair. *Once, Dice, Trice*. Illus. Ben Shahn. Boston: Atlantic/Little, 1958.

Remy, Charlip and Burton Supree. *Mother, Mother I Feel Sick; Send for the Doctor Quick Quick Quick*. New York: Four Winds, 1980. (X)

Rhys, Ernest, ed. *A Book of Nonsense*. Introd. Roger Lancelyn Green. New York: Dutton, 1975.

Roethke, Theodore. *Dirty Dinky and Other Creatures: Poems for Children*. Sel. Beatrice Roethke and Stephen Lushington. Illus. Julie Brinckloe. Garden City, NY: Doubleday, 1973.

————. *I Am! Says the Lamb*. Illus. Robert Leydenfrost. Garden City, NY: Doubleday, 1961. (V)

————. *Party at the Zoo*. New York: Doubleday, 1963. (V)

Sandburg, Carl. *Rootabaga Stories*. Illus. Maude and Miska Petershan. New York: Harcourt, 1922; rpt. 1951, 1967. (X)

————. *The Wedding Procession of the Rag Doll and the Broom Handle and Who Was in It*. Illus. Harriet Pincus. New York: Harcourt, 1967. (X)

Sazer, Nina. *What Do You Think I Saw*. Illus. Lois Ehlert. New York: Pantheon, 1976.

Schmiderer, Dorothy. *The Alphabeast Book*. New York: Holt, 1971.

Scheer, Julian. *Rain Makes Applesauce*. Illus. Marvin Bileck. New York: Holiday House, 1964. (X)

————. *Upside Down Day*. Illus. Kelly Oechsli. New York: Holiday House, 1968.

Schwartz, Alvin. *All of Our Noses Are Here and Other Noodle Tales*. Illus. Karen Ann Weinhause. New York: Harper, 1985. (F)

————. *Buzy Bumblebees and Other Tongue Twisters*. Illus. Kathie Abrams. New York: Harper, 1982. (WP)

————. *Flapdoodle: Pure Nonsense from American Folklore*. Illus. John O'Brien. New York and Philadelphia: Lippincott, 1980. (TT)

————. *Kickle Snifters and Other Fearsome Critters*. Illus. Glen Rounds. New York and Philadelphia: Lippincott, 1973. (A)

————. *Tomfoolery: Trickery and Foolery with Words*. Illus. Glen Rounds. New York and Philadelphia: Lippincott, 1973. (WP)

————. *A Twister of Twists, a Tangler of Tongues*. Illus. Glen Rounds. New York and Philadelphia: Lippincott, 1973. (X)

————. *Unriddling: All Sorts of Riddles to Puzzle Your Guessery, Collected from American Folklore*. Illus. Sue Truesdell. New York and Philadelphia: Lippincott, 1983. (X)

Schwartz, Amy. *Bea and Mr. Jones*. New York: Bradbury Press, 1982.

Sendak Maurice. *Higglety Pigglety Pop*. New York: Harper, 1967. (X)

————. *The Night Kitchen*. New York: Harper, 1970. (X)

————. *The Nutshell Library* (*Alligators All Around, Chicken Soup with Rice, One Was Johnny*, and *Pierre*). New York: Harper, 1962. (X)

————. *Outside Over There* New York: Harper, 1981. (X)

Seuss, Dr. (Theodor Geisel). *See* Dr. Seuss.

Shakespeare, William. *Hamlet, Measure for Measure*, and *Midsummer Night's Dream. Twenty-Three Plays and the Sonnets*. Ed. Thomas Marc Parrott. New York: Scribner's, 1966. (X)

Silverstein, Shel, auth. and illus. *A Light in the Attic*. New York: Harper, 1981. (X)

————. *The Missing Piece*. New York: Harper, 1976.

————. *Uncle Shelby's ABZ Book*. New York: Simon, 1985.

————. *Where the Sidewalk Ends*. New York: Harper, 1974. (X)

—. *Who Wants A Cheap Rhinoceros?* New York: Macmillan, 1983; 1st edition 1964.

Silvis, Craig. *Rat Stew.* Illus. Annie Gusman. Boston: Houghton, 1979.

Slobodkin, Louis, auth. and illus. *Magic Michael.* New York: Macmillan, 1968.

Smith, Louisa and Glen Smith. *The Not Like Any Other Children's Book, Book.* Minneapolis: Smith & Smith, 1982.

Smith, William Jay. *Boy's Blue Book of Beasts.* Illus. Juliet Kepes. Boston: Little, 1957.

—. *Laughing Time* Illus. Fernando Kruhn. New York: Delacorte, 1980. (V)

—. *Mr. Smith and Other Nonsense.* Illus. Don Bolognese. New York: Delacorte, 1968. (V/X)

—, auth. and illus. *Puptents and Pebbles: A Nonsense ABC.* Boston: Little, 1959. (V)

Sorensen, Jim, auth. and illus. *Sons and Daughters of Mystical Creatures: An ABC Guide.* Mercer Island, WA: Peanut Butter Publishing, 1983.

Sperling, Susan Kelz. *Murfles and Wink-a-peeps: Funny Old Words for Kids.* Illus. Tom Bloom. New York: Potter, 1985.

Steig, William. *CDB?* New York: Simon, 1968. (X)

—. *CDC?* New York: Farrar, 1984. (X)

—. *The Zabajaba Jungle.* New York: Farrar, 1987.

Stein, Gertrude. *The World Is Round.* New York: William R. Scott, 1939, 1967; rpt. in *Sharing LIterature with Children: A Thematic Anthology.* Ed. Francelia Butler. New York: Longman, 1977. 411–30. (X)

Steptoe, John. *Stevie.* New York: Harper, 1969. (X)

Stevenson, James. *Could Be Worse!* New York: Morrow/Mulberry, 1987. (F/ TT)

—. *Grandpa's Great City Tour: An Alphabet Book.* New York: Greenwillow, 1983. (X)

—. *The Great Big Especially Beautiful Easter Egg.* New York: Greenwillow, 1983. (X)

—. *No Friends.* New York: Greenwillow, 1986.

—. *There's Nothing to Do!* New York: Greenwillow, 1986.

—. *What's Under My Bed!* New York: Greenwillow, 1983.

—. *Will You Please Feed Our Cat?* New York: Greenwillow, 1984.

—. *Worse Than Willy!* New York: Greenwillow, 1984. (X)

Stiles, Norman and Daniel Wilcox. *Grover and the Everything in the Whole Wide World Museum.* New York: Children's Television Workshop/ Random, 1974. (X)

Stine, Jovial Bob. *Gnasty Gnomes.* Illus. Peter Lippman. New York: Random, 1981.

————. *The Pig's Book of World Records*. Illus. Peter Lippman. New York: Random, 1980.

Stine, Jovial Bob, and Jane Stine. *Bored with Being Bored! How to Beat the Boredom Blahs*. Illus. Jerry Zimmerman. New York: Four Winds, 1982.

Stoddard [Warbug], Sandol. *From Ambledee to Zumbledee: an A-B-C of Rather Special Bugs*. Illus. Walter Lorraine. Boston: Houghton, 1968.

Stoutenberg, Adrien. *American Tall Tales*. Illus. Richard M. Powers. New York: Viking, 1966. (X)

Swift, Jonathan. *Gulliver's Travels*. New York: Oxford UP, 1977. (X)

Talbot, Hudson. *We're Back! A Dinosaur's Story*. New York: Crown, 1987. (F)

Tallon, Robert, auth. and illus. *Zoophabets*. New York: Bobbs-Merrill, 1971 (ABC)

Tate, Carole, comp and illus. *Skipping to Babylon: A Collection of Skipping Rhymes*. New York: Oxford UP, 1986.

Terban, Marvin. *Eight Ate: A Feast of Homonym Riddles*. Illus. Giulio Maestro. New York: Clarion/Houghton, 1982.

————. *I Think I Thought and Other Tricky Verbs*. Illus. Giulio Maestro. New York: Clarion/Houghton, 1984.

————. *In a Pickle and Other Funny Idioms*. Illus. Giulio Maestro. New York: Clarion/Houghton, 1983.

————. *Too Hot to Hoot: Funny Palindrome Riddles*. Illus. Giulio Maestro. New York: Clarion-Houghton, 1985. (X)

Thackeray, W.M. *The Rose and the Ring, or, The History of Prince Giglio and Prince Bulbo: A Fireside Pantomime for Great and Small Children*. 1855. Baltimore: Penguin, 1972. (X)

Thurber, James. *Fables of Our Time*. New York: Harper, 1940, 1968.

————. *The Great Quillow*. Illus. Doris Lee. New York: Harcourt, 1944; 1975. (X)

————. *Many Moons*. Illus. Louis Slobodkin. New York: Harcourt, 1943. (X)

————. *The 13 Clocks*. New York: Simon, 1950.

————. *The White Deer*. Illus. author and Don Freeman. New York: Harcourt, 1949; 1968. (X)

————. *The Wonderful O*. Illus. Marc Simont. New York: Simon, 1957; 1976. (X)

Tolkien, J.R.R. *The Hobbit*. Revised edition. New York: Ballantine, 1982; 1984; 1st edition, 1937. (X)

Travers, P.L. *Mary Poppins*. 1934. Illus. Mary Shepard. New York: Harcourt, 1962. New York: Scholastic, 1972. (X)

Tripp, Wallace. *Granfa' Grig Had a Pig and Other Rhymes Without Reason from Mother Goose*. Boston: Little, 1976. (X)

——. *Marguerite, Go Wash Your Feet*. Boston: Houghton, 1985. (X)

Turner, Ann. *Tickle a Pickle*. Illus. Karen Ann Weinhaus. New York: Macmillan, 1979.

Van Allsburg, Chris. *The Z Was Zapped*. Boston: Houghton, 1987. (ABC) (X)

Viorst, Judith. *If I Were in Charge of the World*. Illus. Lynne Cherry. New York: Atheneum, 1982.

Waters, Frank, comp. *Read with Me: A Classic Collection of Stories & Verse Including Works by Edward Lear, Lewis Carroll, Rudyard Kipling, A.A. Milne, Walter de la Mare, Hilaire Belloc*. London: Chancellor Press, 1985; first pub. under the title *Reading with Mother*. London: George B. Harrap, 1974.

Watson, Clyde. *Father Fox's Pennyrhymes*. Illus. Wendy Watson. New York: Scholastic, 1975; New York: Harper, 1987.

Watts, Alan Wilson. *Nonsense*. Illus. Michel Duttel. New York: Dutton, 1977.

Weiss, Renee Karol. *A Paper Zoo: A Collection of Animal Poems by Modern American Poets*. Illus. Ellen Raskin. New York: Macmillan, 1968; rpt. 1987.

Wells, Carolyn, comp. *The Book of Humorous Verse*. New York: Doran, 1920. (X)

——, comp. 1902. *A Nonsense Anthology*. New York: Dolphin, n.d. (X)

——, comp. *A Parody Anthology*. New York: Scribner's, 1904. (X)

Wersba, Barbara. *Twenty-Six Starlings Will Fly Through Your Mind* Illus. David Palladini. New York: Harper, 1980.

Willard, Nancy. *The Island of the Grass King: Further Adventures of Anatole*. New York: Harcourt, 1979.

——. *Sailing to Cythera and Other Anatole Stories*. Illus. David McPhail. New York: Harcourt, 1974. (X)

——. *Uncle Terrible: More Adventures of Anatole*. San Diego: Harcourt, 1982.

——. *A Visit to William Blake's Inn: Poems for Innocent and Experienced Travelers*. Illus. Alice and Martin Provensen. San Diego: Harcourt, 1981. (X)

Willis, Jeanne. *The Monster Bed*. Illus. Susan Varley. New York: Lee, Lothrop & Shepard, 1987. (F)

Winsor, Frederick. *A Space Child's Mother Goose*. Illus. Marian Parry. New York: Simon, 1958; rpt. 1967. (X)

Withers, Carl, comp. *I Saw a Rocket Walk a Mile: Nonsense Tales, Chants, and*

Songs from Many Lands. Illus. John E. Johnson. New York: Holt, 1965. (X)

————. *Riddles of Many Lands*. Illus. Lili Cassel. New York: Abelard, 1956.

————. *A Rocket in My Pocket: The Rhymes and Chants of Young America*. New York: Holt, 1946. (X)

Withers, Carl and Alta Jablow. *Rainbow in the Morning*. Illus. Abner Graboff. New York: Abelard, 1956. Eau Claire, WI, 1961. (V/X)

Withers, Carl and Sula Benet, comp. *The American Riddle Book*. Illus. Marc Simont. New York: Abelard, 1955.

Wright, Blanche F., ed. and illus. *The Real Mother Goose*. New York: Macmillan, 1916; rpt. 1987.

Yolen, Jane. *Dragon Night and Other Lullabies*. Illus. Demi. New York: Methuen, 1980.

————. *How Beastly! A Menagerie of Nonsense Poems*. Illus. James Marshall. New York and Cleveland: Collins, 1980. (X)

Zelinsky, Paul O. *The Maid and the Mouse and the Odd-Shaped House*. New York: Dodd, 1987. (X)

Ziegler, Sandra K. *Knock-Knocks, Limericks, and Other Silly Sayings*. Illus. Diana Magnuson. Chicago: Children's, Press, 1983.

Bibliographies

Secondary Sources

Note: This bibliography includes a citation for all references in this book and some additional books and articles of use for further research.

Adams, G. B. "Counting Out Rhymes and Systems of Numerations." *Ulster Folklife* 11 (1965): 85–97.

Adoff, Arnold. "Politics, Poetry, and Teaching Children: A Personal Journey." *Lion and Unicorn* 10 (1986); rpt. in *ALAN Review* 14.3 (Spring 1987): 11–12.

Ainsworth, C.H. "Jump Rope Verses around the United States." *Western Folklore* 20 (1961): 179–99.

Albee, Edward. "Which Theatre is the Absurd One?" *American Playwrights on Drama.* Ed. Horst Frenz. New York: Hill and Wang, 1965.

Alexander, Peter. "Logic and the Humour of Lewis Carroll." *Proceedings of the Leeds Philosophical and Literary Society* 6 (1951): 551–66.

Anderson, Celia Catlett. "'O Best Beloved': Kipling's Reading Instructions in the *Just So Stories*." *Proceedings of the Ninth Annual Conference of the Children's Literature Association*, U of Florida, Gainsville, March 1982: 33–39.

Apseloff, Marilyn. "Sense and Nonsense in Text and Illustration." Paper read at Children's Literature Division session on "Nonsense in Children's Literature," MLA Convention, New York City, Dec. 29, 1986.

Asimov, Isaac, ed. *The Annotated Gulliver's Travels*. New York: Clarkson N. Potter, 1980.

Arnstein, Flora J. *Poetry in the Elementary Classroom*. New York: Appleton-Century-Crofts, 1962.

Atkinson, R.M. "Songs Little Girls Sing: An Orderly Invitation to Violence." Northwest Folklore 2 (1967): 2–8.

Attebery, Brian. "Fantasy for American Children." *The Fantasy Tradition in American Literature from Irving to Le Guin*. Bloomington: Indiana UP, 1980.

Bartley, W. W., III. "Lewis Carroll as Logician." *Times Literary Supplement* (15 June 1973): 655–56.

Bergson, Henri. "Laughter." In *Comedy*. Ed. Wylie Sypher. Garden City, NY: Anchor, 1956.

Berkovits, Rochelle. "Secret Languages of Schoolchildren." *New York Folklore Quarterly*. 26 (1970): 127–52.

Bett, Henry. *The Games of Children: Their Origins and History*. London: Methuen, 1929; Detroit: Singing Tree Press, 1968.

————. *Nursery Rhymes and Tales: Their Origin and History*. London: Methuen, 1924; New York: Folcroft, 1924.

Blackburn, William. "'A New Kind of Rule': The Subversive Narrator in *Alice's Adventures in Wonderland* and 'The Pied Piper of Hamelin.'" *Children's Literature in Education* 17. 3 (Fall 1986): 181–90.

Blake, Kathleen. *Play, Games, and Sport: The Literary Works of Lewis Carroll*. Ithaca, NY: Cornell UP, 1974.

Blount, Margaret. *Animal Land: The Creatures of Children's Fiction*: New York: Avon, 1977.

Bohannon, Paul. *Justice and Judgment Among the Tiv*. London: Oxford UP, 1957.

Bolton, Henry C. *The Counting-Out Rhymes of Children, Their Antiquity, Origin, and Wide Distribution: A Study in Folklore*. New York: A. Appleton, 1888.

Bosmajian, Hamida. "Louise Fitzhugh's *Harriet the Spy*: Nonsense and Sense" in *Touchstones: Reflections on the Best in Children's Literature*. 2

vols. to date. Ed. Perry Nodelman. West Lafayette, IN: ChLA Publishers, 1985, 1986. Vol. 1. 71–82.

Brewster, Paul. "Rope Skipping, Counting Out and Other Rhymes of Children." *Southern Folklore Quarterly* 3 (1939): 173–85.

———. "Spelling Riddles from the Ozarks." *Southern Folklore Quarterly* 8 (1944): 301–03.

Brotman, Jordan. "A Late Wanderer in Oz." *Chicago Review* 18: 2; rpt. in Sheila Egoff, G.T. Stubbs, and L.F. Ashley. *Only Connect: readings on children's literature.* New York: Oxford UP, 1969. 156–59.

Brown, Carolyn S. *The Tall Tale in American Folklore and Literature.* Knoxville: U of Tennessee P, 1987.

Bruner, Jerome and N. Jolly and K. Sylva, eds. *Play: Its Role in Development and Evolution.* Middlesex, England: Penguin, 1976.

Buckley, B.R. "Jump Rope Rhymes." *Keystone Folklore Quarterly* 11 (1966): 99–111.

Bullitt, John M. *Jonathan Swift and the Anatomy of Satire.* Cambridge: Harvard UP, 1966.

Butler, Francelia. *Skipping around the World: The Ritual Nature of Skip Rope Rhymes.* Hamden, CT: Library Professional Publications, 1988.

Byron, Thomas. *Nonsense and Wonder: The Poems and Cartoons of Edward Lear.* New York: Dutton, 1977.

Caillois, Roger. "Riddles and Images." *Game, Play, Literature.* Ed. Jacques Ehrmann. *Yale French Studies* 41 (1968): 148–58.

Cammaerts, Emile. *The Poetry of Nonsense.* New York: Dutton, 1926.

Camus, Albert. *The Rebel.* Trans. Anthony Bower. Middlesex, England: Penguin, 1971.

Cazamian, Louis. *The Development of English Humor.* New York: AMS Press, 1965.

Carlson, Richard S. *The Benign Humorists.* Hamden, CT: Archon Books, 1975.

Champigny, Robert. *Sense, Antisense, Nonsense.* Gainesville: U of Florida P, 1986.

Chesterton, G.K. "A Defense of Nonsense." *The Defendent.* New York: Mead, 1901. 42–50. Also in Bone, Raymond T., Ed. *The Man Who Was Chesterton.* New York: Dodd, Mead, 1945. 605–06.

Chomsky, Carol. "Approaching Reading through Invented Spelling." *Theory and Practice of Early Reading.* Vol. 2. Eds. L. B. Resnick and P.A. Weaver. Hillsdale, NJ: Lawrence Erlbaum 1979.

Chukovsky, Kornei. *From Two to Five.* Trans. and ed. Miriam Morton. Berkeley and Los Angeles: U of California P, 1963.

Ciardi, John. *How Does a Poem Mean?* Part 3 of *An Introduction to Literature.*

Herbert Barrows, Hubert Heffner, John Ciardi, and Wallace Douglas. Boston: Houghton, 1959.

Clark, Beverly Lyon. "Lewis Carroll's *Alice* Books: The Wonder of Wonderland" in *Touchstones: Reflections on the Best in Children's Literature*. 2 vols. to date. Ed. Perry Nodelman. West Lafayette, IN: ChLA Publishers, 1985, 1986. Vol. 1. 44–52.

Clarke, Anne. "The Griffin and the Gryphon." *Jabberwocky: Journal of The Lewis Carroll Society* 6.1 (Winter 1977): 16–17 .

Cohen, Morton N. "Lewis Carroll's Letters to Little Girls." Illus. Maurice Sendak. *Harper's* (May 1979): 65–68.

Cortazar, Julio. *Hopscotch* New York: Avon, 1975.

Cott, Jonathan. *Pipers at the Gates of Dawn: The Wisdom of Literature*. New York: Random, 1981; 1983.

Crews, Judith. "Plain Superficiality." In *Modern Critical Views*. Ed. Harold Bloom. New York: Chelsea, 1987. 83– 102.

Crutch, Denis. *"The Hunting of the Snark*: A Study of Fits and Starts." *Jabberwocky: Journal of the Lewis Carroll Society*. 5.4 (Aumtumn 1976): 103–09.

———."Lewis Carroll: Linguist of Wonderland." In *Mr. Dodgson*. Ed. Denis Crutch. London: The Lewis Carroll Society, 1973. 34–37.

De la Mare, Walter. "Lewis Carroll." In *The Eighteen-Eighties*. London: Royal Society of Literature of the United Kingdom, 1930. 218–55.

Derrida, Jacques. "Structure, Sign, and Play." In *The Structuralist Controversy*. Eds. Richard Macksey and Eugene Donato. Baltimore: Johns Hopkins UP, 1972. 247–64.

Dolitsky, Marlene. *Under the Tumtum Tree: From Nonsense to Sense, A Study in Nonautomatic Comprehension*. Amsterdam: Benjamins, 1984.

Dorson, Richard M. *Man and Beast in American Comic Legend*. Bloomington, IN: Indiana UP, 1982.

Douglas, Norman. *London Street Games* (2nd ed., rev. and enl.). London: Chatto and Windus, 1931 (1st ed., 1916).

Douglass, Paul. "Eliot's Cats: Serious Play behind the Playful Seriousness." *Children's Literature* 11 (1983): 109–24.

Duvoisin, Roger. "Children's Book Illustration: The Pleasures and Problems." *Only Connect: readings on children's literature*. Eds. Sheila Egoff, G.T. Stubbs, and L.F. Ashley. New York: Oxford UP, 1980. 357–74.

Eckenstein, Lina. *Comparative Studies in Nursery Rhymes*. London: Duckworth, 1911.

Eiss, Harry Edwin. *Dictionary of Language Games, Puzzles, and Amusements*. New York: Greenwood, 1986.

Esslin, Martin. *The Theatre of the Absurd* Garden City, NY: Doubleday, 1969.

Ferguson, C. A. and M. A. Macken. "The Role of Play in Phonological Development." *Children's Language*. Vol. 4. Ed. K. Nelson. Hillsdale, NJ: Lawrence Erlbaum, 1984.

Fisher, Margery. "Climates of Humour." *Intent upon Reading: A Critical Appraisal of Modern Fiction for Children*. New York: Franklin Watts, 1962. 163–68.

Flescher, Jacqueline. "The Language of Nonsense in *Alice*." *The Child's Part*. Ed. Peter Brooks. Boston: Beacon Press, 1969.

Fry, Edward B., Dona L. Fountoukidis, and Jacqueline K. Polk. "Entertainment: Murphy's Law and Others, Euphemisims, Palindromes, Wacky Wordies." *The NEW Reading Teacher's Book of Lists*. Englewood Cliffs, NJ: Prentice, 1988.

Fry, William. *Sweet Madness: A Study of Humor*. Palo Alto, CA: Pacific Books, 1963.

Frye, Northrop. *Anatomy of Criticism*. New York: Atheneum, 1967.

Gardner, Martin. "A Child's Garden of Bewilderment." *Saturday Review* (July 17, 1965); rpt., *Only Connect: readings on children's literature*. Eds. Sheila Egoff, G.T. Stubbs, and L.F. Ashley New York: Oxford UP, 1969. 150–55.

———. Introduction and notes to *The Annotated Alice*. New York: World, 1963; rpt. 1972.

Garvey, C. *Play*. Cambridge: Harvard UP, 1977.

———. "Play with Language and Speech." *Child Discourse*. Eds. S. Ervin Tripp and C. Mitchell-Kerman. New York: Academic Press, 1976.

Geller, Linda Gibson. *Wordplay and Language Learning for Children*. Urbana, IL: NCTE, 1985.

Gilchrist, A. G. "Notes on Children's Game Songs." *Journal of the Folk Song Society* 19 (1915): 221–39.

Gomme, Alice Bertha. *The Traditional Games of England, Scotland, and Ireland*. 2 vols. New York: Dover, 1964.

Green, Percy B. *A History of Nursery Rhymes*. London: Greening, 1899.

Green, Roger Lancelyn. "You May Call It Nonsense." *The Lewis Carroll Society Magazine* 3 (March 1970): 9–12.

Greenacre, Phyllis. "On Nonsense." *Psychoanalysis—A General Psychology: Essays in Honor of Henize Hartmann*. Eds. R. M. Lowenstein et al. New York: International UP, 1966. 655–77. Also in *Emotional Growth*. New York: International UP, 1971. 592–615.

Greenleaf, Warren T. "How the Grinch Stole Reading: The Serious Nonsense of Dr. Seuss." *Principal* 61.5 (May 1982): 6–9.

Halliwell, J. O. *Popular Rhymes and Nursery Tales*. London: Bodley Head, 1970.

Handke, Peter. *Nonsense and Happiness* [*Als das wuenschen noch geholfen hat*

English and German]. Trans. Michael Roloff. New York: Urizen Books, 1973.

Handley-Taylor, Geoffrey. *A Selected Bibliography of Literature Relating to Nursery Rhyme Reform* (2nd ed). Manchester, England: True Aim, 1952.

Harmon, William. "Lear, Limericks, and Some Other Verse Forms." *Children's Literature* 10 (1982): 70–76.

Herron, R. and Brian Sutton-Smith, eds. *Child Play*. New York: John Wiley, 1971.

Higonnet, Margaret R. "Narrative Fractures and Fragments." *Children's Literature*. 15 (1987): 37–54.

Hilbert, Richard. "Approaching Reason's Edge: 'Nonsense As the Final Solution to the Problem of Meaning.'" *Sociological Inquiry* 47 (1977): 25–31.

Hodge, M. C., Jr. "The Sane, the Mad, the Good, the Bad: T. S. Eliot's *Old Possum's Book of Practical Cats*." *Children's Literature* 7 (1979): 129–46.

Hoff, Benjamin. *The Tao of Pooh*. New York: Penguin, 1987; rpt. from Dutton, 1982.

Hoffeld, Laura. "*Pippi Longstocking*: The Comedy of the Natural Girl." *Lion and Unicorn* 1.1 (1977): 47–53.

Holquist, Michael. "That is a Boojum? Nonsense and Modernism." *Yale French Studies* 43 (1969): 145–64.

Hood, Lois. "The Role of Imitation in Children's Language Learning." *Discovering Language with Children*. Ed. Gay Su Pinnell. Urbana, IL: NCTE, 1980.

Hughes, Ted. *Poetry in the Making: An Anthology of Poems and Programmes from "Listenting and Writing."* London and Boston: Faber, 1967; rpt. 1986.

Huizinga, Johann. *Homo Ludens: A Study of the Play Element in Culture*. Boston: Beacon Press, 1955.

Hurlimann, Bettina. Trans. and ed. Brian W. Alderson. "'Jabberwocky': A Typically English Element in Children's Literature" and "Fantasy and Reality: Nonsense from *Peter Pan* to *Pippi Longstocking*." *Three Centuries of Children's Books in Europe*. London: Oxford UP, 1967.

Jian, Guo. "The Victorious Monkey: Favorite Figure in Chinese Literature for Children." *Triumphs of the Spirit in Children's Literature*. Eds. Francelia Butler and Richard Rotert. Hamden: Library Professional Publications, 1986. 159–63.

Jurich, Marilyn. "Once Upon a Shtetl: Schlimazels, Schlemiels, Schnorrers, Shadchens, and Sages." *Lion and Unicorn* 1.1 (1977): 9–25.

Keith-Spiegel, Patricia. "Early Conceptions of Humor: Varieties and

Issues." *The Psychology of Humor*. Eds. J. Goldstein and P. McGhee. New York: Academic Press, 1972. 4–34.

Kirshenblatt-Gimblett, Barbara, ed. *Speech Play: Research and Resources for the Study of Linguistic Creativity*. Philadelphia: U of Pennsylvania P, 1976.

Knapp, M. and H. "Tradition and Change in American Playgorund Language." *Journal of American Folklore* 86 (1973): 131–41.

Koch, Kenneth. *Wishes, Lies, and Dreams: Teaching Children to Write Poetry*. New York: Harper, 1980.

Kris, Ernst. *Psychoanalytic Explorations in Art*. New York: Schocken, 1964.

Lanes, Selma G. *The Art of Maurice Sendak*. New York: Abrams, 1980.

Lennon, Florence Becker. *Victoria Through the Looking-Glass: Life of Lewis Carroll*. New York: Simon, 1945.

Lewis, C. S. "On Three Ways of Writing for Children." *Only Connect: readings on children's literature*. Eds. Sheila Egoff, G.T. Stubbs, and L.F. Ashley. New York: Oxford UP, 1980. 207–20.

Livingston, Myra Cohn. "David McCord's Poems: Something Behind the Door." *Touchstones: Reflections on the Best in Children's Literature*. Vol. 2: *Fairy Tales, Fables, Myths, Legends, and Poetry*. Ed. Perry Nodelman. West Lafayette, IN: ChLA Publishers, 1987. 173–83. 2 vols. to date. 1985, 1986.

———. "Nonsense Verse: The Complete Escape." *Celebrating Children's Books*. Eds. Betsy Hearne and Marily Kaye. New York: Lothrop, 1981. 122–39.

Loomis, C. G. "Jonathanisms: American Epigrmmatic Hyperbole." *Western Folklore* 6 (1947): 211–27.

———. "Traditional American Wordplay." *Western Folklore* 18 (1959): 348–57.

Loy, John, ed. *The Paradoxes of Play*. West Point, NY: Leisure Press, 1982.

Lucian's Dialogues. Trans. Howard Williams. London: George Bell, 1903.

Lukens, Rebecca. *A Critical Handbook of Children's Literature*. Glenview, IL: Scott, Foresman, 1976; 2nd ed. 1982; 3rd ed. 1986.

Lynn, Joanne. "Aesop's *Fables*: Beyond Morals." *Touchstones: Reflections on the Best in Children's Literature*. Vol. 2: *Fairy Tales, Fables, Myths, Legends, and Poetry*. Ed. Perry Nodelman. West Lafayette, IN: ChLA Publishers, 1987. 4–13. 2 vols. to date. 1985, 1986.

———. "Hyacinths and Biscuits in the Village of Liver and Onions: Sandburg's *Rootabaga Stories*." *Children's Literature* 8 (1980): 118–32.

MacCann, Donnarae. "Wells of Fancy, 1865–1965." *Wilson Library Journal* (1965); rpt. in Sheila Egoff, G.T. Stubbs, and L.F. Ashley. *Only Connect: readings on children's literature*: 133–45. New York: Oxford UP, 1969.

Matthews, Gareth B. *Dialogues with Children*. Cambridge: Harvard UP, 1984.

———. *Philosophy and the Young Child*. Cambridge: Harvard UP, 1984.

McDowell, John. "Riddling and Enculturation: A Glance at the Cerebral Child." *Working Papers in Sociolinguistics* no. 36. Austin, TX: Southwest Educational Development Laboratory, July 1976.

Mikkelsen, Nina. "Richard Chase's *Jack Tales*: A Trickster in the New World." *Touchstones: Reflections on the Best in Children's Literature*. Vol. 2: *Fairy Tales, Fables, Myths, Legends, and Poetry*. Ed. Perry Nodelman. West Lafayette, IN: ChLA Publishers, 1987. 40–55. 2 vols. to date. 1985, 1986.

Millar, Susanna. *The Psychology of Play*. Baltimore: Penguin, 1969.

Monro, D. H. *Argument of Laughter*. Victoria, Australia: Melbourne UP, 1951; South Bend, IN: U of Notre Dame P, 1963.

Muller, Charles A., comp. *Isn't that Lewis Carroll? A Guide to the Most Mimsy Words and Drabjous Quotations of Lewis Carroll's Alice's Adventures in Wonderland, Through the Looking-Glass, and The Hunting of the Snark*. New Market, VA: Trackaday, 1984.

Nash, Walter. *The Language of Humour: Style and Technique in Comic Discourse*. White Plains, NY: Longman, 1985.

Newell, William Wells. *Games and Songs of American Children*. 1903; rpt. New York: Dover, 1963.

Nodelman, Perry. "The Nursery Rhymes of Mother Goose: A World Without Glasses." *Touchstones: Reflections on the Best in Children's Literature*. Vol. 2: *Fairy Tales, Fables, Myths, Legends, and Poetry*. Ed. Perry Nodelman. West Lafayette, IN: ChLA Publishers, 1987. 183–201. 2 vols. to date. 1985, 1986.

Nolton, Lucy. "Jump Rope Rhymes As Folk Literature." *Journal of American Folklore* 61 (1948): 53–67.

O'Hara, J.D. "Gertrude Stein's *The World Is Round*." *Sharing Literature with Children: A Thematic Anthology*. Ed. Francelia Butler. New York: Longman, 1977. 446–49.

Ong, Walter J. *The Interfaces of the Word*. Ithaca, NY: Cornell UP, 1977.

Opie, Iona and Peter Opie. *Children's Games in Street and Playground*. New York: Oxford UP, 1984.

———. *I Saw Esau: Traditional Rhymes of Youth* London: Williams and Norgate, 1947.

———. *The Lore and Language of Schoolchildren* Oxford: Clarendon Press, 1950; rpt. 1959.

———. "Introduction." *The Oxford Dictionary of Nursery Rhymes*. Oxford: Clarendon Press, 1951. 1–45.

Orwell, George. "Nonsense Poetry." In *Shooting an Elephant and Other Essays*. London: Faber, 1945. 187–92.

Partridge, Eric. "The Nonsense Words of Edward Lear and Lewis Carroll." *Here, There, and Everywhere: Essays Upon Language*. London: Hamish Hamilton, 1950. 162–88.

Pflieger, Pat. "Fables into Picture Books." *ChLAQ* 9.2 (Summer 1984): 73–75, 80.

Piaget, Jean. 1959. *The Language and Thought of the Child*. New York: NAL, 1974.

Pitcher, George. "Wittgenstein, Nonsense, and Lewis Carroll." *The Massachusetts Review* 6 (Spring-Summer 1965): 591–611.

Polhemus, Robert M. *Comic Faith: The Great Tradition from Austen to Joyce*. Chicago: U of Chicago P, 1980.

Pietropinto, Anthony. "A Psychiatrist's Case for Jabberwocky and Other Violent Nonsense." *Learning* 2.7 (March 1974): 80–83.

Pinnell, Gay Su, ed. *Discovering Language with Children*. Urbana, IL: NCTE, 1980.

Preminger, Alex, ed. *Princeton Encyclopedia of Poetry and Poetics*. Princeton: Princeton UP, 1974.

Prickett, Stephen. "Consensus and Nonsense: Lear and Carroll." *Victorian Fantasy*. Bloomington: Indiana UP, 1979. 114–49.

Priestley. J.B. *English Humor*. New York: Stein and Day, 1976.

Rackin, Donald. "Alice's Journey to the End of Night." *PMLA* 81.5 (Oct. 1966): 313–26.

Redfern, Walter. *Puns*. London: Andre Deutsch, 1984.

Roberts, Patricia L. *Alphabet Books as a Key to Language Patterns: An Annotated Action Bibliography*. Hamden, CT: Library Professional Publications, 1987.

Romney, Claude. "Of Cats and Bats in *Alice's Adventures* and Its French and German Translations." *Jabberwocky: Journal of The Lewis Carroll Society* 12.1 (Winter 1982/83): 15–20.

Rosenheim, Jr., Edward W. *Swift and the Satirist's Art*. Illus. Rainey Bennett. Chicago: U. of Chicago P, 1963.

Ross, Bruce. "The Poetics of Nonsense: Echoic Abuse and Hyperbole in Lewis Carroll's *The Hunting of the Snark*." Paper read at Children's Literature Division session on "Nonsense in Children's Literature," MLA Convention, New York City, Dec. 29, 1986.

Rowland, Beryl. *Animals with Human Faces*. Knoxville: U of Tennessee P, 1975.

———. *Birds with Human Souls*. Knoxville: U of Tennessee P, 1978.

Sacksteder, William. "Looking-Glass: A Treatise on Logic." *Philosophy and Phenomenological Research* 27 (March 1967): 338–55.

Sapire, D. "*Alice in Wonderland*: A Work of Intellect." *English Studies in Africa* 15.1 (1972): 53–62.

Schneiderman, Leo. *The Psychology of Myth, Folklore and Religion.* Chicago: Nelson-Hall, 1981.

Segel, Elizabeth and Joan B. Friedberg. "From Mulberry Street to Stethoscope Row: Fifty Years of Dr. Seuss." *Carnegie Magazine* 58.6 (Nov./Dec. 1986): 8–15.

Sendak, Maurice. "Mother Goose's Garnishings." *Jump Over the Moon: Selected Professional Readings.* Eds. Pamela Petrick Barron and Jennifer Q Burley. New York: Holt, 1984. 62–68.

Sewell Elizabeth. *The Field of Nonsense.* London: Chatto and Windus, 1952.

———. "Nonsense Verse and the Child." *Lion and Unicorn* 4.2 (Winter 1980–81): 30–48.

Shibles, Warren H. *Humor: A Critical Analysis for Young People.* Whitewater, WI: Language Press, 1978.

Shipley, Joseph. *Wordplay.* New York: Hawthorn Books, 1972.

Shulevitz, Uri. "What Is a Picture Book?" *The Five Owls.* 2. 4 (Mar./April 1988): 49–51.

Siegel, R.A. "The Little Boy Who Drops His Pants in the Crowd: Tomi Ungerer's Art of the Comic Grotesque." *Lion and Unicorn* 1.1 (1977): 26–32.

Smith, Elva A. "Mother Goose Yesterday and Today" in ALA *Children's Library Yearbook* 4 (1932): 27–39.

South, Malcolm. *Mythical and Fabulous Beasts: A Source Book and Research Guide.* New York: Greenwood, 1987.

Spacks, Patricia Meyer. "Logic and Language in *Through the Looking-Glass*." *ETC: A Review of General Semantics* 18.1 (1961): 91–100.

Steig, Michael. "Dr. Seuss's Attack on Imagination: *I Wish That I Had Duck Feet* and the Cautionary Tale." *Proceedings of the Ninth Annual Conference of the Children's Literature Association,* U of Florida (March 1982): 137–41.

Stern, Jeffrey. "Lewis Carroll the Surrealist." *Lewis Carroll: A Celebration.* Ed. Edward Guiliano. New York: Potter, 1982. 132–53.

Stevens, Albert M. *Nursery Rhymes: Remnant of Popular Protest.* Lawrence, KA: Coronado Press, 1968.

Stewart, Susan. *Nonsense: Aspects of Intertextuality in Folklore and Literature.* Baltimore: Johns Hopkins UP, 1979.

Strachey, Constance, ed. *Letters to Edward Lear.* New York: Duffield, 1907.

Sutton-Smith, Brian. "Boundaries." *Child's Play.* Eds. R. Herron and B. Sutton-Smith. New York: John Wiley, 1971.

———. "A Developmental Structural Account of Riddles." In *Speech Play.*

Ed. Barbara Kirshenblatt-Gimblett. Philadelphia: U of Pennsylvania P, 1976.

———. "The Game as a School of Abstraction." *The Folkgames of Children.* Ed. B. Sutton-Smith. Austin: U of Texas P, 1972.

Sutton-Smith, Brian and Diana Kelly-Byrne. *The Masks of PLay.* New York: Leisure Press, 1984.

Swinfen, Ann. *In Defence of Fantasy: A Study of the Genre in English and American Literature since 1945.* Boston: Rutledge & Kegan Paul, 1984. (Includes commentary on Norton's *The Phantom Tollbooth* and Thurber's *The Thirteen Clocks.*)

Taylor, Archer. *English Riddles from Oral Tradition.* Berkeley: U of California P, 1951.

Taylor, Mary Agnes. "From Apple to Abstraction in Alphabet Books." *Children's Literature in Education* 9.4 (Winter 1978): 173–81.

Thomas, Joyce. "'There was an Old Man. . .': The Sense of Nonsense Verse." *Children's Literature Association Quarterly* 10.3 (Fall 1985): 119–22.

Tough, Joan. *Listening to Children Talking.* London: Schools Council Publications, 1976.

Tremper, Ellen. "Instigorating" *Winnie-the-Pooh."* *Lion and Unicorn* 1.1 (1977): 33–46.

Tucker, Nicholas. *The Child and the Book: A Psychological and Literary Exploration.* New York: Cambridge UP, 1982.

Tymn, Marshall B., Kenneth J. Zahorski, and Robert H. Boyer. *Fantasy Literature: A Core Collection and Reference Guide.* New York: R. R. Bowker, 1979. (Includes commentary on Thurber's wordplay.)

Watson, Jerry J. *Reading Nonsense (Poetry) Makes Sense in the Reading Program.* Research report, U of Iowa, 1977.

West, Mark I. "Edward's Lear's *Book of Nonsense*: A Scroobious Classic." *Touchstones: Reflections on the Best in Children's Literature.* Vol. 2: *Fairy Tales, Fables, Myths, Legends, and Poetry.* Ed. Perry Nodelman. West Lafayette, IN: ChLA Publishers, 1987. 150–56. 2 vols. to date. 1985, 1986.

Whalen-Levitt, Peggy. "Picture Play in Children's Books: A Celebration of Visual Awareness." *Jump Over the Moon: Selected Professional Readings.* Eds. Pamela Petrick Barron and Jennifer Q Burley. New York: Holt, 1984. 167–74.

White, Allison. "With Birds in His Beard." *Saturday Review* (Jan. 15, 1966); rpt. in *Only Connect: readings on children's literature.* Eds. Sheila Egoff, G.T. Stubbs, and L.F. Ashley. New York: Oxford UP, 1969. 279–85.

Whorf, Benjamin Lee. *Language, Thought, and Reality: Selected Writings.* Ed. John B. Carroll. Cambridge, MA: Technology Press MIT, 1956,

Willard, Nancy. "The Game and the Garden: The Lively Art of Nonsense." *Angel in the Parlor: Five Stories and Eight Essays.* San Diego: Harcourt, 1983. 258–82.

———. "The Nonsense of Angels: George MacDonald at the Back of the North Wind." *Proceedings of the Fifth Annual Conference of the Children's Literature Association*, Harvard U (March 1978): 106–12; rpt. in *Children and Their Literature: A Readings Book*, ed. Jill P. May. West Lafayette, IN: ChLA Publications, 1983. 34–40.

Willis, Gary. "Two Different Kettles of Talking Fish: The Nonsense of Lear and Carroll." *Jabberwocky: Journal of The Lewis Carroll Society* 9.4 (Autumn 1980): 87–94.

Wilson, Edmund. "C.L. Dodgson: The Poet Logician." *Aspects of Alice.* Ed. Robert Phillips. New York: Vintage, 1971. 198–206.

Winslow, David. "An Annotated Collection of Children's Lore." *Keystone Folklore Quarterly* 11 (1966): 151–202

———. "An Introduction to Oral Tradition among Children." *Keystone Folklore Quarterly* 11 (1966): 43–58.

Wolfenstein, Martha. *Children's Humor: A Psychological Analysis.* Glencoe, IL: The Free Press, 1954.

Wooden, Warren W. *Children's Literature of the English Renaissance.* Lexington, KY: UP of Kentucky, 1985.

Wright, Thomas. *A History of Caricature and Grotesque in Literature and Art.* London: Virtue Brothers, 1865.

Index